Joseph R. Mancuso, Ph.D. is the founder and president of The Center for Entrepreneurial Management (CEM), an affiliate of the American Management Association (AMA). He is not only a respected educator and author but also a compulsive entrepreneur.

In all, Dr. Mancuso has launched seven businesses and serves as a board member and advisor for a score of entrepreneurial ventures.

He holds a B.S.E.E. from Worcester Polytehnic Institute, an M.B.A. from Harvard Business School, and earned his Doctorate in Education from Boston University. He has written and edited nine books, including *How to Start, Finance, and Manage Your Own Small Business* and *The Small Business Survival Guide: Sources of Help for Entrepreneurs,* both published by Prentice-Hall, Inc. He is a regular contributor to numerous magazines.

JOSEPH R. MANCUSO

HAVE YOU
GOT
WHAT IT TAKES?
How To Tell if You Should
Start Your Own Business

A SPECTRUM BOOK

PRENTICE-HALL, INC.   Englewood Cliffs, New Jersey 07632

Library of Congress Cataloging in Publication Data

Mancuso, Joseph.
  Have you got what it takes?

  A Spectrum Book
  Includes index.
  1. Small businesss—Management. 2. New business
enterprises—Management. 3. Entrepreneur.
4. Venture capital. I. Title.
HD62.7.M36   658'.022   81-15686
                                      AACR2

ISBN 0-13-383885-4 {PBK}

ISBN 0-13-383893-5

To Karla Schulz—you've got what it takes.

This Spectrum Book is available to businesses and organizations at a special discount when ordered in large quantities. For information, contact Prentice-Hall, Inc., General Book Marketing, Special Sales Division, Englewood Cliffs, N. J. 07632.

10   9   8   7   6   5   4   3   2   1

Printed in the United States of America

Editorial production/supervision by Cyndy Lyle Rymer
Manufacturing buyer: Cathie Lenard

Prentice-Hall International, Inc., *London*
Prentice-Hall of Austrialia Pty. Limited, *Sydney*
Prentice-Hall of Canada, Ltd., *Toronto*
Prentice-Hall of India Private Limited, *New Delhi*
Prentice-Hall of Japan, Inc., *Tokyo*
Prentice-Hall of Southeast Asia Pte. Ltd., *Singapore*
Whitehall Books Limited, *Wellington, New Zealand*

CONTENTS

THE ENTREPRENEUR'S PHILOSOPHY

PREFACE

Alfred North Whitehead, English mathematician and philosopher, once said, "The greatest invention of all is the invention of inventing inventions." If that is so, the person who often introduces an invention to the world—the entrepreneur—must share that greatness. Much has been written about entrepreneurs—their desires, their motivations, and their characteristics. Unfortunately, although most of this literature has been the result of scientific investigation, the "human" side of the issue has been sadly neglected. Actually, it is very difficult to study entrepreneurs, these people who organize, manage, and assume the risks of business. Many, if not most, are absorbed into the business world and cannot be separated from the whole. This is especially true of the majority of entrepreneurs whose ventures fail. And given the reality that most entrepreneurial ventures do fail, academic studies, which begin with a localized small business directory, are really only studies of success. Thus, most studies have been made of successful entreprenurs only.

Since the late 1950s, I have worked directly with more than 1,000 entrepreneurs in a variety of businesses and industries. I have been their confidant and their sounding board. I have shared both their failures and their success. I have been their friend.

I have worked with winners and losers alike, even though each time I begin a consulting relationship I am confident that I am working with a winner. This is not always the case. Experience has taught me that to predict what makes a "successful" entrepreneur is nearly impossible. It is a good deal easier to predict what causes an entrepreneur to fail.

In June 1978, I founded a not-for-profit enterprise to promote entrepreneurship, called The Center for Entrepreneurial Management (CEM) in Worcester, Massachusetts. It was founded as a membership association for entrepreneurs because I felt that although it was fine to be independent, there was no reason to be alone. Our motto is "While the professional manager seeks to protect resources, the entrepreneurial manger creates them." In December 1979, I merged the business with the not-for-profit American Management Association (AMA) of New York City. The fifty-eight-year-old AMA has just under 100,000 members, and together with CEM it serves small business in a unique manner. I remain as CEM's president, and I encourage you to write to us at 311 Main St., Worcester, Mass. 01608.

The opinions stated here in this book are mine alone. They are not based on any sampling or interviewing; neither are they based on any statistical fact-gathering. They might be called my "gut" reactions after working hand-in-glove with so many different entrepreneurs.

After all, business is not a science with its foundation based on a simply stated formula. A science can be taught by transferring facts from teacher to student. In business, as with other arts, the student must study what others have done and draw his or her own conclusions.

These are *my* conclusions. They may help the individual risking his or her capital, family, career, and personal net worth on a new business venture to recognize what leads to success for some artists of enterepreneurship and failure for others. The budding entrepreneur might even get a couple of chuckles from the foibles of some fellow mavericks.

ACKNOWLEDGMENTS

Thank you, all my fellow entrepreneurs, for your invaluable assistance in preparing this manuscript. The original draft was dictated on a cassette recorder in my automobile. Mrs. Kaiser patiently managed to separate my pearls of wisdom from the honks, roars, rattles, and screeches of traffic. Doris Bergin, Gretchen Schwamb, Mary Eaton, Cheryl Hall, and Gail Perry all typed drafts of the manuscript.

Among these entrepreneurs with whom I have worked and who candidly shared their experiences with me, I would especially like to thank Michael Grant, Bob Schwartz, Murry Rubin, and Fred Adler for their insights.

Have You Got What It Takes? is an outgrowth of my very first book—*Fun and Guts: The Entrepreneur's Philosophy.* (Addison-Wesley, 1969).

Although I claim that these opinions and findings convey a consensus of entrepreneurs with whom I have worked, I take full responsibility for them. The conclusions are mine and mine alone.

1

WHO IS
THE MALE
ENTREPRENEUR?

THE ENTREPRENEUR'S LIFE CYCLE

If a man write a better book, preach a better sermon or make a better mousetrap than his neighbor, though he build his house in the woods, the world will make a beaten path to his door.

RALPH WALDO EMERSON

All successful small businesses start with an idea and proceed through a given life cycle. Following is a curve showing the cycle from early development through idea, start-up, and financing, to growth and maturity. At any point in your entrepreneurial career, you are at a unique position on that curve, and each spot requires special courses of action.

1

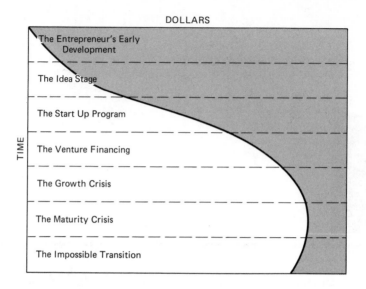

DOLLARS

The Entrepreneur's Early Development

The Idea Stage

The Start Up Program

TIME

The Venture Financing

The Growth Crisis

The Maturity Crisis

The Impossible Transition

ENTREPRENEURS ARE BORN, NOT MADE

There are more horses' asses than there are horses.

A bewildered farmer

Remember the old breakfast cereal commercial about champions? The kicker was the sponsor's claim that the product contributed to making champions. This implied that champions are made and not born. How about entrepreneurs? Are they born or made? What product or process produces this breed of human? That is a question for which there is no once-and-for-all answer.

Just because there is no final answer is hardly justification to neglect the topic. Whenever I am forced to take a position on the made/born issue, I lean toward the born side. On the one hand, I claim entrepreneurs have common characteristics; such as the father being self-employed, the first child being the entrepreneur, and an abundance of energy. On the other hand, I also claim that the aspiring entrepreneur is molded within a rather specialized environment. So, it is a dilemma, with no simple answer. Both sides of the issue are a little bit correct; the question is—which is more correct?

If entrepreneurs are made (not born), we should witness a different pattern to the process of starting, financing, and managing a small business. This story will demonstrate the point and my underlying reasons for leaning toward both sides of the question.

2

While I was consulting with an executive vice president of a major listed company, our discussions frequently evolved around the possibility that he would have his own company. We reasoned that he possessed the management skills necessary to run his own business. But the thought of starting a business from scratch frightened him. He actually shook when he thought about the tedious chores of developing company letterheads, hiring accountants, and setting up new banking relationships. During his professional business career, he had managed these relationships very successfully, but he had never started them from scratch. On several occasions I presented him with entrepreneurial opportunities. With a little bit of capital and a little bit of energy and a little bit of luck, he could have developed these ideas into a business. He had the capital, he had the energy, and he had the desire—but he did not have the one essential element, the entrepreneurial spirit; it was not born in him. As he said over and over, "I guess I'm just a hired hand and my job is keeping someone's farm in shape."

It may be far-fetched, it may be unreasonable, but it does seem that some people are cast forever in the role of the hired hand. The presidents of General Motors, General Electric, and General Mills are hired hands, for that matter, and the plight of the hired hand is not so dreadful in the American business system. But the distinction is made; they *are* hired and fired. How many managers of successful large companies could pick up the entrepreneurial ball and run with it? How many would want to, given the opportunity?

These observations, along with other experiences, have led me to the conclusion that the spark of entrepreneurship is born within some people and is part of their heredity, and or others it is created—therefore, I maintain that entrepreneurs are both made and born. The classic heredity versus environment debate about personality development can be left to the behavioral scientists and scholars, but, as you read through this section about the personal characteristics of male entrepreneurs, remember that you, as an entrepreneur, may be bucking the odds if you are not born with the essential spark and desire, or you are not nurtured in an "entrepreneurial incubator."

Further evidence for my position comes from entrepreneurs who have started not just one, but many businesses. There seems to be a pattern to these individuals. Once they have started one business, they are prime candidates to start another. Some individuals have started five, six, seven businesses. I have started half a dozen myself. So, when thinking about yourself and your possibility of becoming an entrepreneur, keep in mind the characteristics of other enterpreneurs.

However, even if you are not the first child, if your father is not self-employed, if you do not have a master's degree—don't be discouraged. If you are crazy enough to want to try, you could be the next American business hero. Who is to say?

WHAT IS AN ENTREPRENEUR?

Many are stubborn in the path they have chosen, few are in pursuit of the goal.

NIETZSCHE

The entrepreneur, according to the following sources, is defined in many ways.

1. In *Websters Seventh New Collegiate Dictionary,* the entrepreneur is: "entre-pre-neur (f Fr. entreprendre, to undertake); one who organizes, manages, and assumes the risks of a business or entreprise—en-tre-pre-neur-ship/n."

2. In *The Achieving Society,* by Dr. David McClelland (Halstead, 1976), the entrepreneur is defined as "someone who exercises some control over the means of production and produces more than he can consume in order to sell (or exchange) it for individual (or household) income."

3. In *The Organization Makers,* by O. Collins and W. Moore, the academic fathers of entrepreneurship the entrepreneur is identified as "a person who has created out of nothing an ongoing enterprise."

4. In the employees' view, the entrepreneur is the person with the office nearest the front door, whose employees have affectionately changed his (sometimes her) title and name to an age—indicating adjective and initials—from "Dr. John" to "Old J.D."

5. To friends, the entrepreneur is the person who is feverishly writing during an airplane flight while his or her comrades enjoy drinks, movies, and games.

6. An entrepreneur is someone who is confused when responding to the question: "Are you an entrepreneur or are you unemployed?"

7. "Entrepreneurship is the most fun you can have with your clothes on!" (Sven Atterhead of Sweden)

ENTREPRENEUR IS A DIRTY WORD

It's not the critic who counts, nor the observer who watches from a safe distance. Wealth is created only by doers in the arena who are marred with dirt, dust, blood, and sweat. These are producers who strike out on their own, who come up short, time and again, who know high highs and low lows, great devotions, and who overextend themselves for worthwhile causes. Without exception, they fail more than they succeed and appreciate this reality even before venturing out on their own, but when these producers of wealth fail, they at least fail with style and grace, and their gut soon recognizes that failure is only a resting place, not a place in which to spend a lifetime. Their places will never be with those nameless souls who know neither victory nor defeat, who receive weekly paychecks regardless of their week's performance, who are hired hands in labor in someone else's garden. These doers are producers and no matter what their lot is at any given moment, they will never take a place beside the takers, for theirs is a unique place, alone, under the sun.*

Not so long ago, to have been called an entrepreneur would have almost been cause for a duel. It meant that you were overly aggressive and probably not terribly trustworthy; maybe even dishonest. Certainly it meant that you were not the kind of person with whom "good" people associated.

Today, that view is somewhat dated; the volumes of scholarly literature on the subject and the accomplishments of great entrepreneurs have made the word respectable. But it is not difficult to see how such a view became prevalent.

To create a business from nothing—and to succeed at it—requires motivation and perseverance bordering on obsession. It sometimes requires ruthlessness. It nearly always means neglecting your family and long absences from home.

All of this could easily be interpreted as antisocial behavior, and none of it is good for a person's reputation. But of the many entrepreneurs I have known, there are very few I have not been proud to regard as friends. It is through these associations that I began to notice the common backgrounds, .traits, or combinations of them that most entrepreneurs share.

THE ENTREPRENEUR'S CHILDHOOD

Give a man a fish, feed him for a day; teach a man to fish, feed him for a lifetime.

E. JOSEPH COSSMAN

Most entrepreneurs seem to enjoy talking about their childhood. Most of their early recollections are honestly interesting if not downright fascinating.

*Dedication from Joseph Mancuso, *How To Start, Finance, and Manage Your Own Small Business* (Englewood Cliffs, N.J.: Prentice-Hall, 1978).

It is during childhood that entrepreneurial tendencies first show themselves. As early as age four or five, entrepreneurs-to-be are peddling "lemonade" on the sidewalk at a few cents a glass. At age eight or nine, they are delivering newspapers to earn money for a new bike. In their early teens, they may collect coins or stamps or photographs. By the time they reach high school, they may actually be running their own businesses—albeit on a small scale.

In short, most adult entrepreneurs were enterprising children, with their courses already set toward future enterprises The basic charactertistic emerges very early in life, and this is true for both men and women.

THE SONS OF POLYGAMOUS MARRIAGES

Fourteen-year-old Amy, "Knock, . . ."
Venture Capitalist, "Who's There?"
Amy, "Opportunity; it only knocks once."

When you examine entrepreneurial history, two not so surprising findings pop up. First, men dominated entrepreneurship until the 1970s, so most of the historical data are built on case histories of men. Second, the entrepreneurial role model is strongest for men, but is emerging for women.

The data also say that immigrants are more likely to be entrepreneurs. Large numbers of immigrant Irish, Italians, other southern Europeans, Cubans, Japanese, Chinese, and Vietnamese, have started businesses in the United States. The same holds true in foreign countries; certain displaced or disadvantaged peoples in each of the above-mentioned countries are the groups starting businesses.

A key finding that may tap you on the back and make you turn around is that, according to senior members of the Church of Latter Day Saints in Salt Lake City, Utah, the sons of a second or third marriage are generally more entrepreneurial than the sons of a first marriage. In Mormon history this tendency is well documented, almost as well documented as the tendency in the rest of the population for the firstborn to be more of an achiever than the following offspring.

THE FIRST CHILD SYNDROME

The Lord's Prayer contains 50 words. The Gettysburg Address 266, the
Ten Commandments 297, the Declaration of Independence 300, and
the recent U.S. Government order setting the price of cabbage 26,911.

The firstborn child, the eldest offspring in the family, is the one most likely to become an entrepreneur. Vance Packard wrote an article titled "The First, Last, and Middle Child: The Surprising Difference." He pointed out various studies, especially one by behavioral scientist Dr. Stanley Schacter, which showed that firstborns far outnumber later-born children in almost every ranking of achievement. Firstborns are overly represented in *Who's Who* and virtually dominate all such rankings of achievement. George Washington, Abraham Lincoln, Thomas Jefferson, Woodrow Wilson, and Franklin Roosevelt were all firstborn children. Of the first twenty-three astronauts to go on American space missions, twenty-one were either the eldest or the only children. (Remarkable when you consider that later-born children outnumber firstborns by two to one in the general United States population.) And in a recent analysis of 1,618 Merit Scholarship winners, 60 percent were firstborn children.

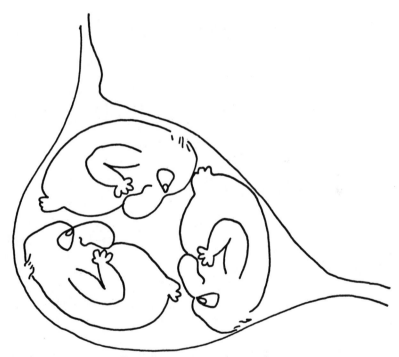

First one out is an entrepreneur!

Later in the article, Packard indicated that firstborns are more likely to accept their parents' standards, to be traditionally oriented, and to call themselves religious. It is the later-born children who are more likely to rebel against the set standards. The firstborns tend to be entrepreneurs.

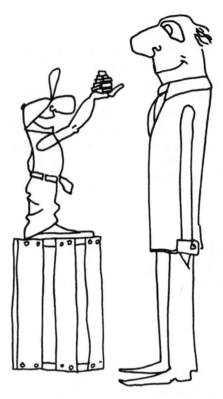

"Look, pop. Today my profits profited, my gross netted and my net grossed, there's a lotta bread in lemonade."

OH DAD, POOR DAD

You never get a second chance to make a good first impression.

The entrepreneur's obsessive need to succeed can often be traced to his relationship with his father. If the two have a "good" relationship, even if dad is not a success, the son strives to prove himself and to make dad proud. Dad's subtlest signs of approval, like a nod or halfsmile, are the son's cherished rewards. A majority of entrepreneurs imitate their fathers and become self-employed.

In cases where the father-son relationship is less cordial even strained, the son may be out to "get the old man" by achieving a greater level of success to prove that *he* is the better man.

If the father is not present during the entrepreneur's childhood because of death, divorce, or desertion, the son may be forced to assume the father's role in the family. He inherits a great deal of responsibility at an early age.

Very seldom, it seems, does the entrepreneur ever have what we would consider your average, run-of-the-mill, subdued oedipal relationship with his father.

THE ORIGINAL ENTREPRENEURS

All you need to grow fine, vigorous grass is a crack in your sidewalk!

In the early days of America, the most prevalent entrepreneurial activity was farming. But, much like the native American, who is seldom given credit for being this country's original inhabitant, few farmers are given much credit for being the original entrepreneurs.

A friend of mine described today's entrepreneurial options in terms of old-time entrepreneurial farming.

First, there is the *crop farmer*. He cultivates the land, plants the seeds, and waters and fertilizes the crop. Depending on his skill and luck, he harvests

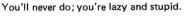
You'll never do; you're lazy and stupid.

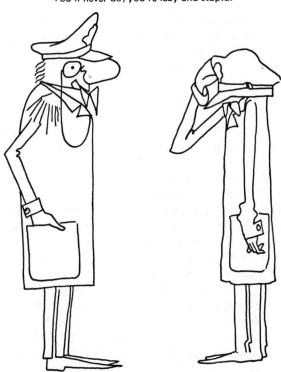

the crop in the fall. He may make a great deal of money or he can lose the whole crop. Big risks and big rewards.

Second comes the *dairy farmer*. This fellow has a lot of capital that he uses to buy cows. He then sells the by-product of his capital investment, milk. This by-product does not deplete his original investment, and he continues to make a level of interest on his investment. Low risk, low reward.

The third type, the *pig farmer*, has an even different outlook. With his limited capital, he cannot afford to feed or house the pigs in any decent style. He feeds them garbage and lets them wander free. After they have grown to full size, if they are still alive, he takes them to market and sells them. Low risk, big reward.

How are your farming skills? Know any small, skinny pigs?

A MATTER OF DEGREES

Knowledge may give weight, but accomplishments give lustre, and many more people see than weigh.

PHILIP DORMER STANHOPE
Earl of Chesterfield

In the January 1971 issue of *Harvard Business Review,* Dr. J. Sterling Livigston the Harvard Business School, president of Sterling Institute, consultant, and world-renowed entrepreneur, wrote: "There is no direct relationship between performance in school or in training programs, and records of success in management."

In *The Enterprising Man* by O. Collins and W. Moore (University of Michigan Research Dept., 1958), the authors conclude that the majority of entrepreneurs have a lower educational base and often are not college graduates. These learned gentlemen have their points of reference, and I have mine. In my experience, and I see this more and more, a great many entrepreneurs, if not the majority in small manufacturing operations, have achieved master's degrees, if not in business, in some technical discipline.

This does not mean that these individuals were brilliant students. In fact, the opposite might be the case. It does, however, indicate a certain level of respect for education—a level that ends abruptly when it comes to taking that extra time to gain a doctorate. For some reason, the master's degree is the most popular highest degree for the New England entrepreneur. Outside of a few professors-turned-entrepreneurs, almost no one chooses to start a business after he has persevered long enough to obtain a doctorate. Rather, these individuals "profess" at a university rather than to practice founding a new business enterprise. This observation is not meant to knock all academics in one damaging blow. It must be pointed out, however, that most academic programs of study leading to an academic degree offer little assistance to the aspiring entrepreneur. Rather than being academically brilliant, the entrepreneur has too much energy to wait at the university before applying his new-found talents in the real world. He does, however, maintain a cordial, though not intimate, relationship with academia. Of course, there are exceptions, and An Wang of the Massachusetts Institute of Technology (MIT), founder of Wang Laboratories in Massachusetts, is one of the most popularly cited.

THE ESSENTIAL INGREDIENT

People can be divided into three groups: those who make things happen, those who watch things happen, and those who wonder what happened.

JOHN W. NEWBERN

If there is any one coefficient of entrepreneurial success it is *energy*. You may have all the ambition in the world, gobs of capital, a gambling man's soul, and business degrees covering an entire wall, but if you are not a human dynamo, forget it!

You must be able to go twenty-five hours a day, if need be, to make the business work, and that takes energy. If you do not have it, all the Wheaties and Ovaltine and little blue pills in the world are not going to help.

A friend responded to my query "Who is the entrepreneur?" in this way: "I do not know who he is, but it seems he is on the 7:00 A.M. air shuttle. The professional manager takes the 8:00 A.M. flight."

THE ENTREPRENEUR'S AGE

I love my job—it's the work I hate!

KARLA SCHULZ

Obviously, the entrepreneurial club has no age limit, but it seems clear that the vast majority of entrepreneurs are in their thirties when they begin their ventures. Some time ago, a study showed that the average entrepreneur is getting younger and that the average age has dropped to somewhere between thirty and thirty-five. Few entrepreneurs begin their ventures after they reach middle age.

This raises an interesting point. Why do people venture forth to start a business at the time when they are most needed by family, religious and civic organizations, when the demands on them are the greatest? Perhaps, the axiom "If you need something done, give it to a busy person" applies here.

ENTREPRENEURS AS INDIVIDUALS

How can you soar with eagles when you work with turkeys?

DR. GORDON BENNETT

I often invite outside guests to speak to the college students in my course in in small business policy at Worcester Polytechnic Institute. My aim is to expose students to a broader view of the entrepreneurial universe than I alone can offer.

One of these speakers is an excellent example of the entrepreneur as an individualist. Every year he repeats, "Small business is not an institution. It's a way of life, and the best teacher of life is personal experience. There is no book, you sort of observe and make your own way."

In another incident, after the course was completed, one of my students came to me and said, "I've listened to every one of our guest speakers, successful and unsuccessful, but I can't figure out the pattern for success. Each speaker was so different." As soon as he completed his sentence, he got the point.

THE OPTIMISTS

To be good is not enough when you dream of being great.

We all know that an optimist views a bucket of water as half-full rather than half-empty, and a person is always viewed as climbing up the rope, never down. We know they view problems as opportunities turned inside out. Another example is Will Roger's well-known story of a child locked in a windowless room that had two feet of horse manure on the floor. Once the child got over the initial shock, the little optimist started digging in the odoriferous stuff, muttering, "With all this manure, there must be a pony somewhere." Entrepreneurs seek out opportunities—and when they do not exist, they create them. Entrepreneurism is a synonym for optimism.

Recently, an entrepreneur managing a business in Florida stayed at my home over the weekend. I pass along this story as another example of entrepreneurial optimism. After he showered and shaved in the morning and just before breakfast, he took out a pair of dice from his pocket and rolled them a dozen times on the breakfast table. My family just watched as though it was some sort of religious ritual equivalent to saying grace before breakfast. Finally, as he put the dice away, I could not resist, and I blurted out, "What are you doing?" He was mildly amused when he matter-of-factly said, "I roll dice every day because I might be lucky and not know it."

Today may be your lucky day, so treat the day as though it is and it will be.

Entrepreneurs Quiz

How do you perceive these objects?
Do you have the entrepreneur's outlook?

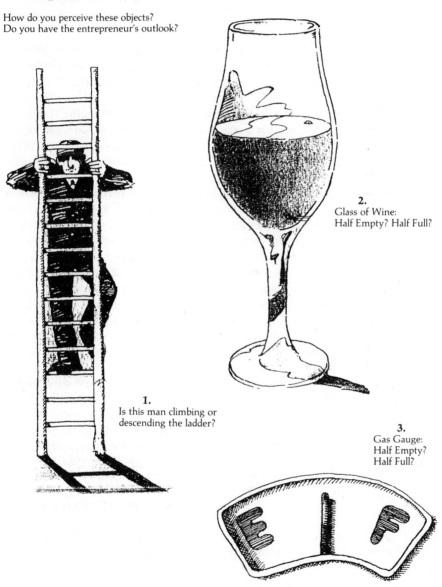

1.
Is this man climbing or
descending the ladder?

2.
Glass of Wine:
Half Empty? Half Full?

3.
Gas Gauge:
Half Empty?
Half Full?

THE LONG SHOT

God made only a few perfect heads ... the rest he covered with hair.

JOE MANCUSO

I have never bet on a horse. I have never played a game of poker or craps for money. I have never bought a sweepstakes ticket or even a state lottery ticket.

Do not take all this to conclude I am a virgin or a prude when it comes to gambling. I have taken many sizable gambles, just never any of the above. Because of my own peculiarity, I have been curious about the behavior that entrepreneurs would exhibit at a horse race. Would they bet on the 20-to-1 shots, the odds-on favorites, or some complicated versions of the daily double? So, in my work with entrepreneurs, I asked questions to learn the answer to the question.

The answers were a bit surprising.

Somehow, I guessed the entrepreneur would be betting on the 10-to-1 shot—you know, the chance to make a killing. I was dead wrong. On the other hand, he would not bet on the house favorite either. The odds were too short.

Entrepreneurs seem to thrive on the 3-to-1 shot; something they feel to be exciting but realistic. Even when our discussions left the topic of horse racing, their attitudes remained the same. They played for the realistic but achievable odds. They set reasonable and obtainable objectives. The philosophy that holds at the track also holds in business. They prefer to bet on the 3-to-1 shot, but then to stand at the rail, shouting and yelling frantically for their horse to run faster. All the noise and commotion seems to help, because the 3 to 1 shots do come in every so often, and it seems to happen more frequently with the support of someone cheering them on.

This brings to mind the story of the blind entrepreneur who walked up to champion golfer Lee Trevino and challenged him to a game. Said the blind entrepreneur, "I'll bet $10,000 that I can win, but you have to let me choose the time and place." Trevino said, "You're crazy. You could never win against me; you're blind! However, for $10,000—you're on!" Said the blind entrepreneur, "Great. I'll meet you tonight at 11:00 P.M. at Pebble Beach!" The perfect long shot.

A WORD ABOUT MOTIVATION

Managers never motivated anyone. When they uncover the rare motivated performer, their task is not to demotivate them.

JOE MANCUSO

Every student of entrepreneurship at one time or another has speculated on what motivates a person to leave a good job and security to start his (or her) own business. Some think the person is basically insecure and must prove his worth. Or he just cannot work for someone else; he has to be his own boss. Others claim that he is bored by the slow pace in a large company and hungers for more action. It has even been suggested that he is motivated by a nagging spouse or the desire to keep up with the Joneses.

Any or all of these factors may influence his decision to strike out on his own. But I think that more often than not it is the realization that as long as he is working for someone else, his employer is getting at least twenty-five percent more worth than what he is paying for. Why shouldn't *he* be getting all that he is worth?

But do not be mislead. It is not the money the entrepreneur is interested in so much as the autonomy of deciding how to allocate his worth. He does not like just anyone mixing in such a personal matter. Money as the sole motivater, in fact, is a poor reason to go into business and is probably the reason behind most failures. Deciding to go into business solely to make money is a mistake.

Most successful companies are founded by someone with an idea, and a dream. Making money and accumulating wealth are usually the by-products for accomplishing some nobler goal. You need an idea or a dream to provide the push for success.

THE ENTREPRENEUR'S BIGGEST ASSET—OR LIABILITY

Of all the home remedies, a good wife is the best.

FRANK McKINNEY HALLARD

There is one thing that can make or break an entrepreneur, given all the other factors I have mentioned. His wife. If a venture capitalist could get to know the wives of all his clients, he would have a far better indication of his clients likelihood of success.

I have toyed with various methods of displaying a wife's value to a small firm on a balance sheet. Which way will she tip the balance? According to research, ninety-nine percent of all entrepreneurs are married, far more than nonentrepreneurs. This is because entrepreneurs need the continuity and stability that marriage can provide.

It is not easy being married to an entrepreneur. You have to live with insecurity and change (often for years), and put up with broken dates, forgotten birthdays, burned dinners, deep depressions, and a multitude of other hardships. But show me an entrepreneur whose wife is content and willing to help her husband, and much more often than not, I will show you success.

An understanding wife gives assurance, consolidation, advice, encouragement, and love. With all that going for you, how could you help but succeed?

I continue to discuss entrepreneurs using the pronoun *he.* The hard facts

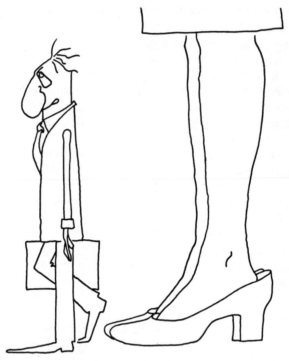

Behind every successful entrepreneur . . .

are that starting, financing, and managing a small business have traditionally been a man's work; women have not chosen to or been encouraged to try in this arena. But this may not be the way of the future. Evidence indicates that more and more women are becoming interested in joining the ranks of entrepreneurs. Hence, this is potentially one of the discipline's most significant changes for the future. The societal changes created by the women's liberation movement are beginning to show up in the small business community. The traits and characteristics of male entrepreneurs, which have existed for centuries, may well change in the near future.

The change may have to do with a growing number of women who seek to start, finance, and manage a small business of their own. It is too soon as yet to determine whether female entrepreneurs will also be overwhelmingly first-born or only children and to know whether they will follow their self-employed mothers as entrepreneurs. (See Chapter 2 about women entrepreneurs and the role of the husband.)

THE BATTING AVERAGE

Babe Ruth struck out 1,330 times in his career.

Every entrepreneur in the course of his career experiences both successes and failures. If you are realistic, you must admit that you cannot strike out every time; neither are you going to clear the fence every time.

Even in his prime, Ted Williams of the Boston Red Sox walked back to the dugout without a hit six out of every ten times at bat. For the entrepreneur, a .400 batting average is not good enough; what he has to do is to get up to bat more often, and thereby get more hits. This does not mean a higher batting average, but it does mean more hits. Improving the batting average is tough; getting more hits just requires more effort.

A friend of mine had the right idea. When asked whether it was better to work hard or to work smart, he said, "I work hard *and* smart. You can't beat that!"

Remember, too, that it is not necessary to choose the best course of action, but you must make the course you choose work . . . and you can do it by getting to bat more often.

THE ENTREPRENEURIAL ROOSTER

Actually, describing an entrepreneur is like trying to describe an elephant when you're standing up close. As you feel and touch the elephant, it's impossible to understand what you're feeling and touching. When you're able to stand back and observe the elephant in perspective, you suddenly discover that that big gray blob of matter is an elephant. The entrepreneur is the same way. We've discussed his traits, his personality, his inner motivation, his secret desires, and all sorts of individual characteristics, but he is a whole human being, who exists more for the value of the whole than the value of the parts.

Let me tell you a story, which I think truly captures the entrepreneurial spirit and one in which you may be better able to visualize the whole person. This tale begins with a farmer who has some chickens, and the chickens are not laying eggs any more. The farmer is disgusted, and he decides to rid his farm of the current crop of roosters. The forty-two roosters are all sent away.

Then the farmer goes to market to buy a new batch of roosters to get his hens laying eggs once again. While the farmer is shopping at the rooster market, a very short, sneaky-looking fellow approaches him and says, "I hear you're looking for forty-two roosters. I think you're crazy because it just so happens that over here in the corner, I got such-a-deal for you. I have a little skinny rooster, an entrepreneur rooster. But I'll tell you from personal experience that this is not an average rooster. This rooster can keep your whole henhouse happy, and they'll be laying eggs again."

The farmer kind of chuckled. "A rooster that size? Do you know how many hens I have?" Finally, when the man offered the farmer a thirty-day, money-back guarantee, it convinced the farmer that he really couldn't go too wrong giving this new rooster a tryout. The farmer took the rooster home, since he had tried just about everything else.

The first few days passed, and the farmer looked out of the window and noticed, much to his surprise, that the chickens were all smiling, happy, and laying eggs. And he was kind of proud of that skinny little fellow, and he said to himself, "By golly, the rooster did the job." After the tenth day, the farmer again looked outside, and not only were the chickens smiling, happy, and laying eggs, but he noticed that the ducks, which were loose in the pond next to the chickens coops, were also smiling, happy, and laying eggs.

A smile beamed across the farmer's face and he said, "By heavens, that little rooster!" A few more days passed and he noticed that not only were the ducks smiling, happy, and laying eggs and the chickens were smiling, happy, and laying eggs, but his very tall ostriches—I mean, really tall, six-to eight-feet high—were smiling, happy, and laying eggs.

In fact, the whole damn farm was smiling, happy, and laying eggs, and the farmer couldn't believe his eyes. This rooster had done the trick and turned the tide. The farmer still kept his eyes on the rooster, just in case. And as the thirtieth day approached, he kept thinking about his money-back guarantee. He looked out of his second-floor bedroom window, but the rooster could not be seen.

The farmer was deeply concerned. So, as he went downstairs toward his pickup truck, he noticed far off in the desert a cloud of dust in the sky, and he wondered what it could be. He hopped into his truck and drove toward that cloud of dust, thinking of that little rooster, and saying, "I wondered how he could ever keep that pace up." As he approached the cloud of dust, he saw a whole flock of vultures circling a limp object laying on the ground. It was the rooster. His feet were up, his tongue was out, and his head was to the side; he looked as dead as a doornail.

The farmer had a double feeling of emotion. On the one hand, he felt that the rooster's death was a tragedy and a waste of an unusual kind of drive and spirit. On the other hand, he remembered that if he didn't get the rooster back in the required thirty days, he was going to lose his money-back guarantee. So he hopped out of the truck, went over to the rooster, and reached down to pick him up to throw him on the truck. Just as he reached down, the rooster turned his head, bit the farmer on the hand, and said, "Shh! This is the only way you can get these vultures."

Here lies the essence of the entrepreneur. A never-ending commitment to go forward when others have stopped. My rooster story, I believe, characterizes the entrepreneur in a single photograph, forever etched on your mind.

A RECAP

One secretary to another: "The efficiency expert has had his eye on me all day. I don't know whether to get busy or act interested."

Now let us put all the traits together to create the whole male entrepreneur. He has a wife, a master's degree, and loads of energy. His self-employed father has made him both an optimist and an individualist. He enjoys talking about his early childhood, which began about 33 years ago as the firstborn child in a middle-class family. He bets on reasonable ventures.

If you do not have this combination of traits, do not despair. Not every entrepreneur has every trait, and if you want to be an entrepreneur, what difference does that make? Just keep in mind the preceding story of the entrepreneurial rooster, which wraps the entrepreneur into a single mental picture. An entrepreneur exists as a whole, not as a sum of the parts.

THE WOMAN
ENTREPRENEUR'S QUIZ

1. A woman entrepreneur is most commodity the--child in the family.

   (a) oldest
   (b) middle
   (c) youngest
   (d) doesn't matter

2. A woman entrepreneur is most commonly:

   (a) married
   (b) widowed
   (c) single
   (d) divorced

3. An entrepreneur is most typically:

   (a) man
   (b) woman
   (c) either

4. An individual begins her first entrepreneurial venture at which of these ages?

   (a) teens
   (b) 20's
   (c) 30's
   (d) 40's
   (e) 50's

5. When does a woman's entrepreneurial tendencies first appear evident?

   (a) teens
   (b) 20's
   (c) 30's
   (d) 40's
   (e) 50's

6. A woman entrepreneur has achieved the following educational attainment by the time she has her first significant business venture:
   (a) grammar school
   (b) high school
   (c) bachelor's degree
   (d) master's degree
   (e) doctorate's degree

7. The woman entrepreneur's primary motivation in starting her own business is:
   (a) to make money
   (b) because she can't work for anyone else
   (c) to be famous
   (d) as an outlet for unused energy
   (e) to obtain a sense of financial independence

8. Primary motivation for a woman entrepreneur's high need for achievement is based upon her relationship with:
   (a) her husband
   (b) her mother
   (c) her father
   (d) her children
   (e) both parents

9. A woman entrepreneur brings which of these items from business to business:
   (a) desk
   (b) chair
   (c) all office furniture
   (d) none of these items

10. To be successful in an entrepreneurial venture, you need an overabundance of:
    (a) money
    (b) luck
    (c) hard work
    (d) good ideas

11. Women entrepreneurs and financiers:
    (a) get along well
    (b) are best of friends
    (c) are cordial friends
    (d) are in secret conflict

12. Successful women entrepreneurs rely on which of these groups for critical management advice:
    (a) internal management team
    (b) external management professionals
    (c) financial sources
    (d) family or friends
    (e) no one else

13. Woman entrepreneurs:
    (a) are best as planners
    (b) are best as doers
    (c) know their astrological signs

14. Female entrepreneurs are:
    (a) high risk takers
    (b) moderate risk takers
    (c) small risk takers
    (d) doesn't matter

15. The only necessary and sufficient ingredient for starting a business is:
    (a) money
    (b) customers
    (c) product
    (d) idea

16. An employee of a woman entrepreneur who reports directly to her should bring the woman entrepreneur/boss which of the following:
    (a) problems to solve
    (b) expense accounts to sign
    (c) business opportunities
    (d) new management practices

17. Which of the following personal characteristics is the best single choice to be possessed by the woman entrepreneur's first mate or right-hand person:
    (a) bright and energetic
    (b) bright and lazy
    (c) dumb and energetic
    (d) dumb and lazy

18. Woman entrepreneurs are:
    (a) life of the party
    (b) a bore at a cocktail party
    (c) will never go to parties
    (d) never fit into a crowd

19. Entrepreneurs tend to "fall in love" too quickly with:
    (a) new product ideas
    (b) new employees
    (c) new manufacturing ideas
    (d) new financial plans
    (e) all of the above

20. All entrepreneurs, at least 99 out of 100:
    (a) keep a dirty, sloppy, and cluttered desk
    (b) are super organized
    (c) are late to meetings
    (d) none of the above

THE WOMAN ENTREPRENEUR'S QUIZ

The following is offered as insight into the question "What makes a woman entrepreneur?" How does her entrepreneur role differ—if it does—from the male? Why is she more at home in a business venture than elsewhere? What makes her willing to spend less time with family, friends, husband? Why can't she be happy working for someone else? Why isn't she more like her mother—or is she? When other girls were practicing for cheerleaders, why was she organizing the prom or developing a stamp or coin collection or selling clothes? What's with her, anyway? Is she really smarter than Wonder Woman, or just some kind of a nut?

What I concluded after research into women entrepreneurs is that these women share many common traits, too many to be coincidental. When I dug deeper into the facts, I developed the following questionnaire based on answers from several hundred women entrepreneurs.

This quiz lacks hard statistical backup, to be sure, but I offer it as insight into the female entrepreneur. Why not try it yourself and see if you've got what it takes to be a woman entrepreneur? You can score the quiz in the privacy of your home or office. No one needs to know the real truth about you except you. These questions should help you to discover whether you have characteristics in common with other female entrepreneurs.

1. A woman entrepreneur is most commonly the _____ child in the family.

   (a) oldest (b) middle (c) youngest (d) doesn't matter

There is no real doubt about this answer. It is (a)—the oldest. All the independently conducted studies agree that entrepreneurs are high achievers, and the same finding holds for both male and female. The oldest child is so often a high achiever because, as the firstborn, he or she is usually showered with vital parental attention early in life. The oldest child in the family inherits the mantle of the family, and when the oldest child is a female, the transference is to her.

About half of all the female entrepreneurs are first children; about two-thirds of all male entrepreneurs are first children. The emphasis is still stronger in the male case, for many reasons, but the female entrepreneur exhibits the same tendencies. Given that about thirty percent of the population are first children, these data are significant. So, it's not just the firstborn son who bears the family heritage, it's the firstborn.

Some other points might be helpful. A high-need achiever is usually, but not always, the first child in the family. Naturally, an only child is also a first child. Some families have children "in clusters." Let's say, for instance, a family has two children, and then a few years pass before a new addition arrives. The newcomer is, in effect, a "second" firstborn child and has about the same likelihood as the "first" firstborn to become an entrepreneur. This is because the real issue is not whether you are the eldest child, but whether your mother and father can expend a proportionally greater amount of energy heaping praise and success on you.

2. A woman entrepreneur is most commonly:

(a) married   (b) widowed   (c) single   (d) divorced

The answer is (a)—married, but interpretation of data on this point varies widely. The question should have been asked in finer detail. Most women in the age bracket of twenty to forty are married. However, so are most women in the United States. While it may be comfortng for chauvinists to believe that most female entrepreneurs are single or divorced, the data do not support this conclusion. In fact, women entrepreneurs who are married are reasonably happily married because they are generally married to supportive husbands, men with enough self-worth to be able to tolerate a two-career family. These entrepreneur wives also make a major contribution within the home.

Although married, entrepreneur women demonstrate greater independence than in most traditional marriages. They are more likely to retain their maiden names rather than adopting their husbands' surnames. It is often common for them to be the bill payer or to have their own separate checkbooks, or to manage their own separate finances. Also, common couple friends for the entrepreneur woman and her husband are likely to be friends from her business associations, not necessarily joint common friends or friends of her husband's from his work. These women like to choose their own friends as a couple as well as individually.

Consequently, the answer is "married," but the details of these marriages are what is truly important.

3. An entrepreneur is most typically _____.

(a) man   (b) woman   (c) either

You might have liked to have answered "woman," but the correct answer is (a)—man. Most entrepreneurs in this country are male. Women are just recently starting their own businesses. Most of the significant entrepreneurial ventures in the country, such as Polaroid, IBM, Xerox, and others, were started by men.

At this count just under 10 percent of American companies are owned and controlled by women. Only one woman controls a venture capital firm out of about 500 companies. There are only a handful of female presidents in *Fortune's* largest companies. There are only seven woman-oriented or controlled banks in the United States, and all have had dismal track records so far. Women are just now being allowed or encouraged to assert themselves in these areas.

Although the answer is still "men," the data are shifting toward a twenty to eighty percent ratio. Women have been successful in a few specific industries, such as cosmetics and food areas, but they are starting to become entrepreneurs in greater numbers. That is why so many books are appearing on the subject and that is why you are reading this quiz.

4. A woman begins her first entrepreneurial venture at which age? (Two answers are possible.)

   (a) teens   (b) twenties   (c) thirties   (d) forties   (e) fifties

The answer is (b) and (c)—twenties and thirties; but the data are a little confusing. In *The Enterprising Man,* in 1958, Collins and Moore said that the entrepreneurial male began his first significant venture around the age of forty. Later, Professor Ed Roberts of MIT discovered that the male entrepreneur starts his own business at the age of thirty-five. My own research revealed that from thirty to thirty-five were the dominant ages. The data for women are confusing because the time of the first venture is not related as much to chronological age as childbearing age. Most married women who become entrepreneurs do so either before or after bearing children, with about a twenty-year gap in between. The women we interviewed were either starting businesses at the age of about thirty-seven, after their children were grown, or about the age of twenty-four, prior to having a family. So, the answer is both twenties and thirties.

5. When are a woman's entrepreneurial tendencies first evident?

   (a) teens   (b) twenties   (c) thirties   (d) forties   (e) fifties

The answer is (a)—teens. Entrepreneurial traits show up early in the life of the enterprising woman. Many of the entrepreneurial women interviewed had started businesses in their teens and surely were into business or into business ventures by the time they entered college. The most common kinds of activity were selling and organizing. They would often organize dances and hops, or solicit groups or church bingos, or they would have some sort of food or collecting specialty, such as rocks, coins, or stamps. Their business enterprises were initially very small, but they were the early signs of their entrepreneurial tendencies. They enjoyed organizing and achieving, and when they began to like such activities more, the rewards were measurable and tangible.

6. A woman entrepreneur has achieved what educational level by the time she has her first significant business venture?

(a) grammar school   (b) high school   (c) bachelor's degree
(d) master's degree   (e) doctorate degree

The answer is (c)—bachelor's degree. Where the majority of male entrepreneur's now hold master's degrees, typically in engineering, the women entrepreneur, at this stage, is more likely to have a bachelor's degree with a liberal arts background. It is probable that as more fields open up to women, and consequently more women venture out into their own businesses, that they, too, will seek higher degrees in more technical areas.

7. The woman entrepreneur's primary motivation in starting her own business is:

(a) to make money   (b) because she can't work for anyone else
(c) to be famous   (d) as an outlet for unused energy
(e) to obtain a sense of financial independence

The tendency for both male and female entrepreneurs is to be one's own boss. But the entrepreneurial woman is often a multifaceted individual, capable, unlike many male entrepreneurs, of working for the right person under the right circumstances. The primary reason she starts her own small business is (e)—to obtain a sense of financial independence. She does not want to be dependent on anyone or a drag on the economic system. She wants to be her own person. Starting her own business is often her outlet to express that need. Her secondary motivation is that she has difficulty working for others.

8. Primary motivation for a woman entrepreneur's high need for achievement is based on her relationship with:

(a) her husband   (b) her mother   (c) her father
(d) her children   (e) both parents

In the man's case, it is the father-son relationship that is the dominant reason for starting one's own business. Consequently, I wondered in my research what was the dominant relationship for a female starting her own small business. I discovered that many of these woman had fathers who were self-employed and who treated their daughters as they would have treated or did treat sons. So, I began to believe that it was the father-daugher relationship, just as the father-son, that made the difference. But in many cases I noticed the presence of a very strong mother, one who was also active in social, charitable, and volunteer work besides raising a family. Therefore, my answer to this question is (e)—both parents. The combination of father and mother convinces the daughter to become an entrepreneur.

9. A woman entrepreneur brings which of these items from business to business?

(a) desk   (b) chair   (c) all office furniture   (d) none of these

The answer for men has been one of Joe Mancuso's trademarks—it's a chair. Male entrepreneurs often enjoy bringing their chairs from business to business. Salespeople enjoy a good comfortable driver's seat (usually a bucket seat) and when they buy a new car, it is not uncommon for them to transfer the old front seat to the new car. I examined this chair/seat issue for females and discovered that most women have not begun starting multiple businesses. Further, I found that most women who start one business do not immediately seek to start another. I am not confident that enough time has elapsed to develop an accurate feel for the preferences a woman may demonstrate in the office furniture area. Compared to women, men seem a little more flighty and prefer to start one business, get it going, sell it, and start another. In these early stages of data collection, I cannot claim that women have carried their chairs from one business to another. So, the answer is (d)—not enough data to know. What I can claim, based on the survey, is that women haven't started multiple businesses.

   10. To be successful in an entrepreneurial venture, you need all four items below, but which one the most?

   (a) money   (b) luck   (c) hard work   (d) good ideas

Most people answer this incorrectly, but it really should be obvious. We all know that money alone is not enough to make an entrepreneurial venture successful. The classic story of Viatron in Boston—where about $50 million of public monies was invested in the early 1970s prior to bankrupty—indicates the ineffectiveness of money alone. Even Ford Motor Company couldn't use its financial muscle to make the Edsel a success. They gave it a $250 million shove, but it still wouldn't start and Ford lost all that money.

   Hard work and a good idea are helpful in starting and succeeding in a small business, but mere hard work can't make a troublesome situation into a success. A good idea offers a greater chance of success as well, but a great many good ideas also end up on the garbage heap.

   But luck—answer (b)—is a different matter. More and more, luck compensates signficantly for other weaknesses. Of the successful entrepreneurs, both male and female, I studied in an eight-year period, everyone agreed that they had been damn lucky. A few key breaks early, according to them, were what made the difference. The data are identical for men and women. Sorry, if you answered this question incorrectly—you just weren't lucky!

   11. Women entrepreneurs and financiers:

   (a) get along well   (b) are best of friends   (c) are cordial and respected friends   (d) are in secret conflict

There is a clear-cut answer for women; (c)—are cordial and respected friends. For men the answer is (d). There is a relationship between women entrepreneurs and financiers that is generally built on mutual respect. Men are more likely to be in secret conflict with their financiers, and often hostile relationships develop between the two.

12. Successful women entrepreneurs rely on which of these groups for critical management advice?

    (a) internal management team   (b) external management professionals
    (c) financial sources   (d) family or friends   (e) no one else

The data on women for this question are not so conclusive as for men. It does not appear that the women entrepreneur depends on external management professionals, at least to any large degree, as men do. She seems not to be as at ease with consultants as her male counterpart; she is not at home with anyone she cannot trust fully. Trust for the woman entrepreneur seems to be a very fundamental issue, and building up trust takes time and experience. She will generally rely only on those people she trusts, such as family or friends, which is the correct answer—(d). Her family and close friends are typically the ones she turns to for personal and business decisions. Usually she is able to choose among family and friends those with significant business experience. This may sound unsound at first, but these people for women are usually more effective than the consultants are for men. They tend to care deeply and personally about the outcome.

13. Women entrepreneurs differ from men entrepreneurs in that they:

    (a) are best as planners   (b) are best as doers
    (c) know their astrological signs

When one of my colleagues read my male entrepreneurs quiz, he immediately remarked that a female entrepreneur was no different in characteristics than the male. She would score the same as a male on the male quiz. The only real difference, he claimed, was that the female knows her astrological sign and the male doesn't! At first, I thought that was merely a funny comment, but it prompted me to check, and lo and behold, almost all female entrepreneurs did know their astrological signs! So, the answer is (c). Further, they were likely to display or discuss the signs (which are often used as guides for decision-making), whereas the few males who did know their signs had to be prompted to reveal them. The female integrates it into her discussion because she attempts to show her ability to be intuitive and logical on certain issues. They say that God created men first because he needed an initial "rough draft."

14. Female entrepreneurs are:

    (a) high risk takers   (b) moderate risk takers   (c) small risk takers
    (d) no risk takers

Males generally are moderate risk takers. They choose realistic but achievable risks if possible. The female entrepreneur is, by comparison, a small risk taker (c); her percentage of acceptable risk is much less than her male counterpart. She is concerned about risk because, in turn, she is concerned about financial independence and is seldom willing to bet on anything other than what she feel is sure. She would rather have a fifty/fifty chance of making $1,000 by spending $100 for a lottery ticket than to spend $1,000 on a fifty/fifty chance of making one million dollars.

15. The only necessary ingredient for starting a business is;

(a) money (b) customers (c) product (d) idea

A business starts with an order and an order only comes from a customer—so the answer is (b). A business revolves around customers, and it begins when someone offers to buy something. Entrepreneurs start with an order. The significant difference between a woman and a man entrepreneur has more to do with the type of ventures they start. A typical male entrepreneur is often dedicated to starting a product or a manufacturing venture in which technology is the key element. A typical female entrepreneur is more likely to be involved in a service-related area. The problem with service-related businesses is that they employ more people. People are expensive, and they seldom produce the amount of work that is necessary for success. They want to take vacations and they want to have holidays. It costs a good deal to employ people. Consequently, the woman entrepreneur is often fruitlessly organizing people to perform a new and better service, like driving kids after school, or a cleaning service, a maid service, a teaching service, or a nursery school service. All of these businesses are people-intensive. Unfortunately, most businesses that are people- or labor-intensive fail, especially in America where wage-based taxes are so high as to stifle labor-intensive businesses. In fact, payroll-related taxes have averaged about 24 percent of payroll, and for a business that seeks to make a profit of 10 percent, these costs are killers.

16. An employee of a woman entrepreneur who reports directly to her should bring the woman entrepreneur/boss which of the following:

(a) problems to solve (b) expense accounts to sign
(c) business opportunities (d) new management practices

The answer to this question for the male entrepreneur is actually funny; really, how can a person working for a male entrepreneur bring a problem to him? A new problem totally absorbs him and gets him uptight and emotionally drained. Never bring a male entrepreneur/boss a problem. He has enough problems of his own. Fair is fair. But it's not the same for a woman. A woman entrepreneur is usually very much at home in solving problems, especially people problems. She is sensitive to people issues. She prefers that people problems be brought directly to her, for her to solve—answer (a). If so-and-so is not getting along with so-and-so, she prefers to know it. She likes to know what is going on in her organization. Consequently, you should bring your problems to your female entrepreneur.

17. Which of the following personal characteristics is the best choice for the entrepreneur's first assistant to have?

(a) dumb and energetic   (b) bright and energetic   (c) dumb and lazy
(d) bright and lazy

The answer is priceless, so pay close attention to this rule. "Dumb and energetic" is a poor choice because this assistant would be forever starting new projects, talking out of turn at meetings, and asking the same question three times. And if she is really energetic, she will drive the whole company—and you, as the entrepreneur—crazy.

"Bright and energetic" has personally characteristics similar to the entrepreneur's. However, she is also a poor choice to join your varsity. This "bright type" usually alienates her peers on her way up the ladder. But you shouldn't keep her on the junior varsity solely because of distrust. If people with these traits aren't their own entrepreneurs, they will soon become frustrated and develop ulcers. And team members must be healthy!

"Dumb and lazy" is the poorest choice of all, because the few tasks she actually accomplishes are done badly. She should not even be in your company, let alone be chosen as a member of the management team.

The fourth choice—and bless this type, because companies are built around them—is "bright and lazy"—(d), the correct answer. She works well with the entrepreneur and does not try to surpass her energies. She will let the entrepreneur put in more hours than she does so that they will develop a mutual respect.

She can be awfully clever at thinking of ways to get out of work and at getting others to do it for her. She is the best choice for your first mate—and let her pick the varsity. The real value of a lazy/bright type is her ability to absorb entrepreneurial energies without budging an inch. The entrepreneur arrives to work at 6:00 a.m. and has all her work finished by the time the workers arrive. She will then charge into the office of the second-in-command and deposit a wad of paperwork on her desk and delegate all the day's work. While the entrepreneur returns to her office, the second lieutenant who is bright and energetic will scamper to attack the immense pile of new work. But the lazy/bright person will let it sit there unattended until afternoon. That is the secret to this type's success. You see, women entrepreneurs, much like their male counterparts, change their mind and their work just before lunch. So, most initial work done to satisfy the entrepreneur is either done three times or not at all. Naturally, a successful entrepreneur desires to have everything going for her, and this is how she overcomes the numerous obstacles. A way of capitalizing on the entrepreneur's inherent inability to delegate is to select this talent in your partners or key employees.

Below is a framework for an enterpreneur to use in picking a first mate.

THE FIRST MATE MATRIX

	Stupid	Bright
Energetic	0	0
Lazy	0	X

Use this matrix when selecting an entrepreneur's management team.

18. Entrepreneurs:

   (a) are the life of a party   (b) are boring at a cocktail party
   (c) will never go to parties   (d) fit into the crowd at a party

You probably guessed that entrepreneurs never go to cocktail parties, but you are dead wrong. These people need socializing just to unwind. They are almost never the life of the party since such people usually drink and talk too much. Entrepreneurs seldom talk too much. They are not traditionally showoffs. If anything, they are a little boring, but that judgment depends on the values of the person engaged in the conversation with the entrepreneur. To many academicians, entrepreneurs are boring misfits and judged as oddballs. But to many others, academicians are eggheads and misfits—so it's a circle with no end. I don't find discussions about a new short cut to work or a new tip on a hot security boring. My life would be over if I couldn't dream of a faster way to go from here to there. So, to me, these people seem to fit into the crowd; to others, they may be boring. But because I put the twenty questions in this quiz together, I'll pick *my* answer as right (d). They just fit into the crowd, which demonstrates another entrepreneurial trait—they don't make mistakes.

19. Women entrepreneurs tend to "fall in love" too quickly with:

   (a) new product ideas   (b) new employees
   (c) new manufacturing ideas   (d) new financial plans
   (e) all the above

Isn't this a fun question? One of the big weaknesses to which many entrepreneurs are prone is the tendency to "fall in love" too easily. They go wild over new employees, products, suppliers, machines, methods, and financial plans. Anything new excites them. These "love affairs" usually don't last long; many are over as suddenly as they begin, rather like a sudden summer shower. The problem is that during these affairs, the entrepreneur may alienate some people, be stubborn about listening to opposite views, and lose objectivity. It is a dangerous trait if practiced with intense passion. A good medicine for this disease is to spend a few moments a day recalling past infatuations. While you are daydreaming about your "love affairs," extend the practice to just old-fashioned daydreaming about anything at all. Daydreaming isn't all bad, as it tends to sharpen subconscious ideas and, in turn, stimulate hunches.

The combination of a woman's intution and an entrepreneur's intuition may be the single greatest asset of the woman entrepreneur. This tendency to be intuitive is not all bad either, and that's why daydreaming is so necessary. The process of guessing right and betting on hunches is a positive feature known as the entrepreneur's intuition. Rather than destroying the sensation of pursuing new problem-solving methods, a wiser entrepreneur would only seek to control or modify her intuitive impulse. A careful program of checks and balances, which is monitored by a good financial officer or an active board of directors, can accomplish this objective. Ignoring the intuition could relegate one of the positive features of entrepreneurs to a neutral status. The controlling mechanism takes some prior planning to get established, but having a monitoring function in place prior to a crisis is the issue of an ounce of prevention versus a pound of cure. Organizing to capitalize on intuitive hunches is a trait well worth acquiring. The answer to this question, incidentially, is (e)—all of the above.

20. Practically all entrepreneurs:

    (a) keep a sloppy and cluttered desk   (b) are superorganized
    (c) are late to meetings   (d) none of the above

You had better pay close attention to this answer. Here is the fundamental law of the entrepreneurial manager, and I've saved the first law for the last question. All entrepreneurs are (b)—superorganized—and that is the big secret that allows them to do tasks faster and better. Some have neat desks, some have cluttered desks, some have both at different times. Most, but not all, are never late for anything, meetings included. Most manage their time very well and that is why they out-perform others. They are usually on time and sometimes a little early.

Answer (b) is a perfect way to end this quiz, for the true entrepreneur, the dyed-in-the-wool captain of the American capitalistic system would never have labored so tediously through these time-consuming twenty questions. Because they are superorganized, they would have discovered that the answers are on the following page!

Entrepreneurs have a system. Some keep index cards or a notepad "jogger" in their pocket or purse on which they list things to do. Then they tick them off, one by one, as they are done. Others keep a neatly arranged "to do" list on their desks with about fifteen items listed. The first four or five items are usually crossed off. Still another type stuffs all pockets with little scraps of paper. To keep track of what is done, they switch the scraps from one place to another. Some even send their lovers or children memos or carbon copies of memos to keep them informed. Can you imagine a memo from Mom that says, "I'll be in Florida at such a number if you need me." Really, aren't they super-organized!

I wish you all good luck, regardless of your score. Below are the answers, so that you can score yourself on the entrepreneur quiz. I have also included a scale so that you can compare your results with those of others.

Answers

1. (a) oldest
2. (a) married
3. (a) man
4. (b) twenties   (c) thirties
5. (a) teens
6. (c) bachelor's degree
7. (e) to obtain a sense of financial independence
8. (e) both parents
9. (d) not enough data to know
10. (b) luck
11. (c) are cordial and respected friends
12. (d) family or friends
13. (c) know their astrological signs
14. (c) small risk takers
15. (b) customers
16. (a) problems to solve
17. (d) bright and lazy
18. (d) fit into the crowd at a party
19. (e) all the above
20. (b) are super organized

Numbers of Questions Answered Correctly
15 or more: Successful Entrepreneur
13-15: Entrepreneur
11-13: Latent Entrepreneur
8-11: Potential Entrepreneur
5-8: Borderline Entrepreneur
5 or less: Hired Hand

THE IDEA STAGE

THOMAS EDISON

*The objective of all dedicated employees should be to thoroughly analyze
all situations, anticipate all problems prior to their occurrence, have
answers for those problems, and move swiftly to solve these problems
when called upon . . . However, . . . when you are up to your ass in
alligators it is difficult to remind yourself that your initial objective was to
drain the swamp.*

Where do good ideas come from? Why do some people have better ideas than
other people? What is creativity? Why are some people more creative than
others? Again, these are universal questions—and again, there are no universal
answers. But there are some clues.

Few thoughts and ideas are actually new. In fact, it is shocking to find how
many are not new at all, but really the same old ideas warmed over and served in
a new package.

There are two schools of thought on entrepreneurial creativity. One says "let us think hard and long for something truly new; let us make a significant breakthrough and be the only ones with our device." The second school tends more toward repackaging, and says that "a frimble works fine in such and such a case; let us see if we can apply it to a new situation." It is more a process of transferring techniques, products, or services from one area to another. The first computer-dating service, for example, was not a new invention, but rather a new use of existing data-processing capability.

Now let us look at what is really new, not just warmed over. Let us face reality and ask ourselves how frequently the opportunity occurs to do something substantially different. I claim that if you were to examine technology and companies you would find that very few new companies are based on new concepts and ideas. Most are based on the repackage of old ideas.

On the other hand, the big rewards and the real excitement come from the breakthroughs of new concepts, such as Polaroid, Xerox, IBM, McDonalds, Kentucky Fried Chicken, and a host of others. Each of these companies was truly new and the success of each is well known. It does appear that many successful new companies started with great ideas that were dramatic departures from the past. The companies with the big winning formulas and the best track records have unique products.

When you look at an idea for a new business, ask yourself whether your idea is really new or whether it is a reworked version of someone else's basic concepts. If you discover that it is not new, you should find it easier to understand why you are having difficulty in bringing the idea to fruition. The reason should be obvious. If you had to choose between investing in Polaroid, Xerox, and IBM or investing in your own company, which would you choose? How much better is your product? How different is it from what it replaces or to what it is most similar?

Watching a new idea blossom into a business is always exciting. There is an unexplainable thrill in working in the area of the unborn. Perhaps it is similar to the feelings of a new expectant mother. What will the unborn be like?

One thing that kills many good ideas is coldly logical reasoning. It is too easy to think of reasons why an idea will not succeed. An individual's prior training can destroy some wonderful thoughts. This is especially true for engineers and scientists. So, do not apply only logical reasoning to new business concepts—it is not fair. The momentous decisions in life should not have to stand up to the test of reasoning—at least not in their beginning stages. The ideas are usually not strong enough at this early stage of life. For instance, you would probably never marry if logical reasoning was the criterion. Most people marry on the basis of plain old emotion. Despite your prior training, the selection of a mate was *not* a scientific calculation.

Starting a new business isn't all that different from starting a new marriage; it is just a little more risky. Let a little emotion enter the decision; there will be plenty of time for cold logic later, after the idea grows into a business. Emotion and creativity are the food for new ideas, and if the idea is fed with hearty food, it can be a truly new notion. That is how people like Thomas Edison can do what he did. It is amazing, truly amazing.

THE IDEA

There is nothing more difficult to take in hand, more perilous to conduct, or more uncertain in its success, than to take the lead in the introduction of a new order of things.

NICOLO MACHIAVELLI
The Prince

Having a business of your own is not too different from having a child. You experience many of the same emotions and problems. And, as with a child, starting one is half the fun. The conception of the business starts with an idea.

Of all the stages in the development of a business, the idea stage is probably the most interesting and rewarding. The world is your oyster and the opportunities seem endless. And they are!

Every business starts with an idea. Successful businesses start with good ideas. Entrepreneurs always generate more ideas than nonentrepreneurs. They're not all good ideas, and for every entrepreneur who builds a business around a good idea, there are dozens of other men who earlier had the same idea. The entrepreneur, however, has the drive and ability to follow through.

Also at this stage the entrepreneur may find that he talks to himself. As a friend of mine once put it: "Small business is a lonely existence, so it's not surprising that you end up talking to yourself." I'd like to add that it's not that you talk to yourself that matters, but rather what you say. So listen carefully. The idea has to make sense to you—and to others, too.

FROGS THRASHING

You can see things, and you say, "Why?" But you see things that never were, and you say, "Why not?"

GEORGE BERNARD SHAW

Do you ever feel you are going backward instead of forward? Ever feel discouraged because your closest friend secretly advised you to throw in the towel? When you need a ray of sunlight, stop for a moment and recall this story of the two frogs who fell into a bucket of cream. For a few minutes both frogs jumped about, trying to swim and stay alive, but the outlook was gloomy. The first frog decided to call it quits, and he slowly sank to the bottom of the bucket. After all, he reasoned, why expend all that effort only to delay the inevitable?

The second frog wasn't as capable a thinker as the first frog, and he just kept on thrashing and jumping. As his body tired, he just moved faster and tried harder. He didn't realize the wisdom of giving up, and lo and behold, all his churning finally turned the cream into butter. He jumped out of the bucket and lived to thrash again another day.

AN ENTREPRENEURIAL
MARKETING ORIENTATION

The most vital quality a soldier can possess is self-confidence—utter, complete, and bumptious.

Author Unknown

A business's success in the marketplace depends on its total commitment to marketing, on whether the organization is entirely embued with the marketing concept or whether it views its marketing as an entity separate and independent of the other divisions. Commitment to a marketing orientation must permeate the organizational whole, from the entrepreneur through every major employee.

Too often, the concept of marketing has been limited to the sole endeavor of selling. Although selling is an integral part of total marketing, it does not encompass the whole of the marketing concept. The essence of marketing is an entrepreneurial venture is evidenced in five major areas of endeavor. To fulfill and utilize the marketing concept to serve the needs of the company and, in turn, increase sales, a marketing organization must do the following:

1. Define its market area.
2. Research consumer needs and wants.
3. Develop and redevelop product and/or service to meet the demand.
4. Recruit, select, and train a work force to deliver the product or service.
5. Develop its sales approach and advertising support.

A person seldom begins a journey unless first knowing the desired desitnation; and if he or she is a careful traveler, the route, the stops, and the time of arrival have been planned, and he or she has determined how much it will cost to get there. If you don't know where you are going, any road will take you there. The lead dog in a sled dog team exchanges an unobstructed view for a willingness to set the course. When the lead dog has a marketing orientation, the team can run swiftly to its destination.

COGNITIVE DISSONANCE

One entrepreneur to another: "I leave my problems at work; I have another set of problems at home."

MATT LORBER

Cognitive dissonance is a term that behavioral scientists may toss about at cocktail parties. Dreamed up by Dr. Leo Festinger of Columbia University, New York City, in the late 1950s, it means that when a person has made a difficult decision, he or she soon notices a sense of discomfort rooted in the fear that the decision was wrong. To alleviate that discomfort, the person searches for anything to confirm the original choice or rationalize it.

Entrepreneurs suffer from the cognitive dissonance disease. After they leave a secure job and steady income to start their own business, the disease sets in. The only way to beat it is to recheck the facts after the decision is made. You will be surprised at the amount of evidence you turn up to support that decision. The greatest danger is that the disease can spread to others less involved in the firm. Remember, cognitive dissonance is contagious.

WHAT IS THE DIFFERENCE
BETWEEN HUMAN BEINGS AND MICE?

The meek have already inherited the Earth; only they don't know it yet.

BUCKMINSTER FULLER

You may initially take this title as a tongue-in-cheek comment, but only after further reflection of happenings in small companies will the concept of mice and human beings be fully understood. What would be different between these two animal species if each were subjected to the famous controlled-maze test?

If a piece of cheese is placed in a maze at the end of the second tunnel and a mouse enters the maze, the mouse will run to the end of the first tunnel sniffing for the cheese; when it fails to discover the cheese, it will travel to the end of the second tunnel, sniff until it discovers the cheese, then sit down and eat it. If you move the cheese to the third tunnel, the mouse will begin by running down the first tunnel, sniffing until it discovers there is no cheese, and then will repeat the process in the second tunnel. When it goes down the third tunnel, it will discover the cheese and eat it. Now, if you move the cheese to the fourth tunnel, the process will repeat iteself until the mouse eventually finds the cheese and eats it. It never fails that the mouse finds the cheese and eats it. There is never an occasion when the mouse will not eat the cheese.

In the case of the human being, when the cheese is placed in the second tunnel, the human being will enter the maze and traverse the first tunnel looking for the cheese; not finding it, he will proceed to the second tunnel, and he too will find the cheese and eat. If that process is repeated several times, the human being will go directly down to the second tunnel, bypassing the first, and look for the piece of cheese. He will begin the searching process immediately at the second tunnel, once he determines that the cheese is located there. Now, if after a pattern of success in the second tunnel is established, should you move the cheese to the fourth tunnel, the human being will immediately bypass the first tunnel and go down the end of the second tunnel to look for the cheese. If it is not there, and if the pattern was established, he will demand to know *why* it's not there! He will stand and shout and yell and complain and gripe that the cheese was supposed to be in the second tunnel and that someone moved it.

The human being will stand in the second tunnel and shout and yell until someone brings him some cheese. He will refuse to move throughout the unending tunnels in the maze to find the cheese because someone moved it and he has come to know that it was supposed to be in the second tunnel. In essence, he believes he is right! The cheese is supposed to be in the second tunnel, and rather than look for the cheese, he will stand hungry in the position of being right.

It would seem from this that human beings would rather be right than have cheese! Being right can be a greater reward than having cheese. There lies the great difference between mice and human beings. Mice will always eat the cheese. Human beings will only eat the cheese when they are also right.

BREAKFAST MEETINGS

Keep in mind the difference between a commitment and a contribution whenever you enjoy a breakfast of ham and eggs. The chicken made a contribution, but the pig made a commitment.

GUY MAINILLA

This may sound unreal, but let me assure you it is true—entrepreneurs hold breakfast meetings. Now we all know they work hard-long hours, holidays, and weekends. But so do the big executives running large corporations in New York, Chicago, and Los Angeles. It is the old puritan ethic—"keep your nose to the grindstone and you will succeed." But our friendly entrepreneur takes this ethic one step further—he *is* the grindstone. He meets his colleagues for breakfast; just imagine. And if he is a real grind, he can go five or six days without taking one meal at home. In fact, the Smaller Business Association of New England (SBANE) holds monthly breakfast meetings. A breakfast get-together is normal for these folks.

I have always wondered how many new businesses were formed out of breakfast meetings. When you are up with the chickens, for some strange reason, the ideas seem to flow more freely.

THE PRODUCT NOTION

When in doubt, win the trick. *

EDMUND HOYLE, 1672-1769

Good ideas are plentiful, but good plans for profitable enterprises are few and far between. Profitable enterprises are all based on good ideas—in a process that roughly follows this sequence:

Idea—bread board—prototype—product notion—first sale—repeat sale—product profitability—profitable enterprise.

It is a long chain with many links and kinks. The danger rests in looking only at one end of the chain.

The chain's weakest link is usually the product notion, not the idea. This is the moment when someone sends a check for your notion. When raising venture capital, success will rest with your projections for enterpirse profitability. But during the idea stage, keep your eye on what it takes to sell the first unit.

Whereas your business plan may predict a going concern with $250,000 and three years, it is all pie-in-the-sky when you have only an idea. The real issue is "how much and how long will it take until the product notion?" That is the apple. Keep your eyes peeled for it.

A FORMULA FOR SUCCESS

Entrepreneurship is a golden glitter by which the rest hope to join the rich.

KARYN MANCUSO

When an entrepreneur is starting a business, the last thought to enter his or her head is failure, which is as it should be. However, keep in mind the wise words of Henry Ford, America's great entrepreneur, who said, "Failure is the opportunity to begin again, more intelligently." One of the ingredients most necessary for success is failure. Entrepreneurs nearly always pass through failure on the road to success. Most do not even try to avoid it, recognizing that it may be only a

*24 Rules for Learners, Rule #12.

necessary detour on the way. Think of failure as a resting place, and you are in the proper frame of mind to start a business.

Remember, too, that success is relative. In other words, you must measure it against a level of accomplishment: such-and-such was more or less successful than something else. To express it another way, success (or lack of it) is what is left after you subtract your total failures from your total successes. It is the remainder that counts.

There is a fundamental law of business, which governs success and failure, commonly known as Murphy's Law. Like the law of gravity, it cannot be fully comprehended; it is just accepted as a universal truth. On the basis of my experience, it is especially pertinent to the entrepreneur. When starting a business, remember Murphy's Law: If anything can go wrong, it will. Mancuso's corollary to Murphy's Law adds: "When it goes wrong for you, it will be when you least expect it." You will see.

Some authorities have held that Murphy's Law was first expounded when he stated that:

If anything can go wrong, it will during the demonstration.

Nothing is as simple as it seems.

Everything takes longer than it should.

The more innocuous a change appears, the further its influence will extend.

Any wire cut to length will be too short.

The necessity of making a major design change increases as the fabrication of the system approaches completion.

Tolerances will accumulate unidirectionally toward maximum difficulty of assembly.

The availability of a component is inversely proportional to the need for that component.

Identical units tested under identical conditions will not be identical in the field.

If a project requires N components, there will be N-1 units in stock.

Firmness of delivery dates is inversely proportional to the tightness of the schedule.

A dropped tool will land where it can do the most damage (also known as the Law of Selective Gravitation).

Dimensions will always be expressed in the least usable term. Velocity, for example, will be expressed in furlongs per fortnight.

An important Instruction Manual or Operating Manual will have been discarded by the Receiving Department.

Probability of failure of a component, assembly, subsystem, or system is inversely proportional to ease of repair or replacement.

A transistor protected by a fast-acting fuse will protect the fuse by blowing first.

Left to themselves, things always go from bad to worse.

Nature always sides with the hidden flaw.

In any given miscalculation, the fault will never be placed if more than one person is involved.

If everything seems to be going well, you have obviously overlooked something.

In any given situation, the factor that is most obviously above suspicion will be the source of error.

Original drawings will be mangled by the copying machine.

The man who developed one of the most profound concepts of the twentieth century is practically unknown to most engineers. He is a victim of his own law. Destined for a secure place in the engineering hall of fame, something went wrong. His real contribution lay not merely in the discovery of the law, but more in its universality and in its impact. The law itself, though inherently simple, has formed a foundation on which future generations will build.

In fact, the law first came to him in all its simplicity when his bride-to-be informed him of the impending birth of an heir to the family fortunes.

YOUR PRODUCT

There is hardly anything in the world that some man cannot make a little worse and sell a little cheaper.

JOHN RUSKIN

Venture capitalists always claim that they bet on management when making an investment. They would like you to believe that the people involved, your investors, future investors, and board of directors included, form the axis about which your success revolves.

I'll take exception to that. Give me a good product every time. I've seen plenty of talented people, who had no trouble raising venture money, fall flat with poor products—and I've seen some no-talents pull one out on the strength of a good product.

Right now, at the first stages of a new venture, remember that the most important ingredient is the product (or service), not the people. Good people will be easy to find later. And don't let the venture capitalists scare you. If they're so smart, how come they only hit about two out of ten?

Of the several hundred small firms I've worked with, the product area chosen has made the difference. The pattern for success begins when someone discovers or identifies a product that has enormous demand—you know, a product for which customers are willing to exchange cash. The enterprise may make all the classic management mistakes, but the product pulls them over the hill. Food management can fail with a poor product, so choose wisely.

I tried forecasting Tops-Down and went broke, but Bottoms-Up is working much better.

THE GOLDEN RULE

I always play to the other team's strength, because if you beat them there, you beat them good.

VINCE LOMBARDI

Launching new products has not been a champagne-bottle busting affair. A new product's success is measured against a previous sales forecast. Sales predictions are the nerve center of the business plan. Of course, new products have no sales history, and forecasting is difficult at best—but a forecast is the foundation for the vital business plan.

There are two basic approaches to predicting sales for new products. The first technique is called *bottoms up*. The bottoms-up technique requires a build-up of sales by identifying potential customers and then summing the customer requirements. Probabilities of buying are acceptable as long as you can pinpoint the customer and the application. Here it is more important to know that the customer *will* buy than it is to know how much he'll buy. Differences wash out if your customer base is above 25 companies.

The second technique, by far the more common of the two, is known as *tops down*. The tops-down technique requires that you estimate the total market and then predict your firm's expected market penetration. This technique has two dangerous weaknesses. First, errors abound in estimating the total market. Second, and more important, accurate penetration predictions are nonexistent. Typical of this technique are business plans for the new products annually introduced in the automotive industry. The sales forecast usually states: "In the U.S.A., nine million new cars are manufactured annually. We anticipate selling our product to 1-1/4 percent of these new car owners. Thus our first year sales will be 112,500 units." Oh yeah?

Just as in life, the Golden Rule is so sensible and obvious. It's the silent secret to happiness and success. Few follow it and, as a result, turmoil reigns. Remember the entrepreneurial Golden Rule—Bottoms Up.

THE
START-UP
PROBLEM

WHAT IS AN ENTREPRENEURIAL VENTURE?

There have been great debates on the definition of "entrepreneur" and "small business." Just what is a small business? Or, better yet, what differentiates a small business from an entrepreneurial venture? Below are three definitions of what is a small business and how it differs from an entrepreneurial venture, from three views—my own, Peter Drucker's, and the Small Business Association.

1. My definition of an entrepreneurial venture is a business enterprise founded by an entrepreneur or an entrepreneurial team dedicated to providing not only employment for the founders, but also for a significant group of other people. Moreover, it accomplishes this good by delivering new and better products or services to the marketplace. In addition, a small business occurs when one person can run the show. Unfortunately, this broad definition allows companies such as ITT to qualify as a small business or an entrepreneurial venture. Yet, by most other classifications, they would not qualify.

2. Peter Drucker's definition of a small business is when one person knows all of the key people. His definition of a medium-sized business is when only your team managers know who the key people are. The definition of big business is when your key people do not know who the key people are.

3. The SBA has a changing set of definitions for a small business. Below is the current definition as provided by the Office of Economic Research, a small business advocacy office in Washington, D.C. It was this definition that came under intense discussion at a recent White House Conference.

SMALL BUSINESS	EMPLOYMENT SIZE	ASSET SIZE	SALES SIZE
Independent Contractor	0	0	Under 100,000
Family size	1-4	Under $100,000	$100,000-500,000
Small	5-19	$100-5,000	$500,000-$1 million
Medium	20-99	$500,000-5 million	$1-10 million
Large	100-499	$5-25 million	$10 million-50 million
Total Small Business	0-500	$0-25 million	$0-50 million
Medium Business	500-999	$25-100 million	$50-250 million
Large Business	1,000+	$100 million+	$250 million+
Government Size Business	10,000+	$2 billion	$2 billion+

Under the SBA guidelines, certain small businesses can qualify for SBA loans. Small businesses that do not meet these loan requirements can also be awarded SBA loans in certain circumstances. SBA used certain criteria for defining small business, number of employees, dollar sales volume, type of business, and nature of business within industry. A manufacturing enterprise is small if less than 250 people are employed, but this varies with the industry, for example, American Motors with 25,000 employees has been classified as small because it has less than five percent market share. A steel-rolling mill is small with under 2,500 employees. A household appliance manufacturer is small with under 500 employees.

In nonmanufacturing, annual sales are used. Retail and service enterprises are small when volume is between $2 million and $22 million, according to the SBA. Manufacturing firms with between 250 and 1,500 employees and construction firms grossing under $9.5 million can qualify as small, depending on the industry.

The SBA revises these figures frequently, so no doubt they will be sliding upward to adjust for inflation.

Given the preceding discussion of the market, I have defined an entrepreneurial venture in a nontraditional manner. Rather than relying on the number of employees or annual sales to identify its market, my definition does not use size as a criterion, but rather the intent of the founder. That is what differentiates an entrepreneur.

To state it simply, no entrepreneur ever starts out to create a small business. It is just that the entrepreneurial venture must initially begin on a small scale before it can grow to fulfill the entrepreneurial vision.

FRIDAY AT 10 O'CLOCK

My theory still holds, reality should be treated as a special case.

PROF. MILTON FRIEDMAN
University of Chicago economist

This bit of wisdom is appropriate only before you start your business. Once you have lived through the start-up problem, the wisdom will begin to make sense. It may even make sense to carry your firm to the growth stage. There is value in thinking through emotional issues before they occur. The environment for the eventual decision is then set and will be more comfortable than if you had not thought about the issue earlier.

We all know the supersitition that Friday the thirteenth is unlucky. But I wonder if you know that Friday at 10 o'clock is the unluckiest moment of all. I am not superstitious, and I do not worry about black cats or ladders, but from my experience, layoffs occur in a week at one hour on one day repeatedly—regardless of company, industry, product, or management philosophy. It is like Fink's Law, which says "a slice of peanut-butter bread will always fall peanut-butter side down." I do not know why it happens, it just does. Regardless of age, seniority, title, rank, length of time with the company, Friday at 10 o'clock is E-hour (entrepreneurs hour) everywhere. It is when employees of entrepreneurs are terminated.

The routine goes something like this. "Because of a drop in company contracts (or sales, if you like), we are going to have to lay off. It is not a result of what you have done for us to date that I am about to let you go. We both know you have been a good, loyal employee. But it is because of circumstances beyond our control." That is the story by many an entrepreneur every Friday at 10 o'clock.

Fortunately, the kind and considerate entrepreneur almost always adds, "Look, why don't you clean up for the rest of the morning and take the afternoon off." I suppose that is the reason they like to terminate you at 10 o'clock instead of 3 o'clock. Out of the kindness of their hearts, they want to give you an extra afternoon off. Whatever you do, don't let it backfire by using the afternoon to go down to the local bar and have a few beers. That is *not* what you need right now. Save that for after a success.

With all my advice for entrepreneurs, a small counterbalance is intended by offering this piece of wisdom to those of you who are employees of entrepreneurs. Whatever you do, do not tell them I told you, but there is a simple way to avoid this catastrophe. The secret is timing. If your timing is right, you will have no problem. Remember that before your boss decides to fire you, he or she must wrestle with a very big and emotional decision. And for that the boss requires at least one rehearsal with a trusted employee and one with his or her mate. So, at a quarter to 10 on Friday, he is all charged up, ready for bear. The secret for you is to go on a little field trip Friday from 10 o'clock on. Come back late Friday, and do your darnest to avoid the boss. If your timing is on, your boss will be all charged up and ready to fire someone, and you will not be around. He or she just might turn to candidate number two—and you might hold your job. It is only a thought and it will not work in every case, but you never know, it could catch on. You know how impulsive the boss can be, right?

But whatever you do, do not mention this strategy to the boss over lunch one day. If you do, your last hope has vanished.

Boys, I'm about to make you an offer you can't refuse.

To the entrepreneur, there is one thing about emotional decisions you should not forget. It is vital, because in your position you will be firing people. You may chuckle at the story about Friday at 10 o'clock, but when you cut away the humor, you will find that we are talking about a serious issue. In fact, it is a *very* serious issue, because it involves the careers of your employees. If it is ever necessary to have a cutback, recall to yourself the reasons that you are doing this. It naturally goes against your optimistic, fun-loving nature to fire people, but, as we both now, it can be necessary for the survival of the business. Do not make a big thing out of the firing. Rather, make a very big thing about the fact that the remainder are still with you. In short, Friday at 3 o'clock call a meeting of all your key employees. Tell them the reasons for your decision to let John Jones go, but also tell them that their jobs are secure. Give them the story straight from the hip. A little pep talk. Congratulate them on still being around and for doing such a fine job. Most of all, ask them to help fill in where John Jones used to make significant contributions. Be sure to mention that by letting some people go now, we may be able to save the entire business and thereby save the rest of the jobs. The time for a pep talk is after you have done the firing. The time is right, and the wise entrepreneur knows when to strike—Friday at 3 o'clock.

PARTNERS—WHETHER OR NOT

If a man does not keep pace with his companions, perhaps it is because he hears a different drummer. Let him step to the music which he hears, however measured or far away.

HENRY DAVID THOREAU, 1817-1862
Walden

A partner can be a blessing or a curse. Whether you take one, or more, into your business venture depends on your needs for additional depth in management, marketing, technology, or financing.

Selecting your business partners is not much different from choosing a wife or husband, and it should be done with the same care; more, perhaps, because the wrong partner can put the entire venture in jeopardy. Marriages are relatively easy to start. And if one fails, you can try again. In business it's not so easy.

I advise finding one partner whose talents complement your own, but whose business philosophy, personality, and background differ. The most succesful companies are formed with two partners whose combined abilities give depth to the enterprise and whose differing backgrounds serve as a buffer against excesses. You both may disagree and have conflicts, but they are usually over business issues, not over personalities.

Honey, will you PLEASE put away Dad's cigar!

A good marketing/financial person is an ideal partner for a strong production/engineering type, but two optimists or two pessimists can kill a business before it has a chance to get off the ground.

Once you have selected your partner, you should immediately agree to disagree. From my experience in mediating between partners. I never become concerned about disagreements. The success of a two-person partnership depends on arriving at sensible business decisions through cooperation and equal participation. Inevitably, however, one of the partners begins to dominate. This happens quite naturally, and usually it's for the best. We can't all be presidents anyhow, so don't fight it.

THE GODFATHER

I am looking for an honest man.

DIOGENES, c. 400-325 B.C.

Every partnership should have a "godfather." Not the kind made famous in the novel and film about the underworld, but one who is trusted and respected by both partners and who can serve as a mediator to help resolve conflicts.

This godfather should be unbiased and have little or no vested interest in the company. He or she can be a business acquaintance, friend, college professor, or someone respected in the technology of your business. Bring the person into the picture right at the beginning and keep him or her informed of what goes on.

If you're lucky, and very unusual, you may never require the godfather to do more than settle minor disputes or serve as a sounding board for new ideas. If it comes to the worst, however, and you must dissolve the partnership, the godfather may be the only one who can keep the pieces together long enough for the company to regain its equilibrium and survive. Remember, nothing lasts forever. But the business, if it survives at all, will most likely outlive the partnership.

A BETTER LEGAL STRUCTURE
FOR A NEW BUSINESS

I came, I saw, I conquered.

JULIUS CAESAR

When an entrepreneur establishes a new business, there are a number of choices for the legal form of the enterprise. They are, unfortunately, as complex as business ventures. The eventual form chosen for your business will depend primarily on the goals of the business and your individual objectives. If you want a small, quiet, mom-and-pop operation, a simple proprietorship may be your best bet. On the other hand, if you're interested in building another General Motors, you should start a corporation structure with section 1244 stock (talk to your lawyer). The question facing all new businesses is how to organize at the beginning for the long-term goals of the enterprise. The advantages of organizing in the most appropriate manner at the beginning is obvious to anyone who thinks ahead. A problem occurs because most businesses begin as proprietorships and, after several growth periods, eventually settle into the right nitch—namely, a corporation.

If, on the other hand, proper care and thought are given at the birth of the new enterprise, it could begin on the right foot and not have to go through changes brought on by experience. In many cases, it is not always best to start with the same legal form of business as you envision for the future. That organizational form may not be the appropriate choice for this moment. That is why the substance of my advice will be to seek legal counsel in this area. A skilled lawyer will help you select the best type of business organization for your objectives by outlining each of your three basic alternatives: proprietorship, partnership, and corporation.

A *proprietorship* is an extension of an individual. It is really the absence of a specialized legal form of business. Your income and that of the proprietorship are married. There are no tax advantages or personal liabilities inherent in a proprietorship. Traditionally, these are effective until your income is in excess of $50,000 annually.

There are two kinds of *partnerships*—limited and general. These forms have been effective for real estate and for accounting and legal firms, and they are becoming serious competitors to the more popular corporate form of business. This is accentuated by the accelerating payroll tax-related expenses suffered by already overburderned corporate forms. Limited partnerships and proprietorships typically do not face these problems. A *limited partnership* is a business association formed by one or more partners. A limited partner will have a liability to a definite prestated amount, usually the amount invested. The limited partners, in turn, cannot participate in the management of the partnership, and that is how they gain their limited liability status. A *general partnership* has unlimited liabilities for each of the general partners, and all the general partners can and should participate in the management of the company. Another of the advantages of both forms of partnerships is that they do not suffer the double taxation of the corporate form of business.

Corporation is the most common form of business enterprise. A corporation is a legal entity and is composed of stockholders under a common name. It has limited liability, which is its greatest attraction, and thus a succession of ownership becomes possible. Under ordinary business law, a corporation is treated as another individual and incurs obligations and privileges similar to those of an individual. The limited liability feature is its greatest single attraction. Of late, its payroll-related tax structure has been a deterrent.

A hybrid form of organization has recently sprung up and has grown in popularity; that is, a limited partnership with a single general partner being a corporation. This structure allows the major advantages of a limited partnership, namely, limited liability and single-level taxation on income, while avoiding heavy payroll taxes. At the same time, this structure protects the general partner from exposure because the corporate structure of the general partner even limits this liability. There are some rather complicated rulings about the process. You should investigate this structure with your lawyer.

A limited partnership with a corporation as the sole general partner can obtain an advanced treasury ruling that it is taxable as a partnership if it meets some basic tests. There are six tests worth discussing in detail with your lawyer and accountant.

Advice on the proper legal form of business is best sought from professional advisors. Discuss with them the possibility of forming your business as a limited partnership with the sole general partner being a corporation. It is a growing trend in entrepreneurial ventures.

THE BOARD OF DIRECTORS

A committee is a group of the unprepared appointed by the unwilling to do the unnecessary.

F. ALLEN

Boards of directors of small companies fall into three categories, with varying degrees of usefulness. Most entrepreneurs don't consider their boards very important; they only appoint them because the laws say there must be at least three directors.

The most common type of board can mislead you about the whole purpose of boards. It usually meets quarterly, and though it appears to be establishing company policy, it's really a social event in diguise. If one member begins to take his role too seriously and actually tries to affect the operation he's considered something of a party-pooper. Since he is spoiling all the fun, he is usually asked to resign.

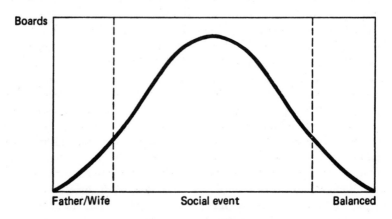

Types of boards of directors.

On one extreme is the second kind of board, consisting of the entrepreneur and his wife and father. This is the most honest kind of board because it doesn't pretend to be anything more than what it is. After all, most entrepreneurs wouldn't heed the advice of a real board, and if any issue ever had to be decided by a vote of the stockholders, the entrerpreneur is usually the majority stockholder anyhow. So who's kidding whom?

But some entrepreneurs go to the opposite extreme and actually appoint a balanced board of seasoned professionals who vote, have conflicts, and determine company policy. This kind of board might decide that the entrepreneur is what's wrong with the company. Of course, if you are the majority stockholder that's not much of a problem, so don't worry.

A balanced board of experienced businesspeople can help maintain a sensible and profitable business plan. They can make valuable contacts for the company and add to its stature in the eyes of the financial community. Pick this kind of board only if you want your company to succeed.

One final word about boards of directors: Good boards have conflicts; bad boards always say yes.

Ahh! I know just what I'll name this baby.

SELECTING THE NAME OF THE ENTERPRISE

A tomb now suffices him for whom the whole world was not sufficient.

Epitaph for Alexander the Great

One of the most important tasks when starting a small business occurs right at the outset, giving the enterprise a name and form. The name chosen soon comes to symbolize the entire enterprise; hence, it is one of the early signs of a company's character. The form will determine how the business is to be established.

My fascination with naming companies stems from the almost endless variety, the brilliant wit, and useful information found in the names people give their businesses. They all fit into one of several categories. The most common category is *ego-trippers*. These are people who just have to claim their little piece of immortality be putting up their own names in lights over the door. In my experience, this is often foolish practice, and most of the time it is downright dangerous. The ego-trippers lose if they win and lose if they lose. This means there are two ways in which to lose. If your business does not make it (loses), having your name on it could be fatal for you (or maybe for someone else), even after the business has passed on. Beside the embarrassment for your business failing while your name is on it, just consider what might happen if it succeeds and you then sell the business, only to find that you do not like what the new owner does with your name. In both cases, you might change your name. I know of three cases where this happened. While visiting the campus of a college in Boston, I was introduced to a bright young undergraduate named Edsel Ford. When I heard his name, I looked up, and suddenly the whole history of the Ford Motor Company's attempts to launch a new line of automobiles flashed before me. Before I even looked at him, I was mentally recalling one of the top half-dozen failures in the business world. And then I saw his face, shook his hand and said, "Are you . . . ." The poor chap.

Further examples of the name problem, although not as colorful as the Edsel case, illustrate some of the problems of mixing your name with your business. Just because the business can win, it does not follow that you will win, too. In fact, you can lose. Here's an example. Jim Pastoriza eventually sold his new business, Pastoriza Electronics, to a highly successful firm started by one of New England's premier entrepreneurs, Ray Stata. Pastoriza Electronics soon became a division of Stata's business, Analog Devices, Inc. (Incidentally, isn't that a great name for a business—Analog Devices? It is descriptive and, thus, helps the customer seeking an analog device to find it.) Anyway, Jim Pastoriza started a second company, Memodyne, and soon became disenchanted with the use of his name on the products sold by Analog Devices. Although Memodyne's products were not similar to the Pastoriza Electronics Division of Analog Devices, Inc., both companies serviced similar customers. Hence, Jim Pastoriza spent a few hours per day explaining the situation to his new group of Memodyne customers. Sounds funny, but it was not.

Another example is Royden Sanders, founder of Sanders Associates in New Hampshire, who had a similar experience. After selling his firm, he became so fed up with the acquiring management's so-called misuse of his name that he eventually brought a legal suit against them. He believed the company's new direction was so opposed to his chances of a successful future that he sought to disassociate his name from his former business. So, you see naming your business after yourself can be a problem.

Then there are those who understand the folly of putting their names on the business, but who cannot quite resist it either. They use their initials (usually B.J. becomes Bee-Jay) or they combine initials or syllables to form the company name. Or they use the name of the street they happen to live on, or their children's name, to identify the business. The best name for a company, in my opinion, is one that tells customers, especially potential customers, what the company does, makes, or sells. In fact, naming the company is the first move of many in which you should keep the customer's needs first and foremost in mind. After all, there is only one essential ingredient for any business—a customer.

A few of my favorite names for the ego-trippers are classics. Do you know that the first multipurpose liquid cleaner, Lestoil, was named for Jacob L. Barowsky's three children—Lenore, Edith, and Seymour. Moreover, Barowsky's business, Adell Chemical Company of Holyoke, Massachusetts, was named for his wife, Adeline. Better yet, it is said that Eugene Ferkauf and Joseph Blumenberg famous department/discount store—E.J. Korvettes—from a Canadian submarine chaser they served on in World War II: the "E" stands for Eugene, and the "J" stand for Joseph, the "K" was changed from "C" and the "S" was added later. Incidentally, William Constantine founded and named Gurnard, Inc., in Beverly, Massachusetts, on a similar basis. He initially wanted to use the name Cunard, based on a pleasure trip he took with the famous shipping line. Cunard said no, and so he named his business Gurnard.

In my home town, small businesses have been named after streets, initials, wives' maiden names, and children. For instance Sherman Olson named his highly successful plastics extrusion business after his daughter, Dana, and called his firm Danafilms. Howard Freeman named the Jamesbury Valve Company after his street, Jamesbury Way. Alan R. Pearlman named his firm, which is the world's leading manufacturer of electronic music synthesizers, after his initials— ARP Instruments, Inc. The same is true of Arthur I. Metzer, whose business is AIM Associates. It has been claimed that ITEK in Lexington, Massachusetts, stands for "I'll Take over Eastman Kodak." I could not confirm this. The list is endless.

My brother, John Mancuso, had to change the name of his entrepreneurial business, Tremont of Connecticut, as part of a trade secrets legal action initiated by his previous employer, Transamerica. So he changed his business's name to Equal, Inc. because so many of his custom-designed, electro-mechanical components were specified on engineering blueprints of original equipment manufacturer's (OEM's). Transamerica had the dominant market share, and millions of blueprints specified by a footnote on the corner of the drawing saying "Transamerica or euqal."

John just sought to capitalize the equal to Equal!

If you are trying to think up a name for a new service-type business, explore combinations of your telephone number, especially if your business is a mail order or telephone-related, service-type business. This is also effective for retail stores, travel agencies, funeral homes, and any business that relies on an initial telephone call to make the sale. You will notice that the telephone is divided into both numbers and letters as below.

NUMBER	LETTER	NUMBER	LETTER
1	–	6	MNO
2	ABC	7	PRS
3	DEF	8	TUV
4	GHI	9	WXY
5	JKL	0	–

Notice that all numbers and letters are not included (no Q or Z) and numbers 1 and 0 have no alphabetical counterpart. Now, since all telephone numbers are basically seven digits, you must spell a seven-letter word. Or, if you are so inclined, also include your area code to make a ten letter word. For example:

SUCCESS is 782-2377
SERVICE is 737-8423
FINANCE is 346-2623
PLASTIC is 752-7842

If the alphabetical combination is easy enough to remember, it can be a great asset for your customers.

The importance of customers is best exemplified by a very successful entrepreneur, Ray Kroc, founder of McDonald's. When accepting induction into the Babson College Entrepreneurial Hall of Fame in Wellesley, Massachusetts, he looked out at a large crowd and addressed his distinguished audience thus: "Hello, Customers."

Incidentally, my favorite name of all is John Hancock Insurance, because just as the insurance agent asks you to sign the contract, he says, "Why not put your John Hancock on the X?" My second favorite name resulted in the merger of two prominent banks in New Jersey. And it clearly demonstrates the importance of naming it right in the first place. A financial institution in Red Bank, New Jersey, bought out a rival in nearby Long Branch, and people in Long Branch have been depositing their checks ever since at the Long Branch branch of the Red Bank bank.

THE DIFFERENCE BETWEEN MARKETING AND SELLING

"Nuts!" Anthony McAuliffe's reply, December 23, 1944, to a German demand for surrender of the 101st Airborne Division, United States Army, which had been trapped for seven days at Bastogne, France.

The difference between a marketing versus a sales orientation can be determined by how management handles the subtle difference between a products feature and the corresponding customer benefits of a product.

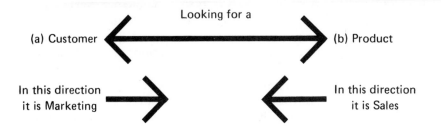

PRODUCT	FEATURE	BENEFIT
Cosmetics	Special fragrance	hope
Drill bits	Characteristics of drill	hole
Encyclopedia	Volumes of information	Knowledge and Intelligence
Computers	Accounts Receivable	Management information systems

An example of this is often highlighted by the quarter-inch drill story. It is estimated that 3,250,000 quarter-inch drills were sold in this country, and the drills have come to represent the product feature. On the other hand, last year customers bought 3,250,000 quarter-inch holes—it just happened that the drill was necessary to produce the hole. If anyone is ever able to package a hole (put it in a small plastic container), customers would begin buying the holes to solve their problems. Charles Revson, the entrepreneur founder of Revolon, the famous cosmetic company, once expressed the same thing in another way. He said, "In my factory we make cosmetics, but in my stores we sell hope." Customers buy benefits while you make features.

A customer benefit is a product feature turned inside out.

A marketing orientation requires a customer looking for a product, while a sales orientation requires a product looking for a customer. It's really only a matter of perception and direction, as can be visualized by the chart.

WHEN IS THE BEST TIME TO SELL?

Failure is a man who has blundered, but is not able to cash in on the experience.

E. HUBBARD

The best time to sell is immediately after you've sold. The theory for this phenomenon, which is generally well accepted by practicing salespeople, is founded in some psychological research conducted by Dr. Leon Festinger of Columbia University, New York City, in the late 1950s. The research comes under the broad category of cognitive dissonance, discussed in Chapter 3. Cognitive dissonance is one of the most popular areas of academic inquiry within the entire marketing profession, as evidenced by the popularity of marketing doctoral dissertations.

Cognitive means being aware and dissonance means being stressed. Therefore, together, it means being aware of internal stress. Every individual who makes a difficult decision, including purchasing decisions, suffers from cognitive dissonance. When the cognitive dissonance reaches an intolerable level, the individual will take action to reduce the dissonance and return to equilibrium and harmony. What action does an individual take to reduce dissonance? Let me offer an example of an automobile buyer.

Assume you are an individual who is torn between purchasing one of two or three medium-sized cars. On a Saturday, you rush first to the Ford dealership and then across the street to the Chevy dealership and eventually down the street to the Plymouth dealership. Because you are a value-conscious buyer, you compare the features and prices of each car, but after comparison you are still undecided on the best value. Finally, as the Saturday wears on and your need for a car increases, you make a commitment with one of the three car dealers— the one you trust. For you, it was a different decision.

This process occurs every day, and because 10 million new cars are sold annually under this back-and-forth dissonance-producing method, many of us have experienced it. Yet, everyone claims to have secured a "good deal." I don't know one person who has every admitted to a "bad deal" during the process. Do you? Can it be so?

This decision is known as a stress decision and the purchaser's dissonance is very high. When you bring the car home, you may take the following steps to reduce that dissonance and justify your purchase.

1. You may inadvertently choose to leave the new car in your driveway rather than the garage. Or, to drive it and park it where it will be conspicuous to your peers.

2. The night you bring home the car, you will undoubtedly read the owner's manual and begin searching for new pieces of information about what a wonderful car you have chosen. You probably will never read the owner's manual again, and you will either lose it or bury it in the glove compartment.

3. You may become extremely receptive to TV, newspaper, and magazine advertisments about the car you just purchased. You will ignore other automobile ads. That car will become the single most exciting thing for you for a period of time. You will reject the chance to read other automobile advertisements, preferring only to read advertisements that reinforce new features about the wonderful car you just purchased. Because motor car companies are aware that you suffer dissonance, the president of General Motors will send you a personal letter congratulating you on your wise automobile choice. The company may even send you a questionnaire seeking feedback information about the purchasing process that occurred during your selection of a car. Beside the value of the information you feed back to them (they can learn these facts through less costly sampling techniques), the questionnaire allows each individual a chance to vent any residual dissonance.

So, the message is simple. The best time to sell is immediately after you've sold. The best time to make a sales call is immediately after you've made the sales. The best time to send a sales message is immediately after you've made a sale. That finding is built on Leon Festinger's concept of cognitive dissonance, and it works.

Several companies have made major efforts to build marketing programs around a dissonance approach. An additional set of dissonance-reducing literature is shipped within the dissonance-reducing product's shipping carton, which is appropriately marked to inform your peers, who may glance at it, that you made a wise choice. Wouldn't it be nice to have the salesperson who recently sold you the what-ever pop in on you one week after you brought it? Isn't that a winning strategy? Why don't you consider adopting it as you improve your entrepreneurial management capabilities?

MARKETING STRATEGY, "THINK SMALL"

No one is such a liar as the indignant man.

> NEITZSCHE,
> *Beyond Good and Evil*, 1885-1886

Developing a marketing strategy is one of the more elusive procedures within the marketing discipline, especially for smaller, less well-heeled companies. A clever strategy, which is traditionally discussed under the umbrella title, "Think Small," may be what David needs to tackle Goliath. A simplified example serves the point better than a statement of what it means.

In the early 1970s, the ten major soap manufacturers were investigating the market for a soap concentrate for home washing machines. They reasoned that the large-size boxes of laundry detergents (Tide, Bold, and others) were unnecessary and could be reduced to the size of an aspirin bottle, while still retaining the necessary cleaning power. In fact, soap manufacturers were shipping a lot of air and water. A concentrate would have the advantages of:

(1) reducing the manufacturing plant, (2) reducing the warehousing, (3) reducing the shipping costs, (4) reducing the valuable supermarket retail space, (5) reducing the storage space in the laundry room. So, the inception of the soap pill began, and one entree was a product known as Salvo (Procter and Gamble). During the marketing research, each of the ten soap manufacturers conducted independent studies to determine the characteristics the soap pill should possess. An element of the research was the suds capacity of the new concentrate. In other words, should it be a high sudser or a low sudser?

On the one hand, the high sudser had the advantage of appearing to be really cleaning because of the high suds. It had the disadvantage of upsetting those concerned about polluting the rivers and lakes, or even their own septic systems. The other alternative, the low sudser had very few pollution disadvantages, but if you opened the top of your washing machine, you might wonder if the pill was lost and not doing the cleaning.

So, it was a fundamental question about the ideal product characteristics, and the research uniformly and independently conducted by all ten manufacturers concluded that eight percent of the housewives wanted a high sudsing tablet. High suds was clearly preferred for its visual cleaning assurances.

Nine of the ten manufacturers interpreted the data and produced the high suds product. They began to fight over that 80 percent share of the market, each eventually settling for an average of about a nine-percent market share. Meanwhile, the tenth company, a clever little marketing-oriented firm, produced a low sudser—one that was a good antipollutant—and they captured 20 percent of the market. The message is simple.

Everyone operates from the same basic marketing facts. But when establishing marketing strategies, you might think about "thinking small" in small businesses.

LAWYERS

Ignorance of the law excuses no man who retains poor counsel.

New York lawyer

The very first thing you should do when starting a new business is see a lawyer about incorporating your company. If you do this in the beginning, you avoid the legal risks and personal liability inherent in a proprietorship. The legal fees for incorporating, only a few hundred dollars, are usually standard. The bar association fee schedule now provides for a $300 fee exclusive of the paperwork costs, which run about $85. But that doesn't mean you can pick just any old lawyer. The lawyer who sells your house or handles divorces should not be the lawyer for your business. Your best bet is to go to one of the biggest and best law firms in town.

Once you've found the firm, you have to choose the right lawyer. Never pick a lawyer whose name is on the door of the firm. It means he (or she) probably has two homes, three cars, and all the clients he wants. The lawyer you want has the office that looks like a converted broom closet at the end of the hall. An up-and-coming junior partner who specializes in the S.E.C. (Securities Exchange Commission) and knows how to take companies public, set up stock-option plans, and avoid catastrophic corporation mistakes—he's your man.

Your lawyer will probably handle some pretty big deals for you, so find one who can gain 100 percent of your confidence. And if he (or she) is young enough and good enough, he will give you 100 percent of his effort. One other point, don't exchange stock for legal advice—free legal service is worth what you pay for it. Moreover, it may lock you into one lawyer just when you need the flexibility to maneuver. Don't take away the option of upgrading your lawyer or accountant.

There exists a set of logic in the entrepreneurial world classically called "mind bogglers." This occurs when you take something that is logical and you turn it inside out. The reciprocal creates enough powerful logic to cause a second reflection, but it is seldom based on sound reasoning.

A third glance will prove it illogical. An example of this occurred when Archie Bunker, television personality in "All In The Family," was asked for his solution to the national crisis that happened during the airplane hijacking scandal a decade ago. It was during this time that an airplane full of unsuspecting passengers was being detoured to Havana, Cuba. If you recall, the country was in an uproar and every solution was being pursued. When asked what he would do to solve the problem, he replied, "It is really very simple. Every single passenger who gets on the plane is given a gun and when he deplanes the gun is taken from him. Now, I ask you what hijacker in his right mind would detour an airplane if every single one of us had a gun?" Isn't that reasoning powerful?

Only those of you who have been involved with lawyers to any great degree will appreciate the simplicity of the following entrepreneurial mind boggler. If the government would pass a regulation that disbarred all the lawyers of the world and prevented them from practicing in any court in the world, there would be no more lawyers. Now at first glance that sounds disastrous. However, if no one could have a lawyer, wouldn't everyone operate at the same so-called disadvantage?

And now, I ask you: Wouldn't it be a powerful world if there were no lawyers? Wouldn't entrepreneurs make great progresss?

This idea was pretested in theory on some entrepreneurs and thought to be foolish, but a few agreed to let it be tried—say for a five-year period. Now, it'll take a fourth glance to undue this logic as it's starting to sound appealing.

ACCOUNTANTS COUNT

Figures can't lie—but liars can figure.

Another person you'll want to get on board at the earliest moment is a top certified public accountant (CPA). Numbers are the language of business management and intelligent decisions require an understanding of the quantitative factors involved.

If you have hopes for expansion or for going public, line up one of the big eight accounting firms. A merely adequate accountant is suicide. A big, well-known firm immediately lends credibility to your numbers and, when the time comes for that public offering, three years of audited statements from one of the big-name leaders adds plenty of status.

Don't worry about a big firm being too expensive. Most of them have separate divisions for small businesses. They will install a one-write check system and accounts payable voucher register, proof your receivables, and set up all the necessary financial controls to help you avoid false starts.

Next, introduce your accountant and your lawyer to your banker. There will be plenty of decisions where their functions overlap, so they should know each other from the outset.

ONE-WRITE CHECK SYSTEM

There are three faithful friends; an old wife, an old dog, and ready money.

BENJAMIN FRANKLIN, 1738

One of the most useful tools for the efficient and accurate operation of a small business is a one-write check system. Rather than opting for the standard bank checks, a one-write system must be specially ordered from a stationary firm. A list of such firms is shown below.

The one-write system has checks with a carbon strip about one-half inch wide running across the middle of the back of the check. This feature allows you to write the check while the carbon strip simultaneously posts the check to the ledger sheet, which is underneath the check. That is why it is called a "one-write" system—you write the check only once. Just about every small business using, say, more than thirty checks a month can justify such a system. The advantages, in our opinion, are as follows:

1. It eliminates posting errors; this is the key feature as the check is the control document.

2. It speeds the bookkeeping process by taking about one-half of the time.
3. The corresponding window-envelope system allows faster mailing, and we recommend using the window envelopes also.

Firms offering one-write bookkeeping systems:

Control-o Fax
Box 778
Waterloo, IA 50704
(319) 234-4651

McBee Systems
151 Cortlandt St.
Belleville, NJ 07019
(201) 759-6500

Ekonomik Systems
Box 11413
Tacoma, WA 98411
(206) 475-0292

Master-Craft Corp.
831 Cobb Ave.
Kalamazoo, MI 49007
(616) 692-0321

NBS Systems
Box 321
Edwardsville, IL 62025
(618) 692-0321

Safeguard Business Systems
470 Maryland Ave.
Fort Washington, PA 19034
(215) 643-4811

New England Business Serv.
N. Main St.
Groton, MA 01451
(617) 448-6111

Shaw-Walker
15 Division St.
Muskegon, MI 49443
(616) 722-7211

S-K Forms
2239 Cambria St.
Philadelphia, PA 19134
(215) 427-8400

Standard Accounting Sys.
P.O. Box 20990
Portland, OR 97220
(503) 661-2323

If you do not presently use a one-write system, give one of our suggested suppliers a call. If your business is too large, the one-write check system may be inadequate for your purpose, but these suppliers can explain the options for you as well.

BANKERS

A banker is a fellow who lends you his umbrella when the sun is shining and wants it back the minute it begins to rain.

MARK TWAIN

Pick a banker, not a bank. If he is with a large bank, or a bank with a captive small business investent company (SBIC), so much the better. Many bankers are really venture capitalists in disguise and can be sorces of valuable financial assistance.

Here, again, forget the big titles and pick a young loan officer or assistant vice-president, then gain his (or her) confidence. Supply him with detailed pro forma cash-flow projections to show what your cash needs will be. Then meet or exceed your projections. Getting financial aid will be easy from then on.

In working with your friendly banker, you'll soon learn that he expects you to personally countersign your company's bank debt. Don't let it throw you. It's the only way he has to certify your numbers and your confidence in what you're doing. But don't take this responsibility lightly either. It's easy for you to be overly optimistic and that can get you into a lot of trouble. Before you sign that note, take a good, hard look at those figures again. That signature on the back of the note isn't an autograph—unless you become very, very famous.

If you have inventory and/or receivables, you may be able to avoid the countersignature, or at least limit your vulnerability to assigning them to the bank. If the worst happens and the bank has to go after your security, better it should be the company's inventory than your wife's or your diamond ring. Most states protect your home from creditors or bankers trying to collect against a bankrupt company, but the diamond ring is sure to go.

I've noticed a small but developing trend that may be of interest to entrepreneurs currently searching for a new banking relationship. My philosophy on this subject has never changed; I have always suggested picking a banker not a bank. Then I usually go on to tell you the qualities of the young loan officer who makes the ideal banker. It's good wisdom.

But, two major changes have occurred in the United States. In 1972 when the Federal Reserve started keeping statistics on such issues, there were fifty-two foreign banks with 100 offices in the United States. By mid-1978, the number of foreign banks had more than doubled to 123, and they operated 268 offices. The assets of these foreign-owned, American-based banks have grown four times over during the five-year-period, and today their assets are more than $100 billion. The second change is the two-tier prime rate structure now being charged to small business. But more about that in a minute.

Why are foreign banks expanding in the United States? There are two basic reasons: devaluation of the American dollar and the ability of these banks to avoid American banking regulations. Because of these factors, foreign banks have generally been taking a more aggressive posture toward loans for ventures. This is not true for every banker at every bank, but it is true in general. So, if you are considering a banking relationship, why not consider Britain's Barclay's Bank, the Bank of Montreal, or the host of Japanese, Swiss, and French banks?

These foreign-owned banks are allowed to open branches outside their countries (American banks are not), and they often have offices in major cities. They are seldom located in small towns, much preferring large cities such as New York or Los Angeles. This ability to operate across counties can also be a feature for your company if they operate in the same cities where branches of your business are located. Besides this benefit, these banks are not required to tie up a portion of their assets with the Federal Reserve System. They most often choose

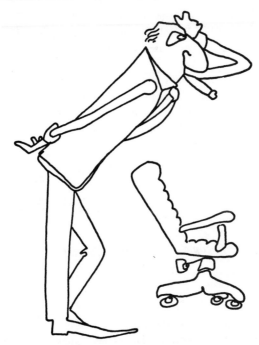

I've got a lawyer and banker, but where do I look for an Indian chief?

to operate under state banking regulations. These two reasons allow foreign banks to be a little more aggressive in securing new business. Hence, it may prove to your advantage to do business with them.

Further, with this expansion continuing, I predict a major overhaul in American banking restrictions to allow them to compete on more favorable terms with foreign banks. If this happens, the opportunity for more aggressive banking will prove to be available only for a short time. When the windows open, the entrepreneurial manager at least pokes his or her head in.

For the foreign bank nearest you, consult the telephone book for the largest city nearest you. And, please remember, I have not mentioned the obvious advantage of doing business with a foreign-based bank if your entrepreneurial venture happens to sell or buy from the host country.

INSURANCE AGENTS

Tomorrow is the first day of the rest of your life.

All of the old jokes about insurance salespeople notwithstanding, a good insurance agent will be another valuable addition to your external team. Pick just one person and let him or her handle the whole package.

The agent will probably recommend key-man life insurance, show and how to get tax advantages with split-dollar plans, and set up funded buy-sell agreements between partners. In these cases, an ounce of prevention is really worth the whole company.

He'll also install group health and accident coverage, insure the company automobiles, set up a workmen's compensation plan, and get you fire and theft coverage. It takes a real pro to do it right, so don't close your door on his foot. If you do, you may be sorry and forget all about the various forms of product and personal liability insurance.

ADVERTISING AGENCIES

The great masses of people . . . will more easily fall victims to a big lie than to a small one.

HITLER
Mein Kampf

Most entrepreneurs tend to avoid advertising agencies or put off hiring one until they hit an impasse in their marketing plans. Then it may be too late. I believe in finding a good, small (no more than ten people) agency early.

With advertising agencies, unlike law firms or public accounting firms, the largest is not always the best for the small businessperson. With a small agency, you'll get the attention of the top, and probably plenty of it.

Once you've found the right people, give them their head. Don't tell them what colors *you* like. Be candid, honest, and give them all the information you can about your product and your markets. The more you give them, the more they'll be able to give you.

When it comes to agency compensation, don't rely on the old fifteen percent-of-media-costs method. First of all, it's impossible for an agency to work profitably on a straight commission basis unless your media expenditures are considerable. Remember, they're in business to make a profit, too. Furthermore, it tends to create a conflict of interest for the agency since it is to their advantage if your ad dollars go into commissionable media. The best course for your company may be direct mail or some other noncommissionable medium. Do you want the agency working for your company or the magazines?

The most practical and fairest method of agency compensation is a monthly retainer fee, which amounts to about ten percent more than the commissions they would receive on forecasted media expenditures. This method eliminates the conflict of interest and lets the agency worry about what's best for you, not what's best for them.

Just think of me as a Doctor of Advertising.

HIRING HELP

If sailing in a big and placid lake's your style, go to work for a large corporation, but if white water canoeing is to your liking, try a small company.

FRED MURPHY

No matter how long you put it off, sooner or later—and probably sooner—you'll have to become an employer. Foreigners refer to this phenomenon as American capitalism. There'll be office help, sales help, and production help, and . . .

When it comes to hiring help, there are two schools of thought. The first says "Let's automate everything we can and hire unskilled, low-pay people for everything else."

Many entrepreneurs go this route in the early stages of company development, figuring it will keep costs down. But before long they see what happens to quality when you hire monkeys.

The second school of thought starts out with good people and pays them good salaries from the beginning. Now there's a school of thought!

My thoughts may not agree with yours on this subject, but I ask you—"How do you motivate employees?"

I have concluded you don't. They motivate themselves. As a manager, your job is not to demotivate them. It's still tough, but it's quite different from trying to motivate them. Rather I'd suggest you select only motivated employees as the single best method of improving your firm's performance.

A fascinating piece of behavioral research was conducted by two Harvard doctoral candidates in the field of education. It's been called the "Pygmalion" or the "late-bloomers" effect. Here is my simplified interpretation about how it was conducted.

All the fourth-grade pupils in the San Francisco, California, public schools were asked to take an I.Q.-type test.

No surprises were discovered. The surprise came later. Harvard researchers sent a personal letter to a random selection of fourth-grade teachers. The letter was short, personal, and to the point. In essence, it said:

> Johnny Jones, who is in your class, is probably not performing at his full potential, according to our testing. We see strong signs that Johnny may be a genius, but that he also appears to be a late bloomer. We judged it best to alert you to this finding, but we suggest you don't share the information with anyone until a future determination can be conducted.

Each letter was typed and personally signed.

One year later, these now fifth-graders were tested again and the academic performance of this random grouping, which were labeled late bloomers, were analyzed against the performance of the group as a whole. I don't really need to tell you the results, do I? The study wouldn't be worth relating to you unless the change was significant, and it was!

The message here, in simple language, is that of the self-fulfilling prophecy. When someone young enough to develop (note the age) is given small signs of encouragement, great developments can occur. The power of words of encouragement toward your younger employees can be staggering. You can actually improve their performance simply by raising your expectations about their possibilities. If you think they are good and communicate this to them, they just might become good. It's darned entrepreneurial!

MANUFACTURERS' REPRESENTATIVES

If Patrick Henry thought that taxation without representation was bad, he should see how bad it is with representation.

From the old *Farmers Almanac*

The manufacturer's rep is the mainstay of the sales force of most small businesses. They are independent businesspeople, entrepreneurs in their own right, selling the merchandise of several manufacturers rather than just one.

Reps don't add to your fixed costs. They are paid on a commission basis according to what they sell. Therefore, you can afford to maintain a respectable sales force until conditions warrant putting on your own people.

The rep is also a valuable source of industry intelligence, a kind of mercenary soldier, stomping through the industrial mud as a commissioned member of several armies. If anyone knows what's going on, the rep does. He's the sage of his industry.

When you latch onto a good rep (there are some poor ones) hold on to him (or her): even when it's time to hire an inside person. Many companies make special arrangements with their best reps to keep them on. It's good for the company and it's good for the rep who lives in fear of selling himself right out of a good line.

THE ENTREPRENEURIAL SELLING MODEL

You should spend every dollar you earn; in that way you will provide the motivation to continue producing.

EDWARD G. ROBINSON

The selling process often follows a specific sequence of actions. There are numerous models or preplanned sequences that describe successful selling. The one I like best is "The six-step selling process. Understanding the process often helps to improve sales performances.

Step 1: Prospecting
Step 2: Approach
Step 3: Qualifying the buyer
Step 4: Presenting the product
Step 5: Handling objections
Step 6: Gaining commitment

Step 1: Prospecting. Without a doubt, for many products, prospecting or determining the location of the most logical customers is the hardest part of the selling process. Once you find the right person, the product can help by taking over. Prospecting is plain hard work and there are no known shortcuts or easy methods to do it! This is especially true for intangible products (insurance, stocks) and services. For tangible products, this is not as crucial.

Step 2: Approach. During the approach, two major actions should occur. First, a salesperson should reduce relationship tension. In other words, you and the customers should feel at ease. Selling is not you doing something to the customer, but a shared experience, where together you solve the customer's problem. Second, the salesperson should simultaneously build a degree of task tension. While reducing relationship tension, there should be a reciprocal concern about the customer's needs, such as, "I understand you don't have a dishwasher. I understand you need a new car. I understand. . . ." The task that needs to be accomplished creates task tension. Selling is not a totally social exchange. You can't just kid yourself and say that you are there just for the fun of it. You're there to represent your products and services. The other person is there for the service or the product you offer.

Step 3: Qualifying the buyer. This is the "hot button," and it focuses on the reason the buyer will eventually buy. In every product or service, there are certain salient features and attributes. Among the product's features, certain benefits are more important to certain customers. Not everyone buys the same product for the same reason. Most of the time the same product is bought by different people for different reasons. The issue is to determine what turns the specific customer on. What button do you push to get the order? What is it that the customer needs? This can only be gained through a very careful questioning of the customer's needs.

Step 4: Presenting the product. Within this sales model, most sales personnel do this step best. They are so familiar with their product, having presented it numerous times, they are almost always able to make a convincing presentation about its benefits. The only issue here is to stress the benefits, which is the perceived value the customer receives from the product versus how your product is made or functions which is its features.

Step 5: Handling objections. There will be some objections or attempts to postpone purchases and some discussion on the weaknesses of your product. How do you handle objection? I offer you a very simple conceptual method, which I call the "feel, felt, found method," and this is how it works:

> When you are given an objection, don't disagree with it, don't be negative. Whatever you do, respond to the objection in a sincere way. Before you do, remember you should do three things: empathize with it: legitimize it; and then introduce some new information to show why that objection is without foundation. On other words, when you're given

the objection, you respond by saying, "I understand how you feel about that. It's very understandable to think that an individual would feel that way about that issue." Then, you say, "I felt that way, too," and you legitimize it—"and my last customer, whom I just visited, felt the same way about that issue, so it is a very legitimate complaint." But now you must remember that you are here for the purpose of making a sale and helping solve this customer's problem. Therefore, you have to introduce new information to more completely inform the customer of the relevant issues. The first two steps reach out and agree with the objection, but the third and final step must change his or her opinion. The mood is set and the guard down, and the objection is about to vanish.

The new information should be introduced something like this: "You are really only partially informed; I want to show you some new test information that we've just completed in the field and that will really put your mind to rest about our products *whatever*." The customer is never wrong. Occasionally, they are partially informed, and that's how you turn your objection inside out. You say, "We found. . . . "

Step 6: Gaining commitment. This has traditionally been classified as the most important sales step. It just is not so. Actually the most vital sales step is qualifying the buyer (Step 3). If that is completed properly and the approach is done properly, gaining commitment is a very small step and actually the least stressing step in the entire selling process. To gain commitment, you may want to create an opportunity to close on an objection. Many times you are given an objection that can be handled by exercising the feel, felt, found technique, and you really want to close the order to get on with other business. How do you do it? I call it a "trial close." Frequently, the salesperson enjoys the selling process so much that he or she goes past the close and keeps presenting the product rather than trying to make the sale. For instance, suppose a customer is buying a house and he objects to the location of the house; he likes everything but the location. You can't do anything about that. Therefore, you are not going to make the sale, and you must realize that you won't make every sale. If, on the other hand, the problem is that the house has no fireplace, and the customer continues to hang on that issue and really wants a fireplace; don't make the mistake of telling the customer that "you don't need a fireplace in today's society; a fireplace takes up the heat," or "it's a poor energy choice." Rather you should acknowledge whatever the customer really wants. If a fireplace is important, don't change his mind; accept the conclusion. The way to close on an objection is to say, "Do you like the location? Do you like the house? Is the price okay?" If the answer is yes, you can say, "You mean you would buy this house if it had a fireplace?" If the customer says yes, you only have to negotiate the price of the fireplace and you have gained commitment.

Selling is the art of reaching agreement. It is a process of building trust and confidence. It is an art and, unfortunately, the reason salespeople are often held in low esteem is that many of them are ineffective artists. This professional salesperson is an artist with a set of listening skills and an inner desire to perform. Selling is fun when you are good at it.

The whole world is your customer and you're selling everyday to everyone—so why not get good at it?

EMPLOYMENT CONTRACTS

I sold my soul and my time to the company for an annual salary and I am buying back my time slowly with good performance.

DR. LARRY FOX

The employment contract protects the entrepreneur from injury to vital spots caused by key employees who try to leave to join or form a competing company.

Just as many businesses are spinoffs from small companies as from large ones. This was verified in a recent study in Palo Alto, California. In a small company, more so than in a large company, it is much easier for even a middle manager to gain valuable knowledge of most intimate secrets. If one of them gets away early in the game, he or she can do a lot of harm.

A good employment contract is the best protection you can get, so establish one for all key personnel. At the same time, have them sign patent forfeiture rights to the company. These are two more areas where your lawyer can provide valuable help and where an ounce of prevention is worth the whole works.

5

THE
VENTURE
FINANCING

MY SON, THE VENTURE CAPITALIST

Boat (bōt) n. a hole in the water surrounded by wood into which one pours money.'

Before you disagree with my notions on venture financing, let me make one thing perfectly clear. My views are in the minority. Venture capitalists don't like or agree with my position. They don't believe in broken-field running, and they don't believe in premature public offering. They don't like what I have to say; they think it's hogwash and possibly they are right. But I am reporting it as I have seen it through the eyes of the entrepreneur, and we can't both be right!

I claim they are wrong and I stand firmly behind that claim. I believe an uneasiness exists venture capitalists and entrepreneurs at all stages. My reasons are straightforward. Each is in a different business; each is from a different

*A sign hanging in Chuck Stein's office.

73

school; each plays a different ball game with different rules. Venture capitalists have seldom had to raise money for a new business enterprise. True, the good ones have had to raise money for their funds, but not for a new business enterprise, not for something with a *product* and a concept. They have raised funds, a few of them, for a *cause* and a concept. I claim that difference is vital.

Entrepreneurs are poor venture capitalists, and venture capitalists are poor entrepreneurs. I claim that each should recognize this phenomenon to be as infallible as the more popular notion that entrepreneurs are poor managers and managers are poor entrepreneurs. The transition between venture capitalists and entrepreneurs is shaky at best. That doesn't mean we shouldn't admire and respect a good venture capitalist. I do, very much. It is truly an unusual talent that enables him or her to invest in people and make money on this basis, but that doesn't make him or her a good entrepreneur.

Here are a few examples of why I believe broken-field running is a necessary part of the entrepreneurial process. I can cite, without naming names (or even calling names), a handful of companies that have succeeded despite the management; they made all the management mistakes; they hired the wrong banker, lawyer, and accountant; yet they have succeeded. I can also cite companies that have failed. Now here's the vital difference: almost every situation that has failed has attracted funds. That's how it got to be a failure. Without funds, the entrepreneur doesn't become a company or even become recognized; it dies at the idea state. Millions of businesses do that every year. To be classified as a failure, you first have to have started.

Venture capitalists have a batting average of less than two successes in ten tries. Consequently, they are understandably familiar with failing; it's part of their business. It happens much more frequently than succeeding. The entrepreneur, however, gets only one attempt—or possibly two—at success. If he fails, it's all over (at least for a while). Now that's a helluva big difference.

To have the opportunity to fail is the yearning of the would-be entrepreneur.

Tennyson said, "Tis better to have loved and lost than never to have loved at all." Loving and starting businesses are both tricky processes. I offer no advice about loving, but to successfully start a business, an entrepreneur must treat a venture capitalist as a resource, just as he or she treats accountants, lawyers, consultants, and bankers. You never fully oblige yourself to a resource; you hire it and you use it. Someday it may be replaced, so don't grow dependent on it; at least no more than on other resources.

A statement of a venture capitalist I admire is more in keeping with my views. He said, "Don't think of this process as me giving you money to start your business; it's more appropriate to think of it as you giving me stocks to buy some of my money." That's the right philosophy, and I would strongly urge every aspiring entrepreneur to consider those thoughts before disagreeing with me and agreeing with the views of the venture capitalists.

GETTING UP THE ANTE

There is nothing I love as much as a good fight! *

The name of the game for every entrepreneur is "raising money." For all but a chosen few, it's the hardest part of starting a business—and the most rewarding when you are successful at it.

People who invest in new business enterprises run the gamut from public investors to doctors and lawyers to "angels" and institutional investors. Each has his or her own special characteristics and peculiarities with which every entrepreneur should be familiar.

At one end of the spectrum is the "itchy" money. These are nonprofessionals who invest with high expectations for quick profit and provide little, if any, management assistance. At the other end are the professionals who seem to worry little about their money, but pride themselves on the caliber of help and advice they can give the management. Somewhere between these two extremes is the happy medium.

BROTHER, CAN YOU SPARE A HUNDRED GRAND?

When they say its the principle, not the money, it's the money.

JOHN DILLON

If you follow the course taken by most entrepreneurs, you will not start out with a public stock offering. You will be making a private placement and will have to negotiate most of the following terms with the individual investors:

1. Registration rights and timetables for selling the investor's stock.
2. Seats on the board of directors, frequently of financial statements, and right of inspection of books.
3. Piggyback features of investors' stock to allow them to participate in a registration at a formula-determined cost.
4. Working capital, net worth, and dividend restrictions.
5. Key-man life insurance for you; property and product liability insurance for the company.
6. Employment and salary agreements for key personnel.
7. The capital to be repaid as debt, if any.
8. Call or conversation aspects of the stock or debt.

*Interview, *The New York Times,* January 22, 1911, Franklin Delano Roosevelt, 1882-1945.

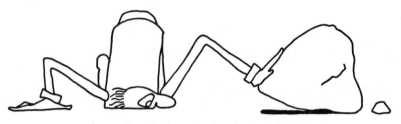

Now, where did I put that hundred grand?

9. Pre-emptive rights; offering new stock to old stockholders first, and penalty and prepayment provisions.

Most investors prefer to invest capital as part equity (stock) and part debt (loan). The equity money provides a base on which the company can build, and the debt money allows the investor to exercise controls over the company's financial activities without being involved on a day-to-day basis. Debt money offers the investor the added benefit of being returned with interest if the venture is successful.

In negotiating these "boiler-plate" provisions, remember that the investor is entitled to certain considerations, and, usually, their requests are reasonable. You may be caring for the garden, but they're providing the fertilizer. Enough of the right type can do wonders for your seeds, even with poor gardening skills. These investors want to make sure that the crop comes in, too. It is also a good idea to enlist the aid of both your lawyer and accountant in drafting the provisions of your deal. They'll catch things that you'll miss.

All types of investors have their own special needs and reasons for making an investment. Your major decision and greatest effort should go toward choosing the right type investor for your needs. If your business is high risk, but with potentially large rewards, you'll probably do best with the "itchy" money. If your situation is relatively stable and secure, the institutional investor might be best.

Pick the right money and you're on your way. The wrong money can mean plenty of headaches. Once you've found it, though, don't haggle unnecessarily over terms, and keep in mind that what's good for the investor can't hurt you. Remember, you're both stockholders in the same company.

VENTURE CAPITALISTS

The men who manage men are the men who manage men who manage things. The men who manage money manage the men who manage men.

BOB McCRAY

Venture capitalists are the people whose business is investing money in starting and expanding businesses. You can't live with them and you can't live without them. However you feel about them, venture capitalists play a vital role in the founding and eventual success of many entrepreneurial ventures.

Usually, the relationship between entrepreneurs and their venture capitalists is tense. Beneath the outward cordiality and comaraderie, the sentiment is often one of mutual mistrust.

You can't blame either of them, really. The venture capitalist, on the one hand, has what must be one of the world's toughest jobs; evaluating the potential of businesses that, in reality, are little more than pro forma cash flows and an entrepreneur's dream. It's risky business.

On the other hand, the entrepreneur knows he or she is going to make the venture capitalist wealthy beyond his fondest hopes and finds it hard to understand the need for so much unnecessary deliberation.

Attracting venture capital has been called a form of Russian Roulette, or the "you bet your company" game. Venture capitalists and entrepreneurs each play the game with their own tools. Venture capitalists bet on people and managements, but entrepreneurs know people and managements are unreliable and they choose to bet on products and technologies. So, the competition is between players with different combat weapons. It's an exciting contest.

The entrepreneur tries to build a company and prove his point. The venture capitalist tries to make money by backing highly speculative enterprises. It isn't difficult to understand why the two don't really fit comfortably together.

Remember, Mr. Entrepreneur, that your venture source, for what may seem the flimsiest of reasons, may suddenly change the terms or even back out of the deal and leave you with nothing. The experienced entrepreneur has a backup venture capitalist warmed up on the sidelines, just in case his original source poops out. Just don't let the number two know he's not on the first team.

Entrepreneurs are poor venture capitalists, and vice versa, but each needs the other. They can coexist peacefully, even profitably, so long as each recognizes the other's objectives. Many bid deals have resulted from such recognition.

ANGELS

Remember, no company ever sells stock. They buy capital. It just so happens that the medium of exchange for the capital is stock.

ARTHUR F. SNYDER

Angels are hard to find, but they do exist. They're those marvelous people who descend from the heavens just to invest in small companies. No, they're not supernaturals. Usually they are just successful, wealthy businesspeople who, instead of putting their money in the stock market, investing in mutual funds, or buying savings bonds, invest a portion of their wealth in young businesses.

This is the best sort of investor. They usually come in at the founding level and stay with the company until it makes a public offering. Often they sit on the

I want you—to take my money!

board of directors and make useful contacts for the company. When more money is needed, they are usually the first to step forward.

Most angels have invested between $100,000 and $200,000 in several small businesses, keeping their stake in each venture below $50,000. They are likely to be the only nonemployee investor in the companies. To top it off, they're usually the salt of the earth. Nice people. But smart. As venture capitalists they are better to do business with than any other alternative. If you can find one (in a city the size of Boston there are probably only 100 angels), you can't go wrong by bringing him or her into your financing arrangements.

THE FOOTWORK NECESSARY

Extreme fear can neither fight nor fly.

WILLIAM SHAKESPEARE, 1564-1616

How's your broken-field running? Raising venture capital often parallels trying to make a touchdown through the best defense in the league. It takes fancy footwork to work your way over that goal line.

Let's say you want to raise $250,000 for twenty-five percent of your company in a private placement. First, you must get a venture capitalist lukewarm about your situation. No one will be really enthusiastic after only one visit. I've heard that Digital Equipment Corporation of Maynard, Massachusetts, shopped around for quite a while before American Research and Development Corporation finally committed itself to the tune of $70,000, an investment that, rumor has it, is worth $200 million today.

Venture capitalists see dozens of deals a day, so it will not be easy to turn them on to your proposition. Besides, they are like sheep. They'd rather follow than lead. You have to be the sheep dog to keep the pack moving.

So, once you've got the first party lukewarm, plan your strategy carefully.

One strategy that usually works begins on the second visit when you say, "I know you're not in a position to go first in this package, but I have a proposition that should interest you. I already have other investors subscribed for the first $200,000. You can have the last $50,000. You don't have to sign anything—just give me a verbal commitment contingent on my getting the other $200,000 first."

If he or she agrees, then repeat your story to anyone else who seems to be lukewarm and proceed to sell the last $50,000 five times. You have to deal from strength.

The example may be a little farfetched, because someone has to go first. He's the one who counts and the hardest one to find—not a sheep but a true *venture* capitalist.

He is the person (who will) set the pace for the rest of the deal. Ask him for some sort of tentative percentages and terms, and, after you've negotiated, get a letter of intent for $50,000 spelling out the terms of the placement. You may have to make a few extra concessions, but once you have his pledge on paper or even verbally, your placement is the bag and you should have the rest within two months. Touchdown!

Always talk to potential investors as if your deal is all but closed and you may have to eliminate two or three investors from the package. Never act as if you need their help or you'll be tackled before you reach midfield; rather, suggest that this one time you'll accept their money. I can't overemphasize the need to deal from strength!

PERSONAL GUARANTEES

It is fatal to enter any war without the will to win it.

FRANKLIN D. ROOSEVELT,
1882-1945, speech

Have you ever been asked to guarantee the debts of your business? If you have, what protection can you take? The first thing you can do is to be sure the lender takes as much security as can obtained for your company's debt. That way, the lender is protected as fully as possible out of your company's assets. If the assets are not sufficient to cover all of your company's indebtedness upon a liquidation, it will be the unsecured general creditors who take the loss, rather than you as guarantor.

Thus, if you are a guarantor of unsecured indebtedness of your company and it subsequently gives security for a debt that is already outstanding, you should be very careful that the lien is perfected under the bankruptcy laws, especially if there is any concern about the continued viability of your company. Otherwise you may find that the security interest can be voided and you as guarantor may have to make up any deficiency to the lender you hoped would be secured.

When is a perfected lien not perfect? When it is less than three months and a day old. If a lender, such as a bank, files a bona fide lien or security interest against your inventory or receivables, and you go into bankruptcy within ninety days of that filing, the validity of the security interest may be challenged. If it turns out that you did not get full and fair value at the time you granted the lien, then the lender loses his preferred position against other creditors as to those pledged assets. Consequently, if you are either a company that has recently pledged some collateral, or a company that gives credit on a secured basis, keep in mind the valuable three-months-and-a-day rule. It can make the difference between a secured and an unsecured position. This rule is part of federal bankruptcy law and is, therefore, the same in every state.

ENTREPRENEURS AS VENTURE CAPITALISTS

It is not possible to fight beyond your strength, even if you strive.

HOMER
The Iliad c. 700 B.C.

Surprising though it may sound, entrepreneurs are usually interesting and compatible people—especially for other entrepreneurs.

Appreciating this fact, I founded a new company in 1968, called Imaginative Investments, Inc. (I.I.I.). The idea was to form a powerful source to raise capital for speculative and imaginative investments.

The company quickly became known as Eye,Yie,Yie. Entrepreneur met entrepreneur and we had excellent attendance at all meetings, averaging 90 percent of the group.

The group functioned well at luncheons, trade shows, and seminars, but when it got down to making some tough, high-level decisions, the cordialities ceased and each member frequently and forcefully voiced his own opinion. We couldn't agree on anything, even when to meet.

In the end, Eye,Yie,Yie was disbanded. Everyone had his initial investment returned and walked away from it none the poorer, save myself.

All of which proves that entrepreneurs make good friends but lousy venture capitalists.

THE BUILDING BLOCK CONCEPT

I Think I Can, I Think I Can, I Think I Can . . . .

The Little Train That Could

Most small businesses that fail, do so because their working capital is inadequate, and they go broke before they can get off the ground.

You can minimize this problem by using the building block concept of planning each action sequentially so that the profits from the first action form a base for the next action. For instance, you employ manufacturers' reps to generate sales and profits so that you can eventually employ direct salespeople. To do it the other way would drain limited capital and jeopardize further operations.

It's easy to become overwhelmed by the sudden infusion of large amounts of capital, as, for example, after a successful placement. Some entrepreneurs and small companies believe this excess capital will let them skip certain building blocks. They hire direct salespeople, for instance, or they buy an expensive piece of equipment that provides capacity that won't be needed for a year. Then, suddenly, the money is gone and so is the business.

The skip-a-step concept is suicide. The building block concept builds a strong foundation for your company, impresses the financial community, and increases your chances for success dramatically.

Most entrepreneurs have the vision needed to see beyond the present requirements of the company, but the financial community, suppliers, employees, and customers don't have that foresight.

The secret to successful financing lies in its execution, not its speed. Perform each step in sequence better than the previous step. Whatever you do, don't try to make some of your decisions in a logical building block manner and the rest as short spurts.

SELECTING THE UNDERWRITER

The entrepreneur's passion for "mattress money" can prevent the deal from happening.

FRED ADLER

An early step in making a public offering is the selection of an underwriter—the firm that actually sells your stock. It is difficult to generalize about the best method of selecting one. Each situation is different and each underwriter has certain advantages and disadvantages for each situation. The most crucial aspect of the selection is to match your company's financial needs to your underwriter's capabilities.

Talk to several underwriters before making a choice. You'll be together for some time and it's a difficult relationship to revoke. At the same time, offering your deal to a dozen underwriters may create an auction-like environment, and could scare away the good guys who don't cherish a bidding war.

Underwriters are compensated in many ways. They often receive warrants and options to buy your stock at lower prices in the future, in addition to the the underwriting discount. Be sure to understand all the levels of compensation before closing your deal.

Your underwriter will choose the best form of public offering from several alternatives, depending on your financial needs and the condition of the stock market at the time of your offering.

When the new issue market is hot, some start-up situations may be better off with fast action and less money. These are usually handled under Regulation A of the Securities and Exchange Commission. Commonly referred to as Reg A offerings, they can generate up to $2 million for a ball park cost of $50,000 in about three months. The Reg A has less stringent registration requirements because it is approved by a regional office of the SEC, not the Washington, D.C., office.

If your company's financial position is more substantial, you may choose an S-1 or S-2 registration. Essentially, an S-1 is a more substantial registration

Eenie, meenie, minie, moe; Uncle Bert or Uncle Joe?

than an S-2. There is no limit on the amount of money you may raise, but the lead time is usually in excess of six months and they are both much more costly than a Reg A.

Throughout a public offering you are regulated by the Securities Act of 1933, which prohibits your promoting or selling stock before it is properly registered. Ignoring this rule is the fastest way to blow an offering (on your company). Your lawyer and underwriter will explain the requirements in detail. Listen hard. It's important.

Finally, the success of your offering may depend on your underwriter, so be sure there is no mismatch before you jump for the much-needed, fresh, new, money transfusion. Also, ask your underwriter about the new S-18 registration procedures. This is another new option for raising capital. In 1979 and 1980, most entrepreneurial ventures, chose this new, less cumbersome form of public registration.

FRIENDS AND RELATIVES

Niccolo Machiavelli (1469-1527), one of the outstanding statesmen of the Italian Renaissance, wrote in The Prince, his classic treatise on the use of power, "The first opinion that is formed of a ruler's intelligence is based on the quality of the men he has around him."

There are nearly as many methods of financing entrepreneurial ventures as there are entrepreneurs and venture capitalists. All venture financings, however, proceed through the same three stages—from seed money to private financing to public offering. Any of these steps can be multifaceted, and having a number of substeps within a stage has become common. the entrepreneur must adapt his or her company structure and financial needs to meet the needs of the investors at each stage. Investors won't adapt for companies.

Seed money financing is the most thrilling and exciting stage of any new venture. Here the investor takes the biggest gamble by supplying the long money at long odds in search of the long gain, usually with a basis no more concrete than an idea or a dream.

The danger that lurks at the seed stage involves the natural tendency of the entrepreneur to look to friends and relatives for seed money. The number of fathers, mothers, uncles, aunts, and neighbors who have backed new business ventures is legion. Because most entrepreneurs are inexperienced and unfamiliar with the footwork necessary when raising capital, they all too often take this route, and all too often it proves catastrophic.

Venture capitalists hope to make money by investing in new businesses, but even they frequently fail to evaluate situations properly. If the professionals have trouble, how can Uncle Bert do better?

If you really believe you have such a good deal to offer your friends and relatives, you shouldn't have much trouble convincing a professional venture capitalist. Remember you have to live with friends and relatives for a long time. Coexistence could be tough if you lost their money.

So, get your capital, especially the seed money, from professionals. If your venture is successful, you can always invite your friends and relatives to buy stock later—and sleep better in the meantime.

THE GROWTH CRISIS

CHEATERS AT THE GROWTH STAGE

You don't have to be nice to the people you meet on the way up if you're not coming down again. *

During the growth stage it is crucial to keep your fingers on the pulse of the business. It is so easy to lose the pulse, and when you do you can lose the business.

In the late 1960s, one of my entrepreneurial whims eventually developed into a business. I was the entrepreneur in a scheme for creating an Alberto-Culber (VO-5 hair spray) in the aerosol business. With some friends and relatives, we raised a small amount of money to develop the product line. Shortly thereafter, in order to attract a quarter of a million dollars in venture capital, I

*From a speech by Daddy Warbucks in the Broadway musical *Annie,* written by Thomas Meehan.

devoted most of my time and effort to this venture. We chose a high flying, fast moving course of action. The choice was not bad; the trouble was our inability to control the choice. So many things can go wrong, as Murphy has said many times. I have to admit that Lanewood (the street that I lived on) Laboratories was a series of mistimed tragedies.

But I do feel an obligation to relate this one tragedy in order to warn you about certain employees. Most of them are very trustworthy. However, there are always a few bad apples. And one bad apple can spoil the barrel.

Lanewood hired a salesman for the New York territory with all the credentials of Mr. Wonderful. He had been an All-American quarterback in college, he was top salesman for his previous employer, and he taught Sunday school. I had entertained him and his family, and anticipated great results from his New York territory. After all, New York held our greatest market potential.

I was flabbergasted when three months later we discovered that he was employed not only by our firm, but by another firm as well. In short, while we thought he was working full time for us, somebody else thought he was working full time for them. Not only did he receive two salaries, he was clever enough to collect double expenses by double reporting—a real shrewd operator who caught us in our growth stage.

As a small company, we could not survive the damage done by this one nonperforming employee. It was not the $10,000 he chiseled from us that hurt (although it stung), but what he did not do when we needed him. That's what made the difference. What we could not withstand was the lack of sales in his territory. It made our high flying course of action look bad.

Lanewood had arranged an incentive program that paid the salesmen when they delivered purchase orders, not when customers paid for the merchandise. Another bad mistake. In a short time, our New York man had booked more orders than any of our other salesmen and gathered in several nice incentive checks. Not until after the merchandise was shipped did we realize that our customers believed they ordered the merchandise on consignment. You can appreciate the impact of this bad mistake.

I doubt whether very many human beings have evil intent. However, greed for money and the pressing weight of other circumstances may force this characteristic on some. And running foul of evil intent at the growth stage can put the business into a downward spiral. Since a business still in the growth stage is not very far above ground zero, it can be a short-lived spiral—with a loud ugly noise at the end of it.

LONG-RANGE PLANNING

It is not doing things right that counts, it is doing the right thing.

PETER DRUCKER

The problems don't stop once an entrepreneur has managed to start a venture, put together a financing package, and build an organization. If anything, they increase in number and complexity. But they are different kinds of problems, more related to internal goings on, and often they are more difficult to solve. With the money in the bank and the production line rollling, cheer up and smile occasionally. Your "guts" have got you this far, and now it's time for some "fun."

For most small companies, long-range planning means thinking at breakfast about what to do after lunch. Stay alive in the short run, the theory goes, and the long run will take care of itself.

On the other hand, Dr. Theodore Levitt, professor par excellence at the Harvard Business School, contends that if you don't know where you're going, any road will take you there. In other words, the company that carefully plans for the future optimizes its chances for success.

No doubt Levitt is right, but for an entrepreneur choosing between survival tactics that long-range planning, it is no choice at all—and here lies one of the fundamental differences between large established businesses and small businesses. The large company has advisors and staff assistants whose major function is to plan their company's every move. Small businesspeople can't afford janitors, never mind planning staffs. The entrepreneur can only choose a course and try to stay flexible enough to consider another course at a moment's notice. It's a choice between thinking and doing. Big companies think; the entrepreneur does.

THE TENDENCY TO OPERATE
A SMALL BUSINESS AT A MINIMUM

Expectation is always greater than the event.

Source unknown

There has been a growing interest of late in the professional services corporation—a business that offers services rather than selling a product. The major advantage of a small organization is its ability to compete with large cumbersome organizations. It is more flexible, quicker to react and more pliable than a larger organization. However, there is one fundamental limitation on the growth of a small organization, especially a small service-based organization. This limitation is fundamental to any growth issue for a small service business, because it is unavoidably part of the business. It just naturally comes with the territory. So, rather than trying to elude it, why not face it straightaway. The change of conquering it is better based upon a direct frontal assault.

See the following page for further insight into this avoidable tendency.

The question is "how do these one person service-based firms become large successful businesses?" The greatest disadvantage of a one-person firm is its inability to function when the one person is not working. There is no continuity and there is no other source of revenue other than this individual's time; so, how does the one-person firm succeed and eventually grow?

Here are some of the inherent problems in attempting to expand a one-person service firm. There exists in nature several happy states. They occur whenever there is a high degree of efficiency. An automobile engine is more efficient (which makes the owner happier) at 55 miles per hour than it is at 65 miles per hour because gas efficiency is better at the lower speeds. So, too, businesses are happier at certain organizational sizes.

Let's look at organizations of people within service businesses. Obviously, the size of "one" is the happiest state in a professional service organization because so many one-person service organizations exist and prosper. The reason is very simple; there is a very nice mix of overhead and labor at the organizational size of one. All the money that is received by the firm goes directly to the one person who produces it. It's easily the happiest state, where there is an unusually high organizational efficiency.

According to my research, the next happiest state occurs at about eight people. At eight people, one boss and seven workers, the ratio of overhead and labor significantly improves and the boss no longer has to perform the actual working functions required when the firm was only one person. Consequently, it would be better for eight one-person firms to merge or for two four-person firms to merge to reach the magic size of eight than it would be for each one-person firm to face the consequences of growing from one to eight. Hence, eight is an optimum. Between any two optimums in a business by definition is a minimum. And most firms work hard to operate at a minimum.

An elusive jellylike concept that evades many an entrepreneur is the quantum-jump concept. Now this isn't a take-off on Einstein's theory. It's really very simple: different optimum sizes exist for each firm. Profit optimums occur at different sizes for different firms. About halfway between two otpimums is a minimum. This is a no-no region. Somehow most firms operate in the minimum while struggling toward a maximum or optimum.

Let's examine an easy-to-analyze firm, which usually is the analyzer and not the analyzee—a management consulting firm. Size could be measured by such variables as plant size, capital stock, and so on, but let's use the number of employees in our example.

Obviously, a one-person consulting firm is one optimum size. That's why there are so many one-person firms. Many consultants find it desirable and profitable to operate as a a one-person firm. From this point, the next optimum

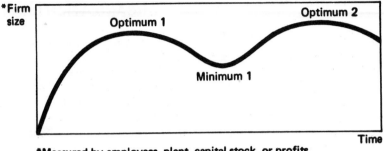

*Measured by employees, plant, capital stock, or profits

would not occur until the firm has about eight employees, at which size a sensible ratio would exist between workers and bosses. The danger for all the one-person optimums is that they lack the resources to make it all the way up the hill to eight employees, and they end up in a valley of three or four employees. Therefore, without appreciating this danger, they begin expanding and run out of resources just as their firm has reached a minimum.

It would be better to stay just where you are than shoot for a minimum. You wouldn't attempt to cross a desert with only enough water to make it three-fourths of the way, would you? Well, neither should you try to make it to the next larger optimum size without sufficient resources. In fact, maybe going back (in size) might bring you to an optimum quicker and cheaper.

FINDING THE MEAT

The entrepreneur is a poet and packager—an actualizer and a visualizer.

BOB SCHWARTZ

Remember the old joke about the gourmet who was asked by the waiter how he found his steak? Peeved by the small portion, the diner retorted, "I just moved a pea aside and there it was."

When it comes to solving internal company problems, the entrepreneur seldom thinks to look under the peas. Instead, he or she tends to look outside the company for solutions that are often right under the nose.

The growing company frequently encounters problems that can be solved just by improving production techniques, inventory control, or purchasing procedures. Remember, saving $1,000 on something like quantity discounts on purchases produces the same level of profit as $10,000 in additional sales.

Why not move a few peas around?

Glory is like a circle in the water, which never ceases to enlarge itself, till by broad spreading it disperses to naught.

WILLIAM SHAKESPEARE, 1564-1616
Henry VI, 1591

An organization chart graphically depicts the relationships between the various functional business areas of a company. By definining the levels of authority it minimizes confusion and optimizes efficiency.

Show me a small company with management trouble and I'll show you a company without a formal, publicized organization chart. An organization chart is effective only as long as the company's structure remains unchanged, and in a small, growing company, the structure changes weekly, sometimes daily. Trying to update the organization chart would be like charting traffic at O'Hare Airport.

But that doesn't mean small companies neglect organization charts. Not at all. They just like to keep them secret. Tucked in the back of the center drawer of every entrepreneur's desk is a penciled sketch (usually on the back of an envelope), drawn for someone who inquired about his organization. It's usually covered with dotted lines and erasures, and a few names magically appear in more than one box.

The entrepreneur *always* knows what his or her company would look like on an organization chart. After all, the organization chart is really the master plan to conquer the competition. He or she would avoid a lot of confusion, improve communications, and stop a lot of internal politicking if the employees were in on it, too.

OPPORTUNITIES VS. PROBLEMS

I know what to do, but I wonder if I can keep it interesting?

Zsa Zsa Gabor's seventh husband

Entrepreneurs discuss opportunities, not problems. In a small company, especially during the growth stage, problems are as plentiful as apples in October. Can you wonder that entrepreneurs would rather talk about opportunities?

Scholars claim that defining the problem is the first step in solving it. With all these apples in the orchard, the solution doesn't rest with definitions, but with enough hands to help in the harvest. There is always plenty for all. If you are an employee of an entrepreneur, there's one fundamental rule you should never violate. Never take to the boss problems, on opportunities. He has problems of his own.

THE 80-20 RULE

He who can, does. He who cannot, teaches.

GEORGE BERNARD SHAW

If one law is universally applicable to business, especially to small business, it is the rule that 20 percent of the customers provide 80 percent of the sales, or that 20 percent of the inventory accounts for 80 percent of the sales; or that—well, you get the idea.

According to one of my associates, an Italian scientist named Pareto first recorded this law in the sixteenth century. It is every bit as valid today as it was some 400 years ago, and the wise entrepreneur will put it to practical use.

HOW TO ESTABLISH CORPORATE STRATEGY

And God created the organization and gave it dominion over man.

Genesis 1, 30A, Subparagraph VIII

No one knows for sure what makes one corporate strategy work and another fail. It is known that those companies that succeed have better strategies than those that fail. It's not known whether the strategy causes success or if the success is a result of the strategy. Consequently, it is difficult to offer reliable advice about setting corporate strategy in entrepreneurial ventures. It's possible to give more tangible advice about incorrect strategies than about correct strategies.

While setting your corporate strategy, you must be able to assimilate in your head the millions of variables that interact simultaneously to contribute to developing a strategy. The responsibility to determine the strategy is a functional only reserved for the top executive officer of a small company. Only he or she can determine what business you are in, It is often said that if you don't know where you are going, any road will take you there. It's the charge of the strategist to determine the road. The top person is the lead dog in the pack, and he or she exchanges an unobstructed view of what's in front for a willingness to establish the course.

Keep in mind that short-term and long-term strategies are not the same. Short-term strategies are often nothing more than tactics that have been improperly labeled. Long-term strategies answer the fundamental question of what business you are in.

A computer will never lose in competition with the world's greatest human checker player. When a computer plays checkers, it will at least draw with the best human beings. In other words, the computer has the capacity to handle the finite number of more in a checker game and it is programmed to win or draw. The best you can achieve against a computer in checkers is a draw.

Not so in a more complex game like chess. A master chess player can beat a computer almost consistently, not an average chess player, mind you, but a master chess player. The reason the computer cannot outthink a master chess player is twofold: (1) the computer can't handle within its memory the capacity a human being can handle within its memory; In other words, our heads store and assess more data of a useful nature than the computer; and (2) an even more important reason is that a computer is unable to develop long-run strategies. A computer must handle each decision in a step-by-step digital basis. An individual can decide on a strategy that encompasses a wide range or series of moves and the master chess player can beat the computer in the chess game.

The leader must assimilate all the data and be a visionary to determine an optimum corporate strategy for an entrepreneurial venture. As the boss can and must articulate a meaningful answer to the question "what business am I in?" The others must follow.

MEETINGS: HOW NOT TO ATTEND THEM

Entrepreneurs emerge from the groups of disadvantaged, or displaced, people.

PROF. ALBERT SHAPIRO

Small companies that experience rapid growth tend to suffer from conflicts among the production, engineering, finance, and sales departments. Each department blames each other for problems, and to resolve these conflicts department heads have meetings.

The entrepreneur should know what goes on in those meetings, but he or she would go right up the wall by attending all of them. One entrepreneur I know appointed one person to attend the meetings for him. This official meeting-attender would sit in on each meeting, take occasional notes for the boss, and in the event of real trouble, would suggest that the boss step in. After the average two-hour meeting concluded, he would stick his head into the entrepreneur's office and neatly summarize the happenings in a few sentences.

MANAGEMENT CONSULTANTS

Transforming the experiences of business into the celebration of life.

MARSHALL THURBER

Entrepreneurs, more than other businesspeople, rely on other people—such as professional management consultants, college professors, other company presidents, or anyone else who can intelligently offer advice and objectivity.

These people serve as sounding boards for the entrepreneur's ideas and help him or her weigh alternatives before making the final decision. In other fields, such as government, the military, and even sports, these sounding boards exist internally in the form of staff assistants.

Since small businesses can't afford droves of staff assistants, they have to rely on external sources, and this has led to the emergence of professional mangement consultants. The M.C. is usually a person with a broad range of knowledge in the management of businesses, and he or she applies that experience to your problems to guide you in the right direction. Ultimately, the decision is always yours, but the M.C. plays a vital role in helping you see the flaws and correcting them before you implement the plan. The M.C. is often the source for new creative concepts, too.

To demonstrate this emergence of the management consultant, I counted the number of consulting firms listed in the Yellow Pages in various cities and noted their increase over the years. The results are shown in the table below. Apparently, there is no other means to prove this point as neither government nor any association compiles the number of management consulting firms by city. I believe the data demonstrates the growth and, thereby, the value of the service.

NUMBER OF MANAGEMENT CONSULTANT FIRMS
IN YELLOW PAGES BY YEAR

City	1951	1960	1963	1964	1965	1969
Boston	17		60			178
Chicago					268	
Los Angeles		112			225	
Philadelphia					108	
Washington, D.C.				111		

City	1970	1974	1975	1976	1978	1980
Boston				365	412	515
Chicago	449				650	750
Los Angeles	337	340			640	773
Philadelphia	158		182		356	445
Washington, D.C.				401	525	685

A WORD ABOUT COMPUTERS

Sell management information systems, but deliver accounts receivable packages.

I.B.M.

Every small business, during either its late growth or early maturity stage, experiments with buying or time-sharing a computer. The word to remember when you get to this point is KISS.

Computers can do beautiful things, but more often they overwhelm the entrepreneur with information he or she is not ready or able to cope with, and they create more problems than they solve.

As one of my entrepreneurial friends learned, you have to take it easy with computers. To remind his people, he would hold up his KISS sign at meetings where things were getting out of hand, especially with regard to the computer reports. They knew what he meant—*Keep It Simple Stupid.*

COMPROMISE

The speed of the leader is the speed of the pack.

DR. DERECK NEWTON

Compromise is mandatory in politics, valuable in negotiating military conflicts, and helpful in solving legal disputes, but it can be dangerous for the struggling small business.

The temptation to compromise in solving a current crisis exists for every entreprenrur. As the problems and decisions become more complex, the temptation grows stronger. I say fight it!

Entrepreneurs seem to possess great intuitive powers, and it's generally best to trust your intuition for those tough decisions.

Entrepreneurs are leaders, and leaders are made or destroyed on the issues they compromise or refuse to compromise. Napoleon said, "I'd rather have an army of rabbits led by a lion than an army of lions led by a rabbit."

You are the one everyone has bet on. They aren't so dumb; they know a good bet when they see it. Think through alternatives, weigh the criteria, and then, once you've given the decision careful consideration—be a lion!

CONVENTIONAL WISDOM

Most entrepreneurial ventures are born within other entrepreneurial companies.

PROF. ARNOLD COOPER
Purdue University

Running a small business successfully requires common sense. Right or wrong? The answer is right most of the time, but not always. When should conventional wisdom be discarded in favor of contrary thinking? Which rules should be followed even though they appear illogical at first glance? When is common sense uncommon?

Here are four rules of unconventional wisdom:

1. Whenever you don't need capital—that is the optimal time to raise it.
2. Whenever your backlog is high—that is the optimal time to call a dealer or representative sales meeting.
3. When shipments and bookings are high—that is the optimal time to advertise.
4. When the economy is choking off small companies and the times appear bleak—this is the ideal time to launch an entreprenurial venture.

Here is the rationale:

1. Bank lines of credit and new equity capital should be arranged whenever you don't need it. This takes discipline and prior skills in financial planning. It's really contrary to what is done in practice—just try to raise capital when you decide you need it, and you'll appreciate this rule.

2. When sales are low, it's a natural time to try and raise sales, but it's the wrong time to call a rah-rah sales meeting. First, a sales meeting calls the salespeople off the road just when you need the effort. Second, when sales are low, the internal reaction of the sales team is often self-defeating. People are down. Third, when sales are high and you don't need more sales—that's the time to hold the meeting to decide how to keep unsatisfied customers happy.

3. When sales are high, this is the best time to advertise. The dealy between advertising and subsequent sales is usually sufficient to warrant an advertising effort during your peak sales month. The results of the advertising will be apparent a few months after the previous peak sales month, and it should occur just in time to keep your sales rising.

4. When interest rates are high and stock prices are low, capital tends to dry up and small companies die. This is an ideal time to start a new business as your eventual birth will be perfectly timed to coincide with the inevitable upswing that follows the recession. You can be swept along by the economy until you become a viable business.

7

THE
MATURITY
CRISIS

FAMILY BUSINESSES

The best entrepreneur I know is Mother Teresa of Calcutta, India.

MARGARET MEAD

Families can get themselves into some pretty unusual and comical predicaments. Family businesses can get themselves into a whole series of comedies and predicaments.

As a consultant, I've enjoyed working for family businesses. Just what is a family business? First, it is a segment of the small business community. So, to begin with, we must define small business. As we noted earlier, the Small Business Administration defines small business in several ways. My definition of small business is one in which the major decisions are made by one person. I am sure that doesn't hold for every case, but, in my definition, any business that can be handled, managed, and operated by one person qualifies. The definition includes one-person proprietorships as well as $20 million corporations.

A family business always falls within my definition of a small business. A family business is one in which the one person who makes the major decisions was preceded by a relative in the job, or who currently has relatives on the payroll. That's a family business. Some family businesses have a long history of a son following a father who followed another father and so on.

The main reasons that family businesses can be a series of comedies is the unique people relationships that develop in families. And I mean families in the best sense of the word. Really, considering the alternatives, you tolerate an awful lot from your children or your parents. Would you ever tolerate that much from a friend or a business associate? Family businesses stretch tolerance beyond reason. On the other hand, stretching these tolerance lines is what keeps the business friendly and homey.

Here's a story with a moral for all of you operating within a family business. In the early 1900s two brothers decided to start a regional chemical manufacturing business. After hard work and high risk of their own capital, they managed to come out of the 1930s depression with a small profitable business. Nothing to get excited about, mind you, but as they phrased it, "It provided a good living for our families." Both brothers married and had children. One had a son, the other had two sons, and eventually all three boys joined the family business. And here was the core of this family's business problem—poor family planning.

When the two brothers left the business, they left their sons in control—what had been a 50-50 ownership was now 50-25-25. Now any business without someone in firm control requires management by compromise—not management by objectives, not management by one person, not management by exception, but management by compromise. With 50-25-25, there's a tendency for one of the two brothers to vote with a cousin to avoid conflict.

When this dilemma arises, the temptation is to concentrate energy on the relationship between the owners and not on the business. Energy is concentrated on the family, not on the business. The best solution is to avoid the catastrophe. Someone should be in control. Someone must be responsible. Someone must have the authority. But for all of those family businesses where there is no clear-cut control, there's a possible solution in recognizing that two are better than three.

You've heard the old story that three's a crowd. Well, it's just as true in the family business. Working as a consultant on this problem, I devised a rotating sheme by which each one of the three sons took a nine-month sabbatical while the other two managed the business. Brother number one left for nine months, while brother number two and the cousin ran the business. Then brother number two took a sabbatical. Then the cousin. Every combination of two had a chance to work together over an eighteen-month period. The process produced harmony in the business and gave each of the managers an opportunity to understand the other relative's function. It worked very well. As a technique, it appears to have promise for those unusual situations. I pass it along because the company and yourself can both benefit by your sabbaticals. When a situation develops where everyone wins, why not give it some consideration. Remember that two is better than three—but one is better than two.

GOING PUBLIC

From each according to his abilities, to each according to his need.

KARL MARX

The entrepreneur who stays with his or her company through the growth crisis is only slightly less rare than the entrepreneur who manages to get his new venture off the ground in the first place. The rate of entrepreneurial attrition between those first exciting days of the start-up and the time when a company is finally out of the woods is legend. So, one would assume, it's all downhill from here.

If actuarial figures exist on the life expectancy of the business that reaches maturity, I believe they would indicate that it can expect to survive for a good many years. But the crises are not at an end, not by any stretch of the imagination.

Every entrepreneur secretly dreams of the day when his or her company can go public. It's the blessed event that comes after a long, trying, and often painful gestation. It makes all the past problems appear small. When the baby comes, you forget the pain.

Let's see . . . maybe my company could be just a little public.

What does a public offering do for the company? It gives it status; it's a scorecard to show the public that you've done more things right than wrong.

Most important, however, is the fact that a public offering provides equity capital, the magic potion that allows the entrepreneur to operate unprofitably while increasing volume. Furthermore, fresh infusions of capital create a fine mist that clouds the real profit potential of the enterprise. Lack of capital enlarges the entrepreneur's mistakes. Its presence covers them up.

Wall Street has an unwritten rule that says a "good" company shouldn't go public until it has reached at least a million dollars in profits on ten million dollars in sales. Most "good" small companies try to adhere to that rule. If capital is short, try to raise it privately and put off that public offering as long as possible.

When you do finally take your company public, there are two important pieces of advice I can offer. First, don't jump at the first underwriter who makes an offer. Although the financial community generally advises against "shopping your deal," I think it's advisable to line up a few alternative underwriters in the event of unexpected trouble with the prime underwriter. On the other hand, you shouldn't shop your package all over the lot, attempting to create an auction environment to raise the stock multiple and per share offering price. That's a no-no, too. In fact, the Securities and Exchange Commission (SEC) gets very upset if your deal is shown to more than twenty-five potential investors. This figure includes anyone shown the deal, not just those that eventually invest.

Finally, going public can make the entrepreneur rich—at least on paper. Except in rare cases the principals can't sell their stock in the first public offering, but every entrepreneur likes to count his or her shares and multiply them by the public offering price amd use the slide rule to calculate personal worth. During all those years in the cellar, when the entrepreneur fought and struggled to build the company, he or she never really knew the value of the venture. Now there is a realistic measure, and it sure feels good just to have a firm answer. Even if it is only momentary.

CASHING IN THE CHIPS

An entrepreneurial "10" (on a scale of 1-10) is a "4" with 6 million dollars.

KEITH VAN BUSKIRK

Many entrepreneurs decide not to take their companies public. They put them on the market in one lump instead of thousands of small pieces. In many respects this can be more desirable than a public offering. The net effect is the same, especially if the buyer (as is often the case) is a larger public company. There is a fresh source of capital, and the entrepreneur gets either cash (better

O.K., where's the $100 window?

than the first public offering) or stock in the purchaser's company. The draw-back is that he or she becomes an employee and loses at least some of the control.

In selling a small business, one very important problem is how to determine its value so that the seller gets what he or she deserves, and the buyer gets what he or she pays for. Following are the three methods generally used to determine the market value of a small company.

Liquidation value is the value what would be assigned to a business being sold to satisfy its creditors. Tangible assets, such as land, usually have a liquidation value close to their market value. Inventories, on the other hand, are usually valued at about twenty percent of cost. To determine the liquidation value, all of the assets are assigned distressed values, and the debts are totaled. The difference between the distressed value of the assets and the actual value of the liabilities is the liquidation value. This method is used only if a company is in serious financial trouble or exceptionally heavy with assets.

Book value is what is shown on the books as net worth, or stockholders' equity. It is determined by subtracting the book value of the assets from the book value of the liabilities. It can also be determined by adding profits earned, or subtracting losses incurred, from the initial total capital investment in the company. In practice, book value is seldom used, although I believe it is as realistic an approach as any to measuring a small company's worth.

Market value is the most common—and the trickiest—method of evaluating a small company. Simply stated, it is the value a willing buyer would pay a willing seller. If the selling company's stock is publicly traded, its value is the traded per share price multipled by the number of outstanding shares. When selling a company, however, the calculation does not mean that someone will pay the per share price for every share. It often happens that the price is inflated or deflated when only a small part of the outstanding stock (float) is traded on the open market. The per share price does suggest a ballpark price/earnings ratio—the price per share divided by the earnings per share. A P/E ratio of about twenty is common for a small growth company. However, this method of evaluation applies only when the stock is publicly traded.

As an example of the complicated figuring that is involved in selling a closely held small company, let's review the case of one of my clients in the chemical business who sold his company. It had annual sales of about $1 million and earned about ten percent after taxes. Both the book value and the assets value were approximately $250,000. There was no debt. The buyer claimed the business was worth $1 million (after-tax earnings of $100,000 multiplied by the price/earnings ratio of ten). His valuation was based solely on the company's earning potential.

My client refused the offer, calling attention to an important fallacy in this technique of valuation. The business, he pointed out, had a net worth of $250,000. Therefore, it had a quarter of a million dollars of borrowing power. Technically, he could borrow that $250,000, declare a bonus after taxes of $125,000 in cash, and not affect the company's earning power except for a small interest charge. According to the buyer's valuation technique, this transaction would not change the market value of the company. So, my client placed a value of $1,200,000 on the company—the original $1 million plus $200,000 for the net worth. In the final negotiations, his argument held water, and he got $1 million. Give a little, get a little!

TURN-AROUND TECHNIQUE

One of the most interesting problems in small business is turning around unsuccessful companies. A condensed story of how Bill Frustajer (the founder of several highly successful businesses) and his consulting team turned around the H. H. Scott Hi-Fi Company in Maynard, Massachusetts, will serve a point. Scott is one of the leading quality manufacturers of stereo equipment in the country. Some years ago the company ran into terrible price competition from foreign suppliers, mainly Japanese, and was teetering on the verge of bankruptcy. Payroll had been paid intermittently, bills were overdue, and the large Boston-based State Street Bank had closed in. Bill Frustajer's first chore was to find out if there were sources of short-term cash. Cash would keep away the creditors and pay past-due payroll to keep the employees working. The technique he used was to uncover a heretofore undiscovered asset. Three years previously, the earnings of the company had been sufficient to warrant paying income taxes of $1,200,000 on what year's profits. The losses the last two years had been staggering, but profits were respectable the preceding year. Frustajer rewrote his financial statements and filed IRS form 1139 in order to go back and get a tax refund against those assets. A tax loss can be either carried forward for five years or back for three years.

Below is a simplified statement of the company's performance.

SIMPLIFIED PROFIT AND LOSS

	1971	1972	1973	1974
Sales	$12,000,000	$13,000,000	$14,000,000	$12,000,000
Profits before taxes	$ 2,400,000	(250,000)	(2,700,000)	–
Taxes	1,200,000	–	–	–
Profits after taxes	1,200,000	(250,000)	(2,700,000)	–

Although the table is simplified to demonstrate the example, income taxes are not due until March 15 of the following year for a company with a calendar year end. Consequently, by filing an amended set of financial statements and tax returns plus IRS from 1139, he was able to obtain a tax refund for the taxes paid in 1971. In the H. H. Scott case, although these are not the actual numbers, the tax refund saved the day and, in turn, the company.

Actually, the turnaround on receiving an IRS rebate is too long (months) ordinarily to save a faltering business. So, Frustajer pledged this refund to the bank along with the documents filed to secure the IRS refund and was able to borrow against this asset, thereby shrinking the processing time to receive the needed cash infusion. He received the funds in less than a month.

Hidden assets don't always appear as financial statements in plain view. Examples of other hidden assets are foreign rights to produce, licensing arrangements, patents, and goodwill.

STOCK OPTIONS

A liberal is generous with someone else's money.

JIM HOWARD

As soon as an enterprise becomes successful, many entrepreneurs want to "share the wealth" with key employees by making the company's stock available to them over a period of time at highly favorable prices. It's a nice thing to do. It's generally well intended. A qualified stock option plan can give a valued employee an opporutnity to increase net worth substantially. It can also tie an employee to a company for a long time, in return for the promise of future capital gains.

If you do offer your key people stock options, which I recommend, don't offer them advice on when to exercise their options. Consider what would happen if you were asked "off the record" to predict the company's future to an employee who was trying to decide when to exercise his or her option. Naturally, you're going to paint a rosy picture, based on your optimistic nature. But what if something goes sour and the stock price takes a dive? Then, to make matters worse, you're forced to let that employee go. Now he (or she) doesn't have a job, and all of his savings are tied up in a depressed stock. And don't forget he's your friend. It can be unsettling on a person's psyche. It's much wiser to send the employee to a professional for that kind of advice. You stay out of it.

Finally, it might interest you to know that a study of new companies in Palo Alto, California, showed that more than half were founded with money generated from stock option programs of other entrepreneurial companies. Your stock option plan could eventually finance some new competition, too. It's a two-edged sword.

STAFF MEETINGS

The entrepreneurial venture fares best with an entrepreneurial team.

PROF. JEFFRY TIMMONS
Northeastern University

An associate likens staff meetings to an experiment he once witnessed in a psychology laboratory. Seven pieces of string, precisely two feet long, were placed side by side on a table. Next to those seven pieces the experimenter placed an eighth piece of string, a clear six inches shorter than the original seven pieces.

Six people were then brought into the room. Five of them were plants, the sixth was the subject.

The experimenter asked several questions, among which was: "Are all of these pieces of string the same length?" To this, the first plant answered with an emphatic "Yes!" Then each of the other plants did the same, in turn, reinforcing the first "yes." In three quarters of such experiments, the subject also answered affirmatively. Wouldn't you?

When the experiment was repeated with just the subject present, the response was "no" in more than nine out of ten tries. Peer influence, according to these data, is very powerful.

I'm sure you've all attended meetings like this one where everyone agrees with the first couple of speakers, right or wrong. Cancel these types of meetings. They're wasting everyone's time.

LOVE YOUR CONTROLLER

I won't invest in a small company unless it has at least one good financial man.

A West Coast venture capitalist

Show me a successful small company with great growth potential and I'll show you a company with a talented financial person keeping his or her thumb on the cash flow—the company controller.

This is the one who passes on all company expenditures, and the one who manages to get the quarterly aduit done, in spite of last quarter's foolish mistakes.

When given the chance, he'll vote "no" eighty percent of the time. He frustrates everyone with his pessimism and is accused of throwing cold water on every good idea. Production doesn't like him because he refuses to sign purchase orders. Sales doesn't like him because he gives them a hard time about expense reports.

The controller is never popular, he (or she) doesn't smile or tell jokes, but he's the one person in the company who can provide the balance it needs. With him, there's temperance. Without him it could be a drunken spending spree that could cripple a small, young company or a growing old one.

ENTREPRENEURS AS PENNYPINCHERS

Character is much easier kept than recovered.

THOMAS PAINE, 1737-1809
The American Crisis, 1783

Entrepreneurs hate to make out expense reports—and when they do they are always wrong. It's not because they're trying a little petty thievery either—quite the contrary. It's just very hard for an entrepreneur to separate company finances from personal finances, so he or she tends to treat the company's money as personal and vice versa.

You see, he (or she) signs all the checks, and the impact of having more or less money in the company checking account is an everyday sensation. As a result, he never fills out his expense reports, and often he doesn't report many of his personal expenses. I've known entrepreneurs to carry this to an extreme, holding several dozen uncashed paychecks rather than deplete the company checking account during tough periods.

I can't sign any expense checks right now, I'm busy.

The only paperwork chore an entrepreneur despises more than filling out his expense report is signing an employee's expense report. It's a failing of many entrepreneurs that they can't understand why every employee doesn't have their same desire to conserve the company's cash. Putting down every $1.25 cab fare or $1.95 lunch galls the hell out of them. As an employee, you might be better off biting the bullet for a few bucks rather than creating all that anxiety.

FORECASTS AND BUDGETS

Academic entrepreneurial programs are expanding while college enrollments decline.

PROF. KARL VESPER
University of Washington, Seattle

A realistic sales forecast or budget for a small company with a new product is almost impossible. If you're dealing with a new product and a new technology it's ridiculous to waste time on these obstructions. For a new company, then, forecasts and budgets are meaningless. The situation changes dramatically from day to day, and therefore no forecast or budget could be used as a planning tool for more than one day. Right? Wrong!

Entrepreneurs like to work with ballparks and guesstimates. The financial community, on the other hand, likes to work with budgets and forecasts.

Learn to do them; then learn to use them. Eventually one is going to be on the nose, and that's when you'll know you're really moving.

WHAT TO DO IF THE PLAY IS BUSTED

I don't plan to participate in the upcoming recession.

BILL DEVINE

Always have a reserve strategy to use for that tough or unexpected situation when the risks are high and the information low. One example of a reserve strategy popular among entrepreneurs is, "When in doubt, do nothing. Eventually, the situation will resolve itself." Another, used by a conservative M.I.T. graduate who successfully started three small companies, is "When in doubt, go for the green—conserve cash."

Take your reserve strategy from your hip pocket once in a while and dust it off—you never know when you'll need it. A rusty, dusty reserve strategy can make you look silly, dilly—and you wouldn't want that, would you? So besides dusting it off occasionally, try it out now and again and keep it well oiled, just in case.

HOMEWORK

The business plan is the grammar of an entrepreneurial venture; without it you cannot construct coherent thoughts.

NED HEIZER

Entrepreneurs seldom read books or magazines; they never read just for fun. They rely on two sources for information about the world around them and the business world—the daily newspaper and trade journals. Mostly trade journals. They read them at home, in the bathroom, on the subway or plane, anywhere they find an unoccupied moment.

Eventually, however, about the time their businesses reach the maturity stage, they begin to look for books that can help them solve their business problems. They learn that others have had similar problems before them and that their experiences can be enlightening—even profitable. They now ask, "Why reinvent the wheel?"

Many entrepreneurs wouldn't be caught dead without a copy of one of the prestigious academic journals such as the *Harvard Business Review* or *Fortune* on their desks. Most use them for window dressing, a sort of status symbol. A few read them, but not many. For the current subscription price, I consider both a "best buy" for anyone interested in the latest views on business management.

Sources of help at the end of this book list some of the best books and articles I have unearthed to help the entrepreneur. They cover a wide range of subjects and can provide a useful source for expanding your knowledge and improving your skills.

A little homework never hurt anyone. But it does require effort.

This may sound incidental at first, but it's not. I know of a source of information that will list all your customers for you free of charge. It's an even better listing of all your customers than *Thomas's Registrar* or *Moody's* or *Standard and Poors* or *Dunn and Bradstreet*—because it's organized by major cities. And I restate, it's free from the asking. Give your local telephone company a request for the Yellow Pages of the cities of interest and you'll be the proud owner of a complete list of present and potential customers. And, best of all, it even gives their telephone numbers.

THE NEW MBA'S

Life is good!

MARSHALL THURBER

Entrepreneurs hire business school MBA's (Master in Business Administration) in droves. They tend to be infatuated with the MBA type—the brash kid in his late twenties who knows all the answers and all the buzz words like "game plan" and "M.B.O."

The trouble with most of these graduates is that they have more answers than there are questions. It may sound strange, but too many solutions can create a problem. Furthermore, it's claimed that they get too much money and change jobs too often.

In my experience, I find that they spend most of their time analyzing their employers and the companies. The ones who excell in small business management are running their own companies. They won't work for entrepreneurs; they *are* entrepreneurs. Think twice before you offer that kind of money for a would be soothsayer.

If you must hire one, try to find an MBA who is in his or her second or third job. A little experience under the belt could do you a lot of good.

EAVESDROPPING

In the factory we make cosmetics; in the store we sell hope.

CHARLES REVSON
Revlon, Inc.

It's vital for the boss to know what is going on in his or her company. As the entrepreneur's business grows, however, it gets harder and harder to keep up with the day-to-day goings-on. In the beginning he knew everything that happened; now things are actually happening without him. It's worrisome and unsettling.

Have you ever seen the boss "accidentally" pick up the phone while the sales manager was talking to a customer, or surreptitiously leaf through the invoices on the billing clerk's desk when he or she was out to lunch? How about when he regresses to the early days of the start-up and asks to be allowed to open the mail?

Really! You don't have to sneak to get the information you need. Set up a system with your staff so that you get daily reports on the things you want to know, such as what the day's receipts were or how many shipments were made yesterday. That's the way to run a business. Not by eavesdropping.

THE LUCK OF THE FALL

All societies have hero myths. Theone who slays the dragon, searches for the holy grail or the golden fleece, removes the sword, unties the knot is the entrepreneur.

I enjoy the story of the little boy on his way to attend religious services. In each hand he held a nickel, one for the church basket and one for candy after the service.

As he crossed a little wooden bridge spanning a brook, he tripped and fell, and one of the nickels squirted out of his hand and into the deep water below. Looking up toward the sky he murmured, "I guess you're not very lucky, Lord. Your nickel fell into the water."

In the introduction to *Fun and Guts,* I stated that the one ingredient that is both necessary and sufficient for success is luck. It is more than good timing, it's control over the unavoidable. It is something that mysteriously follows some and is never known by others.

If you're successful, Mr. or Ms. Entrepreneur, don't take all the credit. You couldn't have done it without a lot of luck. If you fail, don't blame yourself. Luck just wasn't with you this time.

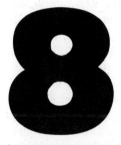

THE IMPOSSIBLE TRANSITION

THE ALARM CLOCK

There are three distinct human needs: power, affiliation, and achievement.

DR. DAVID McCLELLAND
Harvard University

It's ironic, isn't it, that the entrepreneur who starts out attempting an impossible dream, and then succeeds, faces what I call the Impossible Transition. It would appear he (or she) faces a series of impossible tasks, regardless. Succeeding at the first half of this impossible duet usually means failing during the second performance. The limitation of originators should be recognized from the origination. It's very rare, indeed, when someone is both an originator and an administrator. The experience of a bachelor friend presently on his third business dramatizes the difficulty of this transition. In the mid-1960s, along with a college roommate, he started his first small company in the electronics industry. The two-man team built the company to a modest size and then sold it to a major electronics corporation.

Their initial capital was $3,000 each, and the company's sale returned them about $50,000 each. While building this company, they forfeited salaries, worked hard and long, and in doing so made all the management mistakes possible. It was a typical first entrepreneurial experience. Not a big success, not a big failure. After selling the company, it became apparent that bigger goals were on the horizon for the dynamic duo. Neither had realized the complete fulfillment of the impossible dream. Together they invested $100,000 and began a new company. This new company followed the same patterns as their first company. Only this time they chose a winning market area and had a winning product. Only this time they were a bit more seasoned and experienced. Only this time they made it and made it big. My friend sold his share of the company about four years later at a very nice gain of several million dollars. His roommate remained behind to hold the house together.

My friend claims he sold because in his role as president of a $10 million company his talents were a mismatch. Unfortunately, at the time, the same held true of his roommate. But with a clever twist, they agreed to hire an outsider to assume the presidency. The technique worked for a few years, but eventually fell apart and the roommate assumed his proper position as the ship's captain. My friend assumed an inactive role in the company.

But now the fun began. My friend was footloose and fancy free with several million dollars in cash, in his early thirties, a bachelor, good-looking, and available to the world. Many people in this predicament would have spent the rest of their time lounging on the Florida beaches, drinking scotch, and playing tennis. My friend tried those things. They satisfied him for about six weeks. Somehow, he managed to stretch his period of idleness out to eighteen long months, largely by indulging in his whims. For example, he rose early one morning and went to a department store to do some shopping. He planned to buy everything of interest to him in the store—items that he had always wanted. He bought a color television, a stereo, a pair of walkie-talkies, a battery charger for his car, expensive clothes, and a range of nonuseful items. One thing he always wanted, but had never owned, was a special AM-FM radio digital-alarm clock, which also plugged into the coffee maker and turned on the lights. He had always wanted to wake up to soft music and a hot cup of coffee.

As he lived through the year and a half of purposeless existence, he developed a guilt complex about doing nothing. After all, he reasoned (and rightly so), isn't every red-blooded American boy supposed to be working hard every day? Isn't that the American ideal? One morning at 7 o'clock, he reached over and grabbed his multipurpose alarm clock and threw it out of the third-story window to the street below, coffee pot and all. The darn alarm clock kept waking him up at those ungodly morning hours, and he really had nowhere to go. It made pretty music, but it wasn't as sweet as the old $1.95 buzzer alarm that

Either I'm an entrepreneur or I'm unemployed.

he carried in his suitcase. As he expressed it, "It was the most lonely moment of my life when I realized I had no place to get up and go to in the morning. I'd lost my purpose."

It seems a pity that those of us who are temperamentally suited to making a lot of money aren't able to adapt ourselves to enjoy it, while those of us who are psychologically suited to enjoy a lot of money aren't oriented toward making it. Well, anyway, the impossible transition can be shocking to average folk, so don't underestimate it. Before you face it, prepare for it by talking with others who have survived the process. They can help you just as former alcoholoics help new members of AA.

DOER OR THINKER?

An engineer is a man who knows a great deal about very little and who goes along learning more and more about less and less until, finally, he knows pratically everything about nothing.

A salesman is a man who knows very little about many things and keeps learning less and less about more and more until he knows practically nothing about everything.

A purchasing agent starts out knowing everything about everything, but, due to his association with engineers and salesmen, ends up knowing nothing about anything.

Source unknown

Starting a business is one thing, but running it successfully is something else altogether. All it takes to get a business going is a customer. To keep it going and to make it grow require a whole new set of expertise and skills. And don't forget luck.

Businesspeople, unlike most other professionals, require enormous breadth of experience to be successful. In law, medicine, science, and engineering, the trend is toward specialization, and the person who succeeds in one of those fields has usually attained a high degree of skill in a narrow segment of it. He is a *heart* surgeon, or a *criminal* lawyer, or a *microwave* engineer.

When it comes to running a large business, however, the best professional manager is a generalist—a person with a broad range of experience and knowledge he or she can draw on to solve any problem from manufacturing to marketing.

For most entrepreneurs, this transition from specialist to generalist is impossible. He or she just can't make the switch from doer to thinker and planner. The skills needed of a good manager don't fit his or her personality, and the entrepreneur either realizes this early on or fails. The strengths of the orginator are in creating.

ABDICATE OR DELEGATE?

No man can serve two masters: for either he will hate the one and love the other or else he will hold to the one and despise the other.

Matthew 6:24

In managing a business, a delicate balance exists between delegating and abdicating. It is a problem that plagues all businesspeople.

Entrepreneurs accomplish most tasks better and faster than their employees. It stands to reason—they have all the facts at their disposal and they have the authority, so there's no need to communicate with others to resolve a problem. They know what to do, so they just do it—and at least three times faster and better.

Such behavior not only eats up the valuable time to the person who should be involved in other, more productive tasks, but it also tends to destroy em-

Of course I delegate; I don't take my business everywhere I go.

ployee morale. Managing requires "skill in accomplishing tasks through other people."

So delegating isn't abdicating. A good manager knows that and uses employees to perform the work he or she has invented, leaving the entrepreneur free to think up more work for them to do.

Try it this way. You may get to like it. It's healthier for you, and for your company.

ENTREPRENEURS AS MANAGERS

If you giggle, you are not into power.

JUDITH ROSS

Entrepreneurs have difficulty in managing people. They have neither the patience nor the inclination to get down to the nitty-gritty of motivating an employee to perform. Perhaps it is because they tend to be more creative, or perhaps they are too self-centered, or perhaps they are too busy. Whatever the reason, they are not good at it.

The same problem shows up in the sports world. A good player does not necessarily make a good manager. Likewise, many great managers never attained great stature as players. For instance, these men were not great players, but they are generally considered to be among the top of the list as managers:

Basketball: Red Auerbach.
Football: Vince Lombardi, George Allen.
Baseball: John McGraw, Casey Stengel.

Sport is a competitive game, and at the end a winner is declared—but this is not so in the competitive world of small business. Some of the findings in sports can be transferred to other management disciplines. Small business seems to be such a case. Although only a few will agree on who was the greatest athlete, there is fairly good evidence to suggest that the most successful sports managers were not great players.

A great manager is seldom a great individual performer in the specific sport, whereas entrepreneurs are universally great as individual performers. It is rare to find them successful as managers, teachers, or trainees.

In the case of a teacher, the ease of performing well with a minimal effort stands in the way. Often a teacher lacks the proper patience and self-discipline to bring the younger players along. "But how can that be?" you may ask. The reason is simple. The skills needed to be a good manager are not the same skills needed to be a good player. And in business, the skills needed by an entrepreneur are not the same skills needed by a manager.

So, the transition from entrepreneur to manager is seldom made successfully. And therein lies the tale of many business failures. Why fight it? The most successful entrepreneurs, like Dr. Land of Polaroid, recognize their managerial limitations early in the game and hire others to fill the gaps.

This course allows the entrepreneur to capitalize on personal strengths to the greater benefit of the company. Give it some thought. Why buck the odds? Play from your strengths and hire others to compensate for your weaknesses.

MORE PROFITS VS. MORE SALES

Anyone who tries to understand the money question goes crazy.

FRANK VANDERLIP

Every business enterprise eventually has to choose between bigger sales or bigger profits. Most entrepreneurs choose sales (bigger sales = bigger profits?).

Sales are, after all, the most visible sign of a company's success and draw the most applause from spectators. Outsiders seldom know a firm's level of profitability. What they know is what they see—a new and larger building, fancier offices, more and more employees. But what do you want—nice offices or a good return on investment and a bigger net worth?

Profits are what keep a business healthy and growing. In the early stages, sales growth may attract capital, but only rarely can a company consistently have sales growth and profits.

So, when the business reaches that point, the entrepreneur is usually the wrong person to be making the choices ... the monster he or she created is larger than he or she can handle. The entrepreneur will surely opt for sales growth and blow the whole shebang.

NO DESK?

If the boss is thought of as the shepherd of the flock, I guess that makes us the crooks on his staff.

DR. ALBERT J. SCHWEIGER

Executives in large firms are always bothering about the material appearance of their offices. Upward movement on the corporate ladder allows more furnishings. The junior executive starts out in a cubby hole and works up to the penthouse. Success for the senior executives in large firms is two telephones, a rug and drapes, a water pitcher, and most of all, a nice large, wooden desk. Right?

How about the big executive in a little company? What is his or her reward? What does he seek? Does he want a big office or a little room? Naturally, it is difficult to generalize because, in both cases, what I've just claimed isn't always true. On the other hand, we do know that the entrepreneur is different—and that's a starting point and a step forward.

A rather unique solution was generated by an entrepreneur in the discount store business. Thus far, I believe it has caught only his fancy and mine. But, as with many good things, it may only be a matter of time before the wisdom spreads.

My friend has no office. It's not that he is poor; in fact, he is a millionaire, but he has no office. He claims, "When I had an office, I'd get up every morning and drive there without asking myself why. Next I'd shuffle papers all morning and look busy. Desks are magnets for paper."

"Now," he continues, "I have no office and no desk. Naturally, I have no more paperwork. Every morning when I leave the house I must decide where to drive. Instead of going to my office I usually go to one of our stores. After all, that's where the action is—right?

GET UP FROM THE TABLE

It's okay to be independent, but there is no reason to be alone.

JOE MANCUSO

Starting and managing a small business is similar to two dissimilar American pastimes: motherhood and gambling. Like a mother with her child, the entrepreneur becomes emotionally attached to the business, and just as it isn't easy for a mother to untie the apron stings, the entrepreneur hates to let go of the "baby." Often this attitude prevents the enterprise from realizing its full potential. On the other hand, a business is often like a card game, and the entrepreneur who can adopt the card player's attitude will be better able to cope with the inevitable separation.

In a card game, the player places his (or her) stakes on the table and plays as best he can. He may win, break even, or lose. But the wise player knows when to quit—when he's obtained the maximum possible leverage from his capital and his talent, or when he's taken enough abuse. There's no room for emotion here.

So it should be in business. Leave emotion behind and, at the appropriate time, get up from the table. Don't be ashamed to take your winnings, and be courageous enough to walk away from your losses. There will be another game another day.

"DEAR ABBY . . ."

When a man comes to me for advice, I find out the kind of advice he wants and I give it to him.

JOSH BILLINGS

Every entrepreneur needs good, competent advice from time to time. Of course, there's usually plenty around—from friends, family, and associates. And for the real deep stuff there are consultants, lawyers, accountants, and bankers. Everybody knows about them. But here are a couple of generally unknown sources of help and advice.

The Bums Club. In Boston, we have an informal club of former entrepreneurs who have successfully started, managed, and left their own small businesses. they built their companies to a sizable volume, found the problems beyond their scope, and then sold the company. Typically, they've stayed on for some time as consultants, and then left for greener pastures.

They've come to be known as the BUMS (Boston Unemployed Men's Society, and they make up one of the most socially elite "clubs" around.

These are mostly operating people, capable of putting together people, technology, ideas, and profits, and they often show up as consultants and friends to businesses in trouble.

There are BUMS or their equivalents everywhere, and no entrepreneur should overlook this source of help. You can usually find them in the Yellow Pages under *management consultants.*

Psychologists. Bruce Patterson defines a psychologist as a man who, when a beautiful girl enters a room, watches everybody else. Could be, but when they're not watching the girl-watchers, professional psychologists are playing an increasingly important role in small business. More and more, entrepreneurs use their services to help them over tough spots.

Entrepreneurs are often driven by deep-seated desires and experience periods of deep frustration and depression. A competent psychologist can do them a lot of good. I've known several entrepreneurs who have gained valuable insight into their own motivations and drives with psychological assistance, and improved their own situations in the process.

So, if you ever feel the need, don't be ashamed to call on a psychologist. They don't perform miracles, but in the process of getting to "know thyself" better, you can relieve some of the tension and frustration experienced by both successful and unsuccessful entrepreneurs.

After I made the first million I just didn't have a valid excuse to work anymore, and that's when these funny pains. . .

If you're so smart, how come you're not rich?

An obnoxious success

Unfortunately, many times small companies employ small practices. They usually shy away from large-company corporate espionage, but as a substitute, entrepreneurs often engage in the foolish practice of swapping key personnel with their competitors. A vice president of engineering who has been tutored by the other fellow is the entrepreneurial version of industrial espionage. And just as with any infectious disease, once it starts it's hard to stop.

A sign of small business maturity is when you, the entrepreneur, discover the long-run plan to develop an organization that brings forth good people. Then, if one of your talented employees changes allegiances, your organization can bring along another. Whatever you do, please *don't* hire away the key personnel from your competitor. You'll only end up with the losers, because, by definition, the good guys are unavailable.

The danger of this swapping technique was highlighted a few years ago by two small electronics competitiors—call them A and B. A appeared to get the best of the people-swapping and B was left with both his and A's rejects. To even the score, B decided to make an acquisition out of the electronics industry and, of all surprises, he purchased control of a janitorial service—the one that did the floors, cleaned the offices, and looked after A's place of business. He had bought into what modern management people like to call a "management information system." The best source was the waste baskets, if you're interested in such details.

As with all good things, this couldn't last forever, and eventually A uncovered the scheme. Was he ever mad! He hired enough lawyers to bankrupt most firms, but he discovered that, from a legal point of view, he had a weak case. What could he prove? But he was mad, and I do mean mad, and he had no apparent outlet for this emotion.

Finally, out of desperation, A called together all the former employees of B who now worked for him and asked their advice. The result of this meeting was an anonymous phone call to the IRS, offering some inside information from a former accountant on some questionable tax write-offs. At last A had vented his emotions.

After the IRS investigated B, the tables were turned as a result of another anonymous phone call with some inside information. They made a thorough check of A, too.

I could go on with the story, because it doesn't end here, but I think the message is clear. Maybe industrial espionage as it is allegedly practiced in larger corporations is the lesser of two evils. But, I ask, why engage in either?

BRINGING THE HEIR INTO THE BUSINESS

The money that men make lives after them.

SAMUEL BUTLER

Nearly every entrepreneur whose company reaches maturity eventually faces the decision of encouraging or discouraging his or her children to join the family business. Each case must be decided on its own merits, but you can apply one

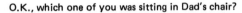

O.K., which one of you was sitting in Dad's chair?

generalization to every case. At least three-quarters of the time, when a son joins the business he does so prematurely and for the wrong reasons.

Whenever possible, the children should start their careers elsewhere to broaden their experience. This gives them a perspective that they'd never develop working for Dad (or Mom) from the start, and it makes them more valuable to the family business when (if) they do join up.

So don't push your offspring into the family business. In fact, don't push them at all. Let them know that if they want it, it's there, but not as an easy way out. Make them work. You did, and it did you a world of good.

HOW TO BUY OR SELL A BUSINESS

Business is a combination of war and sport.

ANDRÉ MAUROUS

Eventually, most entrepreneurs reach the point where they want to buy or sell a company. Since the 1970s, this sport has challenged baseball as the national pastime, so important that numerous publications, monthly bulletins, and books discuss the subject.

I'll tell you what they'll tell you—get outside assistance.

First, explore the logical avenues for prospective buyers or sellers—your largest supplier, customers, or your smallest competitor. Then talk to a broker. Business brokers make their living in the marketplace, and if anyone knows who's buying or selling, they do. Remember, too, they make their commission only if they're successful in finding a buyer or seller, so the bad ones don't last too long.

Here, in order of importance, is a list of business broker sources:

1. Management consultants.
2. Venture capitalists.
3. Stock brokers.
4. Bankers.
5. Certified public accountants.
6. Legal firms.
7. Financial/business editors.
8. Publishers of trade periodicals.
9. Advertisements in the *Wall Street Journal* and your local newspaper.
10. Manufacturers' representatives.
11. Insurance agents.
12. Advertising agencies.
13. College professors.
14. Local business directories.
15. Telephone book.

If you can't stand the heat, get out of the kitchen.

HARRY S. TRUMAN

Chapter Eleven is a legal state that can do wonders for small companies in financial troubles. It's a form of bankruptcy, not a chapter of some book.

You probably always thought that bankruptcy was bad. Not necessarily.

As I discussed earlier, the name of the game in small business is raising the venture capital. Successful companies raise the right amounts of money at the right times. This capital, among other things, helps cover up problems and hide mistakes. The company that is unsuccessful in raising capital leaves all its mistakes hanging out for the whole world to see.

If you go down the tubes, the IRS gets the prime cut and the stockholders get the gristle.

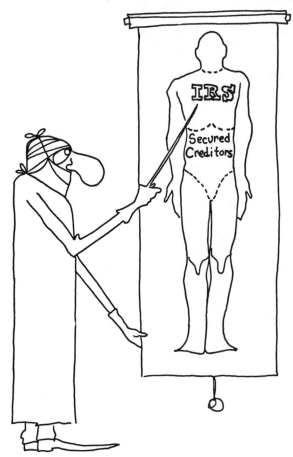

Many small businesses fail because a planned financing collapses, a public stock offering doesn't come off, or someone backs out of a private placement. If the company has been spending freely, anticipating the new capital, it may find itself deep in the hole.

That's when they should seek cover behind the skirts of Chapter Eleven. It gives them time to work things out and have another go at it.

Bankruptcy can be voluntary or involuntary. Chapter Eleven requires that if fifty-one percent of the creditors, by dollars and by number, agree to settle for a portion of what the company owes them, then the other creditors must accept the deal made by the majority. Since not all creditors think alike, this task may not be as easy as it sounds. The small ones tend to be aggravations; the big ones worry. They all want their money.

But Chapter Eleven and a new financial plan can salvage the company and provide a chance for it to continue in business, and maybe someday make amends to its creditors, rehire its employees, and, eventually, make a profit for its stockholders.

Alternatively, you can try to operate with insufficient capital and continue to pile up debts until forced into bankruptcy, and the company, its creditors, employees, and stockholders are all wiped out.

Unfortunately, most entrepreneurs do not consider Chapter Eleven bankruptcy as a viable alternative. Nevertheless, in fiscal 1979, 7,750 Chapter Eleven petitions were filed in the United States. Can anything that popular be all bad?

Don't Quit

When things go wrong, as they sometimes will,
When the road you're trudging seems all uphill,
When the funds are low and the debts are high,
And you want to smile, but you have to sigh,
When care is pressing you down a bit—
Rest if you must, but don't you quit.

Life is queer with its twists and turns,
As every one of us sometimes learns,
And many a fellow turns about
When he might have won had he stuck it out.
Don't give up though the pace seems slow—
You may succeed with another blow.

Often the goal is nearer than
It seems to a faint and faltering man;
Often the struggler has given up
When he might have captured the victor's cup.
And he learned too late when the night came down,
How close he was to the golden crown.

Success is failure turned inside out—
The silver tint of the clouds of doubt,

And you never can tell how close you are,
It may be near when it seems afar;
So stick to the fight when you're hardest hit,—
It's when things seem worst that you musn't quit.

Author Unknown

FEDERAL REFORM OF BANKRUPTCY CODE

The Bankruptcy Reform Act of 1978 became effective October 1, 1979. This long-awaited revision of the bankruptcy code has many advantages for creditors. It might be wise to review the code in total, and use this excuse to re-examine your firm's credit policies. Here are some of the highlights of the changes.

1. Previously, Chapter 10 was used for larger, publicly held companies and Chapter 11 for small enterpreneurial ventures. The reorganization effectively eliminated any distinction among business entities. Hence, Chapter 11 can now be available to publicly owned companies and or partnerships and sole proprietorships.
2. The bankruptcy court has greater power and can settle a greater range of issues than previously had to be heard in other courts. In addition, procedural delays have been removed, no longer requiring cumbersome mechanics to become operational.
3. Either a creditor or a debtor can petition for the debtor's reorganization; previously, debtors were the only ones to petition for reorganization and creditors had to petition for liquidation.
4. A creditor can reclaim goods from an unpaid invoice from an insolvent buyer within ten days of sale. This now corresponds with the Uniform Commercial Code (U.C.C.). For a free copy of the Bankruptcy Reform Act, P.L. 98-598, write:

House Documents Room
8226 Capitol Building
Washington, DC 20515

1244 STOCK

If a small company fails, the entrepreneur can still offer the stockholders one benefit—provided that his or her lawyer was on the ball in the beginning and used Section 1244 of the Internal Revenue Code. This section, established to encourage investments in small business, gives stockholders the right to write off against ordinary income up to $100,000 on a joint return ($50,000 on a single return) of any loss due to the failure of such a company during any tax year. Prior to the tax act of 1978, these numbers were $25,000 on a single return and

$50,000 for a joint return. If the loss is sustained by a partnership, the $50,000 (or $100,000) limit is determined separately for each partner.

The ordinary loss deduction is treated as a business loss—it an be carried back three years and forward seven years. Any loss over the $50,000 (or $100,000) limit comes under the less favorable rules for capital losses. An individual can only write off up to $3,000 annually as a capital loss against ordinary income.

Remember, however, that the $50,000 (or $100,000) limit is a yearly limit and not a limit on total losses from Section 1244 stock. If the losses can be spread over more than one year, more than $50,000 (or $100,000) can qualify for ordinary loss treatment.

For example, if a single person invests $200,000 in a business that proves unsuccessful and eventually sells the stock for only $50,000, he or she suffers a $150,000 loss. That person can take an ordinary writeoff of $50,000 each year for three years, for a total of $150,000. Also, 1244 stock can now be issued in a capitalization of up to $1 million instead of the previous $500,000.

Qualifying for this special break merely requires certain language to be included in the corporate minutes when the stock is originally issued. Since there is very little to lose and everything to gain, every small business corporation should automatically include this language in the minutes when organized or issuing new stock.

Under the previous law, a corporation had to offer stock for sale within two years after adoption of the written plan to qualify to issue 1244 stock. Moreover, no prior stock offerings could be unissued at the time the written plan was adopted. The new law repeals these restrictions. Under the new rules, a corporation may issue 1244 stock without adopting a plan, but only the first $1 million of common stock may qualify as 1244 stock. Consequently, there is no longer an equity ceiling on qualifying for 1244 stock. But no matter how much, common stock will be classified as 1244 stock.

A REAL LAUGHER

Small business is often a sad process, and any literature that passes along entrepreneurial wisdom while making you chuckle is worth mentioning. And this is a free plug, as I don't personally know the author.

Many times the sadness creeps into a venture when what starts out as a perfect dream turns into an imperfect reality. This book does not fix imperfections; it only makes them less painful.

The beauty of dreams and the reason entrepreneurs enjoy dreaming is their lack of complications. Within a dream, there is no need to worry about how to get there or how to get home, or about money. It's Utopia. Reality has to deal with all these miserable other considerations. J. Phillips L. Johnston's book, *Success In Business Is a Laughing Matter,* is sort of a dream, or a cure for reality.

Rather than describe this 212-page hardcover book, below is a quote from page 20.

> A friend and I plan to invest in a large cat ranch near Karmossille, Mexico. We would start rather small, with about one million cats. Each cat averages about twelve kittens a year; skins can be sold for about twenty cents for the white ones and up to forty cents for the black. This will give twelve million cat skins per year to sell at an average of around thirty-two cents, making our revenue about $3 million a year. This averages out to $10,000 a day, excluding Sundays and holidays.
>
> A good Mexican cat man can skin about fifty cats a day at a daily wage of $3.15. It will take only 663 men to operate the ranch, so the net profit will be over $8,200 per day.
>
> Now, the cats will be fed on rats exclusively. Rats multiply four times as fast as cats. We will start a rat ranch right adjacent to our cat farm.
>
> Here is where the first-year tax break really comes in. Since we will be utilizing the rats to feed the cats, we can expense the entire first batch of rats purchased just prior to the year's end. If we start with one million rats, at a nickel each, we will have a whopping $50,000 tax deduction for the year even though the "cat rat food" will be used to generate income in the next year.
>
> The rats will be fed on the carcasses of the cats we skin! This will give each rat one quarter of a cat per day. You can see by this that the business is a clean operation, self-supporting, and really automatic throughout. The cats will eat the rats, and the rats will eat the cats, and we will get the skins and the tax benefits! Incidentally, our ecology consultants think it's great.
>
> Eventually, we hope to cross the cats with snakes. Snakes skin themselves twice a year. This will save the labor cost of skinning and will also give us a yield of two skins for one cat.

Now, that's a sample of the medicine called humor and it's priceless! Johnston does a number on all the classics. For some yet-to-be-explained reason, when God created animals, he created only one species who creates business and one species who laughs. No other animal, other than man, either laughs or creates business. While this may be an unfair observation of God's creations, when you are creating an entrepreneurial venture, you get to believe that God purposefully allowed laughter for humans just to help the people who manage business.

Johnston is a millionaire and a Horatio Alger type. Besides being a lawyer, he is Chief Executive Officer of Currier Piano Company, R.L. James & Son, Inc., Johnston properties, Chantry Ltd., and holds several directorates. I loved his writing style. The publisher is small, and I doubt whether the book will receive much press, but it's $14.95 and available from:

Moore Publishing Company
Durham, NC 27705

A NEW WAY TO THINK
ABOUT RETURN ON INVESTMENT

Never invest your money in anything that eats or needs repainting.

BILLY ROSE

I recently attended a seminar on venture capital in New York City. One of the speakers was from Peat, Marwick, & Mitchell's small business division. Jim Walker, CPA, spoke about measuring performance in entrepreneurial ventures. His message focused on going beyond measuring performance by the classic measures (such as growth or profits as percentage of sales) used by big companies. He talked about measuring success by comparing return on investment or return on equity.

Everyone agrees that return on capital is really the most significant measure of an entrepreneurial venture's success. However, the way Walker expressed return on investment was interesting. He called it the DuPont method. Although DuPont is a big company, the DuPont method seemed to apply most appropriately to a small company. He said that return on equity can be expressed as profits over investment or profits over equity. However, it also can be expressed as the asset turnover ratio, times the profit margin, times leverage.

Let's look at that again. The asset turnover ratio is the sales divided by the assets. The profit margin is profits divided by sales, and leverage is assets divided by equity.

A little arithmetic will show very quickly that this is the same as saying profits over equity. However, by thinking of it as three multiplication factors—(1) asset turnover, (2) profit margin, and (3) leverage—it helps entrepreneurs to focus on what they ought to be maximizing. Maximizing each of these three independent variables will, in turn, maximize the return on investment.

The first two, asset turnover and profit margin, are really inside, internally controlled issues, whereas leverage is an outside, externally controlled issue.

Return on investment is effective when it is expressed like this:

asset turnover × profit margin × leverage = ROI.

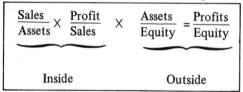

$$\frac{\text{Sales}}{\text{Assets}} \times \frac{\text{Profit}}{\text{Sales}} \times \frac{\text{Assets}}{\text{Equity}} = \frac{\text{Profits}}{\text{Equity}}$$

Inside   Outside

THE ENTREPRENEUR'S PHILOSOPHY

This final chapter contains all of the difficult-to-classify bits and pieces of entrepreneurial wisdom that I have accumulated in my dealings with small businesspeople. Here are the answers to many of the questions I am asked by my clients, which I have asked myself, and with which nearly every small businessperson should be familiar. Remember, the entrepreneur's philosophy is Fun and Guts.

TWO NOTIONS

A decision is the action an executive must take when he has information so incomplete that the answer does not suggest itself.

ARTHUR WILLIAM RADFORD

My comments to introduce the entrepreneur's philosophy will be brief, but, in my judgment, they represent two crucial notions. Adapting the entrepreneur's philosophy as your own requires you to throw off the security of a guaranteed annual income. Your pacifier as substitute for this lost security blanket is Fun and Guts. For some, the fun may be more important than guts. For others, it works the other way. Notion one is to keep a balance between Fun and Guts. There is a magical synergy to the combination. Either alone is meaningless; together they make for a whole entrepreneur. Do your best to keep them in balance.

Notion two comes to the fore when I am asked by college seniors and by young executives making job changes, "Should I go to work for a big company or a small one?" The answer is either. Both roads can lead to a successful career and to entrepreneurship. It is using big or small as a criterion for choosing that is wrong.

The proper choice should not involve company size, type of industry, or other similar variables. It should be based on the talents of your prospective boss. Choose to work for a boss you can trust and learn from. Your boss will be your teacher. The training he or she provides can be invaluable in either a small or large company. That is how to choose—whom you will work with and for, not by company size.

THEORY X VS. THEORY Y

When it comes to personal policy, there are two basic philosophies from which the entrepreneur must choose. First, conceptualized by Dr. Douglas MacGregor in his book, *The Human Side of Enterprises,* they have come to be known as Theory X and Theory Y.

Theory X states that employees are bad and must constantly be pushed and goaded to perform. Theory Y assumes that employees are good and only need the proper motivation to perform.

The ideal, of course, is to attain a Theory Y environment in your company. Most entrepreneurs try to do this, but often end up with a cross between the two—they seek a Theory Y environment, but employ a Theory X method of establishing it.

My advice is to go all the way with Theory Y. Give your employees the benefit of the doubt. Trust them. Give them their heads. In the long run you'll be well rewarded, and you can always sift out a laggard along the way. This may be the way of the future, and entrepreneurs who are successful at it will uncover new horizons.

THE THREE GREATEST ENTREPRENEURIAL LIES

What most astonished me in the United States was not so much the grandeur of some undertakings as the innumerable multitude of small ones.

ALEXIS DE TOCQUEVILLE
Democracy in America, 1840

We all the know the three greatest lies in the world, or at least our localized version of them. Recognizing this phenomenon, I sought to uncover the three most popular entrepreneurial lies. Unpublished until now—here they are:

1. The check is in the mail.
2. I am from the government and I am here to help you.
3. Sure, I will still respect you in the morning.

THE BASICS OF KNOWLEDGE

He knows so little and knows it so fluently.

ELLEN GLASGOW

Philosophy, goes the old saw, is like searching for a black cat in a dark alley at midnight, and theology is like searching in a dark alley for a black cat that isn't there.

Economics, in this view, is like searching in a dark alley at midnight for a black cat that isn't there—shouting all the while, "I've got it, I've got it!"

Econometrics—the mathematical modeling and prediction of events in the real world—provides a way to produce computer generated pictures of the cat you say you've caught, built solely on your description of the beast.

Management is the art of having someone who lost a black cat in a dark alley look under the street light for the cat because it's too dark in the alley.

Venture management is trying to figure out how to make money once the cat is in the alley by having corporate management try to coax the cat out of the dark alley back into the light!

Entrepreneurship is going into the back alley alone and empty handed and trying to create a black cat from nothing.

ENTREPRENEURSHIP AND EMPLOYMENT

Statistics are like alienists—they will testify for either side.

FIORELLO H. LAGUARDIA

In March 1978, Dr. Edwin V. M. Zschau, chairman of the capital task force of the American Electronics Association (AEA), presented data on the effect of employment of entrepreneurial ventures to the House Committee on Ways and Means. When he is not heading this committee, Zschau is chairman of the Board of Systems Industries of Sunnyvale, California, an entrepreneurial venture manufacturing mini-computer peripheral equipment and employing several hundred people. AEA, a trade association, is composed fo 900 high technology companies in thirty-seven states. While the membership employs more than 1 million people, most members are small companies of less than 200 employees. A survey of the 325 AEA member companies accounting for more than $45 billion in 1976 revenue was conducted in 1977. A total of 269 companies (which represented about forty percent because of plant duplication) responded to the survey.

This was one of the major conclusions draw from the young growth companies responding: an average of $14,000 of risk capital was required to create each of the 131,000 new jobs generated since 1955.

The study indicated that, on an average, of the companies founded since 1955, each new job created required $32,700 of assets. These assets were financed in three basic ways.

1. Retained earnings.
2. Debt.
3. Equity (risk capital).

In practice, a combination of the three sources was necessary to create the 131,000 jobs. But, young growing companies seldom generate sufficient retained earnings or borrowing to sustain their growth, so equity, or risk capital, is often their only realistic alternative. For the 276 young companies studied, an average of $14,000 of risk capital was required to create each of the 131,000 new jobs generated since 1955. In contrast, these jobs continue year after year and are not based on a continuing government subsidy to provide employment. The notion is best expressed by the often-quoted phrase, "Give a man a fish, feed him for a day; teach a man to fish, feed him for a lifetime."

The creation of jobs is not the only benefit from this productive employment of risk capital, as the resultant company growth is also a source of foreign sales, R&D expense, and tax revenue. Following is a chart by Dr. Zschau offering these data based upon the AEA survey.

An MIT Program on Neighborhood and Regional Growth conducted a comprehensive study for the Department of Commerce's Economic Development Administration and published the results in a report entitled "The Job Generation Process." The results of this separate and independent study confirm the AEA data.

The MIT study claims that between 1969 and 1976, small concerns (companies with twenty or less employees) provided 66 percent of all new jobs (for the entire United States). For the Northeast, 99 percent of all net new jobs were contributed by small business. In addition, the study found that 80 percent of all net new jobs came from businesses four years old or less.

BENEFITS IN 1976 PER $100 OF RISK CAPITAL INVESTED

Years in which companies were founded	Total number of companies in sample	Average foreign sale	Average R&D sale	Average federal corporate tax	Average state and local tax	Average personal income tax	Average total federal tax revenue
1956-60	26	$91	$19	$ 7	$3	$12	$19
1961-65	38	89	18	9	5	13	22
1966-70	135	57	20	12	4	11	23
1971-75	77	70	33	15	5	15	30
1956-75	276	$76	$20	$10	$4	$12	$22

THE ENTREPRENEUR'S PILL

Yesterday's time is a cancelled check. Tomorrow's time is a promissory note. Today's time is ready cash—Use it!

An anonymous philosopher

We all know that an entrepreneur is a person who creates an on-going business enterprise from nothing. To succeed at such a business venture requires motivation and perseverance bordering on obsession. It requires total dedication to the cause. And, as such, it is often characterized as the American Dream. I have toyed with a very exciting new product, which I call the Entrepreneur's Pill. I considered marketing it as a cure for a disease that is called "I want to start my own business." A potential entrepreneur would take this pill once a day, everyday at eight o'clock in the morning, and it would guarantee to decrease the desire to want to start a business.

I've often dreamed of the good this pill could do for society. So many new businesses are started by entrepreneurs without proper, prior experience. Consequently, many are undercapitalized, and many fail. Failure brings tragedy to so many people. The employees lose, the stockholders lose, the customers lose, the suppliers lose, and the families of all these groups lose. The entrepreneur's pill could offer great hope. The pill, when perfected, could decrease the desire of people to want to start a business. Only those people who were able and had a reasonable probability of success could start businesses. I've had this entrepreneur's pill under development for a few years, but I've never been able to offer it to the general public.

The reason I can't offer it as yet, despite the wonderful results it could achieve, is that it has one undesirable effect, and to some degree, the side effect may be worse than the actual disease. While it will decrease your desire to want to start your own business, unfortunately, it simultaneously increases your desire to be a venture capitalist, or to invest money in other people's businesses.

My entrepreneur's pill must just sit idly on the shelf. Should you ever want a bottle and be willing to withstand the great temptation of investing into other businesses, just write me at The Center for Entrepreneurial Management, 311 Main Street, Worcester, MA 01608, and I will rush you a free bottle of our wonderful device called The Entrepreneur's Pill. But don't blame us if you actually invest.

RICHARD FAULKNER'S PHILOSOPHY

People still remember Ty Cobb, who stole 96 bases out of 134 tries (70 percent). But they have forgotten Mar Corey, who stole 51 bases out of 53 attempts (96 percent).

In his farewell letter to friends, Richard Faulkner summarized a lifetime of findings and conclusions, some of which follow:

>Analysis is important, except when applied to people . . . (where it's useless).
>
>Now that we've checked out our roots, we should concentrate on our branches.
>
>After one fails to corner the market on '51 Fords and '64 Dodges, mere possessions become meaningless.
>
>The most important control I ever had was over myself—it's also the only control I ever had.
>
>Stewardesses are people from Georgia who couldn't get elected or appointed.
>
>Camping out should be reserved for masochists and incorrigible felons.

THE HEART AND BRAINS OF A SMALL BUSINESS

The two most vital elements in managing an entrepreneurial venture are the heart and brains of a small business. When the heart and brains are functioning, the organism is healthy. While both a sound heart and brain won't assure long life, without them there can be no life. The *heart* of a small business is the nature of what you take to market. The *brains* of a small business is the price you sell it for. The control of your heart and your brain in an entrepreneurial venture should never be left to someone else or delegated to outside subcontractors. To live, the entrepreneur must remain in charge of both the heart and the brains.

THIRTY LOVE

Creditors are a superstitious sect, great observers of set days and times.

BEN FRANKLIN

Most entrepreneurs treat their corporate bills as if they were their own. They pay their personal obligations in thirty days and try to do the same in their business.

Sometimes they begin to appreciate the need for financial trade-offs in a small business and realize that it may not be the wisest choice to pay every bill in thirty days.

One entrepreneur resolved the dilemma this way. "When I had $250,000 in the bank and $20,000 in bills, I decided not to pay the $20,000 in thirty days. I paid most of it by sixty days, and some I held for ninety days. I found that most suppliers expect that a small company will pay late. They're shocked if they get their money in thirty days.

"I never know when my business will have to use creditors as a source of working capital. If my suppliers get used to getting our check in thirty days, and then we are late, they get nervous. Then the phone calls start coming—right in the middle of a financial crisis. Now I pay all my bills in sixty to ninety days, but never more than ninety days."

Remember, it's better to pay late than not pay at all. Every supplier will agree with that.

YOU AND THE IRS

A minister of finance is a legal authorized pickpocket.

PAUL RAMADIER

As an employer, you are charged by the federal government to collect a portion of each employee's income tax and Social Security (FICA) tax. In addition, there are state taxes that are deducted from an employee's paycheck and must be remitted periodically to the Internal Revenue Service or other collecting agencies such as a bank.

The result is that the money withheld from the employee's paycheck remains in the company's checking account for between several weeks to several months, creating an inflated checkbook balance.

The danger lies in forgetting that this isn't your money and drawing on it "temporarily" to solve some current financial need. Boy, can you get into a mess of trouble! First, there are penalties for late payment of withholding taxes, and we all know that the tax burden is heavy enough without adding penalties. Second, you as the president, officer, or board member can be held personally liable for those taxes.

If you're ever tempted to tap that source for a little extra cash, take a cold shower and then try to find the money somewhere else.

DISSECTING THE CORPSE

The harder you fall—the higher you bounce.

AMY MANCUSO

In line with the preceding discussion, you should be aware of the pecking order of creditors should your business declare bankruptcy.

1. The Internal Revenue Service gets first cut. Any taxes owed to them must be paid, and they always get what's owed to them. If they can't get it out of the company, they can go after the principals. So, don't take your responsibility as president or treasurer lightly.

2. Creditors with a secured interest on the company's assets, inventory, or accounts receivable, (such as the bank that loaned you that $10,000 to tide you over a period of slow collections) are licking at the heels of the IRS.

3. Unsecured creditors get a cut only after the IRS and secured creditors have sliced away as much as they can. These include most of your suppliers who hounded you to pay those invoices or suffer the consequences. Now they suffer, too.

4. The last to be paid in a bankruptcy are the stockholders. Poor folks. You can imagine what's left for them, and that may be the cruelest cut of all for you. But then, they knew the risk involved.

Another interesting fact you should know regards credit cards. If you issue company credit cards to your employees and they lose one, you and the company are liable for $50 of unauthorized charges as long as you notify the credit card company within the specified period. However, if you declare bankruptcy, and the credit card company doesn't get its money out of the business, they can go after the employee to whom a card was issued for the full amount due. Consider that before you get too generous with those little plastic cards.

Your lawyer can provide you with all of the gory details, and you should know them. Forewarned is forearmed.

THE BIG DISADVANTAGE OF BEING LITTLE

To open a shop is easy; the difficult thing is keeping it open.

Chinese proverb

A sizable number of entrepreneurs relish the idea of keeping their businesses small, manageable, and uncomplicated. They believe that if their companies grow too much, all the fun and romance will be lost. They don't want the baby to get too big.

To a certain extent they are right, and there are advantages to being small when it comes to attracting people, introducing new products, instituting new production techniques, and simply keeping tabs on everything that goes on.

The one big disadvantage of being small is that you can't make too many mistakes, and the one's you do make had better be little ones. Big companies have a higher tolerance for mistakes. They can write off losses, lay off employees, and get back on track.

The small company doesn't have a cushion to fall back on. Its mistakes can wipe it out just as finally as anything. Ford managed to survive Edsel; you couldn't, so keep your mistakes small, few, and far between. Give this notion some consideration as you try to keep the baby in diapers too long.

WORKING FOR AN ENTREPRENEUR AIN'T EASY

Life is what's happening while you're planning for other things.

A friend

Entreprenurs work hard. The forty-hour week is something they've only heard of. That's all well and good, you may say, but if you've ever worked for one, you know that they expect little less from their employees.

In this regard, I will tell the story of a friend who learned the hard way what it's like to work for an entrepreneur.

His career began when he joined a large company right from college. He worked diligently and did very well. His only problem was his desire to participate in extra-career activities—like his family, church, and community. He wanted to be able to have something other than the business to talk about at cocktail parties. When five o'clock rolled around, he'd head for the hills.

In the big company he got away with it. He always got his work done, and then some. He organized his time efficiently, didn't read the *Wall Street Journal*, avoided coffee breaks, and kept his desk free of clutter. With this technique he was able to rise to vice president of the company before he decided to leave for a position as an executive vice president for a small entrepreneurial concern.

Naturally, he repeated the work habits that brought him success in the big company at his new job. Within eight weeks he was fired. His entrepreneur boss wasn't impressed with how much he could accomplish in eight hours, but rather his unwillingness to dedicate his full time to the job.

Unreasonable? Probably. But if you want to enjoy the excitement, exhilaration, and potentially high rewards of working for entrepreneurs, you'd better be willing to do it their way. It ain't easy.

HEROES

Admiration: our polite recognition of another's resemblance to ourselves.

AMBROSE BIERCE

Nearly every profession has its heroes. Visit any graduate school of law and you'll find portraits of Daniel Webster, Clarence Darrow, and other luminaries of the legal profession hanging in the halls. In medical schools there are bound to be portraits of Hippocrates, Pasteur, or Paul Dudley White.

Do you know the name of the president of General Motors, General

Foods, General Electric, or General Mills? I'll give you a hint; none of them are generals. Still don't know, do you?

With business there are no universal heroes. The presidents of the biggest corporations are usually uncelebrated and unknown. The only portraits on the business school walls belong to the faculty.

Heroes in business are personal heroes. Nearly every entrepreneur has one—a person whose career the entrepreneur has followed, whom he or she admires and tries to emulate. It may be only the neighborhood druggist or the operator of a taxi, but he's a hero to some entrepreneur somewhere.

Find the identity of an entrepreneur's hero and you'll learn a lot about the entrepreneur.

TAKE A PROFESSOR TO LUNCH

A professor is one who talks in someone else's sleep.

W.H. AUDEN

Entrepreneurs like college professors. College professors like entrepreneurs. Professors can be an inexpensive and reliable source of information, and since they're seldom in it for the money, they are generally above suspicion or corruption.

If your business is located near a school, and especially if it's your alma mater, it won't hurt to establish good relations with one or more of the faculty and get them interested in your business. You could even appoint a professor to the board to provide a new and different viewpoint, as well as balance. So, even though there are still a few pages left in this book, put it down and call a professor.

LOVE AFFAIRS

Love is the state in which man sees things most decidedly as they are not.

NIETZSCHE

One weakness to which many entrepreneurs are prone is the tendency to "fall in love" too easily. They go wild over employees, products, suppliers, machines, and methods. Anything new excites them. These "love affairs" usually don't last long; many are over as suddenly as they begin.

The problem is that during these affairs, the entrepreneur may alienate some people, be stubborn about listening to opposite views, and lose objectivity. It's a dangerous trait, so try to cool your passion whenever possible. A good medicine for this disease is a few moments a day recalling those past "puppy love" affairs.

THE ENTREPRENEUR'S SECRETARY

A friend is one who does not laugh when you are in a ridiculous position.

SIR ARTHUR HELPS

I've stated my opinion about your relationship with your parents and your children; I've analyzed and described your motivations for founding the firm; I've commented about your wife or husband; and I've stuck my nose in just about every aspect of your business.

Is nothing sacred?

Yes, your secretary. Why don't *you* bring *her* (or *him*) coffee for a change?

BE APPRECIATIVE

Ask not what your country can do for you, but what you can do for your country.

JOHN F. KENNEDY

Employees of entrepreneurs have to take a lot of guff. They are subjected to and affected by your highs and lows far more than employees of a big business. Most of all, more is asked of them.

An employee who can put up with an entrepreneur boss and still perform well deserves a pat on the back for a job well done. Too often, entrepreneurs fail to realize, or just plain forget, this little nicety of employee relations. Many a talented employee has been lost by inconsideration when just a simple sign of appreciation such as a word of praise would have saved him or her.

Good people are hard to come by, so let them know they're appreciated. Remember Theory Y! Keep a little checklist in your drawer, and each day thank one employee for a job well done.

THE ENTREPRENEUR'S LUNCH

It is taken for granted that by lunchtime the average man has been so beaten down by life that he will believe anything.

CHRISTOPHER MORLEY

One of the best established and most honored business traditions is the businessman's lunch. You may ask, "What's different about entrepreneurs at lunch?" They eat just like any other businesspeople—right? The entrepreneur's lunch is the same as for other businesspeople, only quicker and cheaper (as is everything else he or she does), like gluping down a sandwich in the elevator.

When you have got a thing where you want it, it is a good thing to leave it where it is.

SIR WINSTON CHURCHILL

Most entrepreneurs are well organized when it comes to planning the use of their time and getting chores done. They all have a system. Some keep index cards or a pad on which they list the things to do and tick them off one by one as they're done. Others keep a neatly arranged "to do" list on their desks with about 15 items listed. Still another type stuffs all pockets with little scraps of paper on which he or she records ideas, things to do, and shopping lists.

Faster than a foreclosure
More powerful than an interoffice memo
Able to buy tall buildings with a single check, and who, disguised as a mild-mannered. . .

Take away the system, and you'll throw the enterpreneur off stride for days. But don't knock it. Entrepreneurs almost universally possess the ability to tackle far more than the ordinary person, and its usually because they're super-organized.

BALANCE

We didn't lose the game, we just ran out of time.

VINCE LOMBARDI

Over the course of the entrepreneurial life cycle, the entrepreneur faces an average of about two major and ten minor problems a day. He or she has to choose among alternatives, develop criteria, and guess a lot.

However you look at it, it's a hell of a load. Whether you make your decision from a gut reaction, with eyes closed and teeth clenched, or decide on the basis of solid research, there is a way to optimize success.

When given the choice of doing eighty percent of the job with 100 percent effectiveness, or 100 percent of the job with eighty percent effectiveness, shoot for the latter. You don't have to do everything to perfection, just do everything. Leave no area uncovered. Neglect no detail.

That's what I call balance. It helps minimize failure by inaction, and that's a cardinal sin of entrepreneurship.

EXECUTION

Winning isn't everything—it's the only thing.

VINCE LOMBARDI

One of the most useful and enlightening books you can read has nothing to do with business. It was written by Vince Lombardi the late, great coach of the Green Bay Packers football team. Called *Run for Daylight,* it details his philosophy of winning in professional football. His record speaks for itself.

Lombardi was a master of strategy. While the other coaches were concentrating on super-duper, razzle-dazzle plays, he was working with the fundamentals over and over again. He ignored popular strategies like multiple offenses and defenses, flea-flickers, or excessive red-dogging that other coaches counted on to outfox the competition—and seldom did.

The packers were drilled in blocking and tackling. Lombardi's philosophy was that the team that could block and tackle best would win the game. It was simple, but it worked.

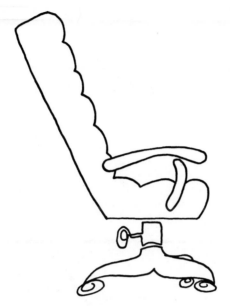

Home, Sweet Home, Inc.

Remember, Entrepreneur, concentrate on executing the fundamentals well, and you'll increase your chances of winning many fold—and winning's the name of the game.

APPENDIX

A. AIRPORT LOUNGES

If you wait between planes at an airport, have a delayed takeoff, or arrive early to relax or complete paperwork before departure, airline lounges provide quiet comfort, reading materials, complimentary coffee or soft drinks, TV and cocktail service. Lounges can be found at most airports.

You can join one or more clubs by writing for a membership application to one of the following:

The Admirals Club: American Airlines; $45 per year or $450 lifetime membership; Write: P.O. Box 61616, Dallas Ft. Worth Airport, Dallas, Texas 75261. Phone: (214) 267-1151.

The Council Club: Braniff International; $35 per year, $90 for 3 years, or $300 for lifetime membership. Write: P.O. Box 61747, Dallas Ft. Worth Airport, Dallas, Texas 75261. Phone: (214) 357-9511.

The Presidents Club: Continental Airlines; $65 first year membership $35 each consecutive year thereafter. Lifetime membership is $300. Write: Contnental Airlines c/o Karen Lemons, 7300 World Way West, Los Angeles, Ca 90009. Phone: (213) 772-6000.

The Ionosphere Club: Eastern Airlines; $40 per year, $160 for five years, or $400 for lifetime. Write: Miami International Airport, Miami, Fl 33148. Phone: (305) 873-3000.

The Clipper Club: Pan American World Airways; $50 annually, $135 for three years, $500 for a lifetime. Senior Citizens lifetime membership $300. Write Pan Am Building, New York, NY 10017. Phone: (212) 752-3151.

The Ambassador Club: Trans World Airlines, Inc.; $35 annual membership or $500 for lifetime. Write: 605 Third Avenue, New York, NY 10016. Phone: (212) 290-2121.

The Red Carpet Club: United Air Lines, Inc.; rates are $35 annually or $525 for lifetime. Spouse's card $10 or $150 lifetime. Initiation fee is $50. Write; P.O. Box 2247, Boston, Ma 02107. Phone: (617) 482-7900.

The Horizon Club: Western Air Lines, Inc.; $40 annual, $10 for spouse card. Write: Box 92005, Los Angeles, Ca 90009. Phone: (213) 776-2311.

*Spouses and/or guests may also enjoy the convenience and comfort offered by these airline lounges. If you travel frequently for business or pleasure, you may enjoy the benefits of a private airline club.

B. BANKRUPTCY

Bankruptcy is a process created by law to solve in a fair way the interest of both the creditor who is owed the money and the debtor who is not able to pay his debts. In 1978 President Carter signed a major amendment to the bankruptcy law, and bankruptcy laws have changed dramatically. The changes were all fundamental improvements. Although it may be depressing to have a section of this appendix entitled "Bankruptcy," it would really not be a complete source guide without it.

Bankruptcy sort of sneaks up on entrepeneurs like a summer cold. And once you get it, it is hard to get rid of. Just like the common cold, there are really no cures—only aspirin to help relieve the symptoms. The sources of help here will familiarize you with the various issues in bankruptcy. Many small businesses find themselves or their customers or their suppliers in bankruptcy and are totally unable to cope with the problem. Unfortunately, many entrepreneurial ventures never come out of a Chapter 11 and die without a second birth. Roughly, half of the small companies in the country are unable to survive a Chapter 11. Yet, keep in mind that Henry Ford, the premier entrepreneur, who started the Ford Motor Company, failed twice before he succeeded. Bankruptcy is really not a bad thing, but it does hold bad connotations.

Kits of bankruptcy forms are available from:

American Bankruptcy Council   Dephic Press
2525 Van Ness Avenue   Belli Building
San Francisco, CA 94109   San Francisco, CA 94111

Bankruptcy: Problems, Process & Reform integrates bankruptcy with other economic and social events. It sets bankruptcy into proper perspective in the American scene. The Brookings Institute is a high-quality source of original information about economic issues and this book is an excellent reference. Write:

The Brookings Institute
1775 Massachusetts Avenue, N.W.
Washington, D.C. 20036

The Complete Guide to Getting Yourself Out of Debt is a practical manual for everyone who needs urgent relief from the tensions of debt. The author, president of Family Financial Planners, explains how to stop bill collectors, suits, garnishments, and wage attachments; how to wipe out old debts without borrowing or bankruptcy—and retain AAA credit; how to set up a workable family budget—and much more. It's especially helpful for an individual. Write:

Frederick Fell Publishers, Inc.
386 Park Avenue, South
New York, NY 10016
(212) 685-9017

The Credit Executive is published by the New York Credit & Financial Management Association exclusively for its members; the subscription charge is included in the membership fee. Occasionally, special provisions are made for universities, government agencies, or even an interested individual. The publication features articles of interest to middle and top executives in commercial credit and finance. It also has articles legislation and court decisions having a bearing on these fields.

A number of handbooks are also available to the general public. Current titles are listed as follows:

1. A Practical Guide to Chapter XI of the Bankruptcy Act.
2. What the Businessman Should know About Commercial Arbitration.
3. What the Business Executive Should Know About the Uniform Commercial Code.
4. Guarantees and Subordinations.

Write:

>   Credit Executive
>   71 West 23rd Street
>   New York, NY 10010
>   (212) 741-4743

The Guide to Personal Bankruptcy is a workbook for bankruptcy. Complete with sample forms and copies of actual forms needed to be used for filing, it's a step-by-step workbook of the bankruptcy process. Its common language makes it worth reading. Write:

>   Crown Publishing Company
>   419 Park Avenue, South
>   New York, NY 10016

How to Get Out if You're in Over Your Head is a large workbook with practical advice on how to get out of debt. Write:

>   Ted Nicholas
>   Enterprise Publishing
>   1000 Oakfield Dane Field
>   Wilmington, DE 19810

The National Bankruptcy Reporter is an interesting newsletter that exists to inform you of business bankruptcy filings above a certain size all across the country. It lists the vital data on each new filing. It's expensive, over $1,000 annually, but it provides useful data on a subject that can be hard to learn or acquire information about. Write:

>   *National Bankruptcy Reporter*
>   Andrews Publications, Inc.
>   1634 Latimer Street
>   Philadelphia, PA 19103

Strategies and Techniques for Saving the Financially Distressed Small Business, written by a practicing attorney, shows business people how to protect themselves from overzealous creditors and how to turn their business adversity around. It offers an overview of some of the remedies that are available. With this information, businesses that can survive will learn, in fact, how to survive. Write:

>   Pilot Books
>   347 Fifth Avenue
>   New York, NY 10016
>   (212) 685-0736

Ten Cents on the Dollar is an extremely easy to read and understandable book on the ins and outs of bankruptcy. Its light touch is valuable because it offers an insight into why 10 cents on the dollar is a common slogan for bankruptcy. Write:

Ten Cents on the Dollar
Simon & Schuster
Rockefeller Center
630 Fifth Avenue
New York, NY 10020

Federal Reform of Bankuptcy Code

The Bankruptcy Reform Act of 1978 became effective October 1, 1979. This long-awaited revision of the bankruptcy code has many advantages for creditors. It might be wise to review the code in total and reexamine your firm's credit policies. Here are some highlights of the new procedures.

1. Previously, Chapter 10 was used for larger, publicly held companies and Chapter 11 was for small entrepreneuiral ventures. The reorganizatin effectively eliminates any distinction among business entities. Hence, Chapter 11 can now be available to both publicly owned companies, to partnerships, and to sole proprietorships.

2. The bankruptcy court has greater power and can settle a greater range of issues that previously had to be heard in other courts. In addition, procedural delays have been removed, no longer requiring cumbersome mechanics to become operational.

3. Either a creditor or a debtor can petition for the debtor's reorganization whereas previously debtors were the only ones who could petition for reorganization and creditors had to petition for liquidation.

4. A creditor can reclaim goods from an unpaid invoice from an insolvent buyer within 10 days of sale. This now corresponds with the Uniform Commercial Code (UCC).

We suggest that you send for a free copy of the Bankruptcy Reform Act T.L. 98-598 by writing:

House of Documents Room
8226 Capital Building
Washington, D.C. 20515

The barter clubs and publication listed below are geared primarily to the self-employed or small businesspersons and offer an alternative to increasing your cash outlay. For exchanges with subsidiary offices in several states, the address of the exchange's headquarters is listed. These offices can be contacted for more information about barter clubs in your area.

Atwood Richards, Inc.
99 Park Avenue
New York, NY 10016

Business Exchange, Inc.
4716 Vineland Avenue
North Hollywood, CA 91602

Barter Billionaire
Lock Box 983, Dept. E-1
W. Caldwell, NJ 07006

Business Owners' Exchange
4901 W. 77th Street, Suite 123-B
Minneapolis, MN 55435

Barter Communique
6500 Midnight Pas Road
Penthouse Suite 504
Sarasota, FL 33581
(813) 349-2242
This is a quarterly barter
   publication with a
   circulation of close to
   50,000.

Exchange Enterprises
159 West Haven Avenue
Salt Lake City, UT 84115
Attention: Ross Rigby or
   Gaylen Rigby
(Branch offices in 14
   western and mid-
   western states, Alaska,
   and Hawaii.

For more information about an office in your area, write to the exchange headquarters at the address above.)

Hilton Exchange
5034 Lankersheim Boulevard
North Hollywood, CA 91601
Attention: M. Hilton

International Trade Exchange, Inc.
7656 Burford Drive
McLean, VA 22101
   Attention: Clyde Fabretti,
   Director of Marketing

The parent company has issued licenses to owner-operators in 40 cities throughout the country and is planning offices in several other cities in the near future. For further information about an exchange office in your area, write to the ITE headquarters at the address above.

Mutual Credit Buying
6420 Wilshire Boulevard
Los Angeles, CA 90048
Attention: Tom Skala, President

Useful Services Exchange
c/o Wellborn Company
1614 Washington Plaza
Reston, VA 22090

The Learning Exchange
Box 920
Evanston, IL 60204

D. BEST-SELLING BOOKS

Below is a list of the all-time best selling self-development books and the authors. These books are readily available in any library and are listed under both author and title. They are all great, not good, because they have stood the test of success in a free marketplace. They have been "noted" as the best because more people have bought or read them.

All-Time Best-Selling
Self-Development Books

Think and Grow Rich by Napoleon Hill
Laws of Success by Napoleon Hill
Psycho-Cybernetics by Maxwell Maltz, M.D.
Success Through a Positive Mental Attitude by Napoleon Hill and W. Clement Stone
The Success System that Never Fails by W. Clement Stone
The Power of Positive Thinking by Dr. Norman Vincent Peale
The Greatest Salesman in the World by Og Mandino
How To Win Friends and Influence People by Dale Carnegie
Your Greatest Power by J. Martin Kohn
How I Raised Myself from Failure to Success in Selling by Frank Bettger

E. BUSINESS PLANS

A document written to articulate the directions of a growing business enterprise is a business plan. These road maps are often written to raise new money for an expanding business. Internal and external entrepreneurs write them to show the obvious strengths of their business. Below are discussed several sources to help in the preparation of these plans.

One of the finest pieces of information for understanding financial statements is offered free of charge by the world's largest securities firm, Merrill Lynch, Pierce Fenner & Smith. This 24-page book, entitled *Understanding Financial Statements* is so good it is often used as a free handout in graduate-level college finance courses. It offers an understanding of three basic financial tools: Balance Sheet, Cash Flow Statement, and Profit and Loss Statement.

You can call your local Merrill Lynch office, which can be found in your local directory, and ask for a copy.

Several excellent articles on developing a business plan are contained within the books offered by the most professional source of venture capital information, Capital Publishing Company. Although these books are a bit expensive, some of the articles on the business plan are truly excellent because the tips are practical and worthwhile. Write:

Stan Pratt
Capital Publishing
2 Laurel Street
Wellesley Hills, MA
(617) 235-5405

The Entrepreneur's Handbook is an excellent book of readings for entrepreneurs. This two-volume handbook is described as excellent because the books contain all the good articles on business plans (plus other entrepreneuiral subjects) ever written. There are six articles on how to prepare a business plan in these two volumes. Write:

Artec House
610 Washington Street
Dedham, MA 02026
(617) 326-8220

The Center for Entrepreneurial
    Management
311 Main Street
Worcester, MA 01608
(617) 755-0770

The Small Business Administration offers several excellent pamphlets on writing a business plan. These are very inexpensive and surprisingly good. They even offer further information on where to obtain information on writing a business plan. Contact your local SBA field office for current information.

Small Marketeer Aid #153
Business Plan for Retailer (24 pages)
Small Marketeer Aid #150
Business Plan for Retailer (24 pages)
Management Aid for Small Manufacturers #218
Business plan for small manufacturers (22 pages)

A new center was established in February, 1978 to speed up the delivery process of SBA pamphlets. All requests to this high-speed center should be on SBA form 115A, which is a list of available SBA publications. Form 115A can be requested from the center. Write:

The Small Business Administration
Box 15434
Fort Worth, Texas 76119

The nationwide toll-free Watts number 800-433-7272. In Texas call 800-792-8901. The telephone recording service is available 24 hours per day, seven days per week.

Another source of information on a business plan's development is a two-part document. Part I is a five-page approach to developing a business plan, and Part II describes how to prepare a business plan.

Institute for New Enterprise Development
385 Concord Avenue
Belmont, MA 02178
(617) 489-3950

An excellent guide to developing a business plan was prepared by A. David Silver for his company Competere Group, In. It is a photocopy of a loose-leaf notebook. Write:

A. David Silver
Competere Group Inc.
140 William St.
Penthouse
New York, N.Y. 10038
(212) 619-1020

F. ENTREPRENEURIAL EDUCATION

A small but fascinating school for entrepreneurs is housed in a quaint inn in the beautiful village of Londonderry, Vermont. It's headed by two men:

1. Brian Smith head of the business department at Franklin Pierce College, founder of a New England-based electronic medical instruments company and a former IBMer.

2. James S. Howard founder of the Country Business Brokers in Brattleboro, Vermont, and a former public relations executive on Madison Avenue.

The seminar program they offer is couple-oriented, with small classes appropriate to the charming setting. The fee is $260 per couple for a weekend. Couples are recruited primarily through newspaper advertisements, and the operations of the inn are often cited as an example of those of a small business of your own. For more information write to:

The Country Business Brokers
225 Main Street
Brattleboro, VT 05301
(802) 254-4504

The School for Entrepreneurs
Tarrytown, NY

About four years ago, Mr. Robert Schwartz, the owner of the twenty-six acre magnificent estate known as the Tarrytown Conference Center in Tarrytown, NY was interviewed by an aggressive reporter on behalf of a small magazine based in Boston, MA known as "New Age Journal." The interview resulted in a cover story for this magazine (circulation of about 30,000 to a somewhat avant-garde readership), where Schwartz expounded upon the values of entrepreneurship as a way of life. The new generation had traditionally been turned off to business and turned on to new and greater sets of social values. The notion proposed by Schwartz was that through the entrepreneurial role of starting your own business, new expressions can take place in society. The new generation can make its greatest impact as change agents not as renegades, claimed this unusual innkeeper.

The message was so powerful in this journal that Schwartz received thousands of telephone calls and letters and this article moved him to consider starting a school for entrepreneurs.

Being the owner of a conference center twenty miles north of New York City, he concluded that two weekend sessions, back-to-back, to sharpen their entrepreneurial skills would have the most immediate appeal. After counseling with academicians, entrepreneurs, and a host of others, he introduced the first school for entrepreneurs in 1976. Since that time, approximately 500 people have graduated from his school, including myself. The school has been written up in "Psychology Today", TWA's "Ambassador Magazine" and a host of other prominent magazines and journals. The reason for the school's success to date is Robert Schwartz, the colorful founder of The School of Entrepreneurs. An entrepreneur himself, he sees the school as a vehicle for expressing a number of his innovative ideas. While some of the more traditional entrepreneurial courses in universities look to The School of Entrepreneurs as something close to "touchy-feely," in fact, it is really a combination of EST and entrepreneurship what I call "entrepreneurism." Schwartz not only imparts how to make money values and the importance of a business plan, but he also imparts a significant message about how to get your life together. A bit of an inspirational thinker and a philosopher, Schwartz is the main star in the revolving cast at the school.

The school is composed of games, tests and the development of a business plan. It is highlighted by the presentation of a specific business plan to Alan Patricoff, a venture capitalist in New York City. That is followed by an exciting party which centers around Bob, his life and the people who surround him. It is an interesting school worthy of note.

The man who has earned the right to talk about entrepreneurship, Robert Schwartz, is a businessman who has a knack for putting together ventures that are not only profitable, but also exciting. According to an article in TWA's "Ambassador" in-flight magazine, "his ideas are tacked up on the bulletin boards of "Fortune 500" companies as well as in Vermont communes. He synthesizes the value systems of people who would not normally talk to each other, and he is respected in both camps."

As a businessman, Bob Schwartz is the sole owner of the multi-million dollar Tarrytown House Executive Conference Center. As a writer and publishing executive, he has been a national magazine journalist on the staff of "Harper's". He has served as the New York Bureau Chief of "Time", was "entrepreneur-in residence" and assistance to the publisher of "Life" and has been a part owner of "New York Magazine".

As a humanitarian, he is a former board member of the Association for Humanistic Psychology and the Humanistic Psychology Institute. As a concerned citizen, he has been on boards ranging from Amnesty International to the National Commission on Resources for Youth. As a speaker, he has addressed international audiences including Swedish industrialists, the Direct Mail Marketing Association and the World Affairs Conference at the University of Colorado. As an orchestrator of social change, he is President of The Tarrytown Group, a forum for high-level dialogue about emerging planetary concerns which was originally conceived by the late Margaret Mead.

As an entrepreneur, he has built unlikely hostelries like the Japanese-designed "Motel on the Mountain" and America's first executive conference center at a hilltop estate in Tarrytown, NY, which has played host to seminars and training sessions of over 2,000 corporations.

Interested? Write:

Bob Schwartz
The School for Entrepreneurs
Tarrytown House
East Sunnyside Lane
Tarrytown, NY 10591
(212) WE 3-1232
(914) LY 1-8200

SBA Study of Educational Entrepreneurship Programs

Entrepreneurship is really coming into its own worldwide. In China, for example the elder, "retired" population is being encouraged to start their own one-person businesses, with over 20,000 springing up throughout mainland China in recent months. The communal farmers are growing their own crops separate from the community gardens and reaping profits.

Needless to say, the entrepreneurial bug is firmly entrenched in the U.S. with growing educational recognition given on the college level in the form of entrepreneurial courses. This has prompted a nationwide survey conducted by the Office of Management Assistance (SBA) in conjunction with the American Assembly of Collegiate Schools of Business (AACSB), and the American Association of Community and Junior Colleges (AACJC) to gather all available current information on course descriptions and syllabli in the area of small business management.

As a result of this survey, two series of booklets, one for four-year schools and the other for two-year schools, were developed. Each series consists of three booklets, in which the information is categorized by geographical locations. If you would like a copy of this study, write to:

Philip A. Sprague
Associate Administrator for Management Assistance
U.S. Government Small Business Administration
Washington, D.C. 20416

Another school of entrepreneurs is headed by William J. McCrea, the chairman of the Entrepreneuriship Institute. This school moves from city to city and offers weekend training seminars entitled "How to Create and Manage Your Own Business." For a schedule, call or write to:

The Entrepreneurship Institute
90 East Wilson Bridge Road
Suite 247
Worthington, OH 43085
(614) 885-0585

Dr. Leon Danco of the University Services Institute in Cleveland, Ohio, offers a host of interesting family-oriented business seminars. Dr. Danco is one of the finest authorities on the father—son team and on issues of families within small business.

University Services Institute
5862 Mayfield Road
Box 24197
Cleveland, Ohio 44124
(216) 442-0800

A group of intense, get-away-from-it-all seminars is offered by Marshall Thurber entitled "Money and You." The seminars are usually one week long and intense, but always very good. Write:

Marshall Thurber
1288 Rimer Drive
Morage, CA 94556
(415) 376-2827

If you have ever felt that penetrating the U.S. government was like kicking a two-hundred-foot sponge, help is now available. The Small Business Administration (SBA) appointed an exceptionally qualified individual to its newly created post of Small Business Advocacy. This means that his taxpayer-funded job is to champion entrepreneurial causes. He will tell you where the SBA is offering seminars in your area. Do you need help of any kind or do you offer positive suggestions? Write:

> Chief of Advocacy
> Small Business Administration
> 1441 L Street, N.W.
> Washington, D.C. 20416

Help From Colleges
for Small Businesses

University Business Development Centers (UBDCs) are funded by government agencies (usually the Small Business Administration (SBA)) and are affiliated with local universities. They are charged with helping small businesses grow and prosper within a specific region. They can be of specific assistance, especially in the development of a business plan, and they are currently operational at the following colleges. As this listing goes to print, other colleges are launching SBDCs, so be sure to inquire in your area. This is an outgrowth of the SBA's Small Business Institute (SBI) program. Under the SBI program, locally colleges and the SBA send 5,000 to 10,000 student teams to help small businesses annually. They can help and they are free, so it may pay to find out about the SBI college serving your area.

Also, in each of the 10 regions of the United States, as segmented by the SBA, a faculty member at a specific university is the regional coordinator of the SBI.

An excellent newsletter exists on the SBI program and provides continuing help for entrepreneurs:

> Small Business Institute
> Directors Association
> Editor, Dr. Kenneth D. Douglas
> University of Northern Colorado
> School of Business
> Greeley, CO 80639

The National Science Foundation (NSF) under the direction of Robert M. Colton has been the champion of this worthwhile cause. The NSF has sponsored three university-based innovation centers. While these centers have an engineering overtone, they do indeed assist the entrepreneur.

A copy of an evaluation report of the three existing innovation centers can be obtained from:

Research Triangle Institute
P.O. Box 12194
Research Triangle Park
North Carolina 27709
(919) 541-6000

Below are the innovation centers currently operating:

Dr. Gerald G. Udell
Univeristy of Oregon
Eugene, OR 97403
(503) 686-3111

MIT, School of Engineering
77 Massachusetts Avenue
Cambridge, MA 02139
(617) 253-1000

Prof. Dwight M. Bauman
Carnegie-Mellon University
Frew Avenue
Margaret Morrison
Pittsburg, PA 15213
(412) 578-2000

Small Business Development Centers

Anyone interested in help in managing their entrepreneurial venture may avail themselves of assistance from a Small Business Development Center (SBDC). The SBDC Program is sponsored by the U.S. Small Business Administration as a cooperative effort by universities, the Federal Government, state and local governments, and the private sector to provide small business management techniques and technology to the small business community.

The following is a list of the 15 Small Business Development Centers at colleges throughout the country:

Mr. Frederick H. Greene, Jr.
SBDC Director
University of Southern Maine
246 Deering Avenue
Portland, Maine 04102
(207) 780-4423

Mr. Gerald W. Hayes
SBDC Director—School of Business
  Administration
University of Massachusetts
Amherst, Massachusetts 01003
(413) 549-4930 - Ext. 304

Mr. Roland Crump
SBDC Director
Rutgers University
Ackerson Hall—3rd Floor
180 University Street
Newark, New Jersey 07102
(201) 648-5627

Ms. Susan Garber
SBDC Director
University of Pennsylvania
The Wharton School
413 Centenary Drive
Philadelphia, Pennsylvania 19104
(215) 243-4861

Mr. Warren Van Hook
SBDC Director
Howard Univeristy
2361 Sherman Avenue, N.W.
Washington, D.C. 20059
(202) 636-7187

Mr. W. F. Littlejohn
SBDC Director
College of Business Administration
University of South Carolina
Columbia, South Carolina 29208
(803) 777-5118

Mr. Larry Bramblett
SBDC Director
University of Georgia
Brooks Hall, Room 348
Athens, Georgia 30602
(404) 542-5760

Dr. Fred Myrick
SBDC Director
The University of Alabama in
   Birmingham
School of Business
1000 South Twelfth Street, Suite F
Birmingham, Alabama 35294
(205) 934-7260

Professor Allan B. Cowart
SBDC Director
University of West Florida
137 Hospital Drive—Suite H
Fort Walton Beach, Florida 32548
(904) 243-7624

Dr. Robert Pricer
SBDC Director
University of Wisconsin
One South Park Street
Madison, Wisconsin 53706
(608) 263-7794

Dr. Dwaine Tallent
SBDC Director
College of Business
St. Cloud State University
St. Cloud, Minnesota 56301
(612) 255-3215

Mr. John Killingsworth
SBDC Director
University of Arkansas
1015 West Second Street
Little Rock, Arkansas 72203
(501) 370-5381

Mr. Robert E. Bernier
SBDC Director
University of Nebraska at Omaha
Omaha, Nebraska 68182
(402) 554-2521

Mr. Richard Haglund
SBDC Director
Graduate School of Business
University of Utah
Salt Lake City, Utah 84112
(801) 581-7905

Mr. Gene Hansen
SBDC Director
441 Todd Hall
College of Business & Economics
Washington State University
Pullman, Washington
(509) 335-1576

Entrepreneur's Education

Karl Vesper of the University of Washington in Seattle has the enviable record of being three professors in one: mechanical engineering, business administration, and marine biology. However, he is best known for his work as scorekeeper of academic courses of small business and entrepreneurship. He recently surveyed 610 schools of business and 243 schools of engineering and based on a response of 61% and 48% respectively, here is what he found:

These are data for teaching new ventures, not the more popular small business management type of course. There are about 30 schools of engineering that teach entrepreneurship, according to Vesper. The remainder are business schools.

TOTAL NUMBER OF SCHOOLS OFFERING COURSES IN NEW VENTURES

Year	1968	1970	1972	1974	1976	1978	1980
	8	29	47	75	105	137	215

Vesper distributes a detailed list of schools and course descriptions that is available by writing to:

The Center for Venture Management
207 E. Buffalo Street
Milwaukee, WI 53202

Furthermore, as the scorekeeper, Vesper has begun keeping score of the emergence of academic chairs in dual fields of entrepreneurship and free enterprise. According to Vesper's early data, the endowed chairs are primarily in the field of private (free) enterprise, with a minority in the field of entrepreneurship.

Colleges and Universities with Established Entrepreneurial and Free Enterprise Chairs and Programs

American International College
Appalachian State University
Augusta College
Babson Institute
Baylor University
Birmingham-Southern College
Brescia College
Brunswick Junior College
George Peabody College
Georgia State University
Harding College
John Carroll University
Kent State University
Lamar University
Lambuth College
Loyola University of Chicago
North Georgia College
Northeast Louisiana University
Ohio State University
Purdue University
Samford University

Southwest Baptist College
Texas A&M University
Texas Christian University
University of Akron
University of Indiana
University of Oklahoma
University of Tennessee, Chattanooga
University of Texas, Austin
University of Wisconsin, Madison
Washington University
Wharton School
Wichita State University

Further information about endowed chairs like these is available from two sources. Richard Emerson and John L. Ward, School of Business, Loyola University, 820 North Michigan Avenue, Chicago, IL, 60601, have prepared a paper summarizing chairs in existence or being planned at 59 colleges and universities. Craig Aranoff is President of the Association for Chairs of Private Enterprise, centered at the School of Business, Georgia State University, Atlanta, GA 30303.

The Entrepreneurs Hall of Fame

While college enrollment in general has been on the decline, enrollment pertaining to entrepreneurship and small business has been on the rise. One of the many schools with established chairs and programs in entrepreneurship is the Babson Institute in Wellesley, Massachusetts. Babson College instituted the Entrepreneurial Hall of Fame in 1978.

Recipients for 1978. Kenneth H. Olsen is the president of Digital Equipment Corporation, which was founded in 1957. It was a new idea to start a company at this time of recession when a number of new companies were in trouble. With only $70,000 to work with, every dollar was carefully watched and most of the work from cleaning the floors to making their own tools was done by Olsen and his associates. He started with the ideas of no government funding for their research, and they sought to make a profit from day one.

Berry Gordy, the president and chairman of Motown Industries, Inc., loved writing and creating songs. His first record store in Detroit was opened in 1953, and in 1955 he was bankrupt. After not being able to collect from a publisher who owned him $1,000, he decided to start a company for young writers. He was told that he could not do it. That was all he needed to hear, and Motown was born. He believes that you must first consider happiness before success so that success does not destroy you later.

Royal Little is the former chairman of Textron, Inc. He used his textile business to expand into more diversified areas of industry. He believed that if one business is not performing, get out—sell it, and then buy another one. His idea worked, and this started the conglomerate trend in the United States.

Ray Kroc, chairman of the McDonald Corporation, started out with the Lily Cup Company, and sold paper cups for about 17 years. As a salesman for a multiple milkshake mixer, the Multi-Mixer, he heard of an operation in California run by the McDonald brothers. Their stand was using eight of these mixers, making up to 40 milkshakes at one time. After his association with the McDonalds, Kroc felt that he was growing faster than they were, and in 1954 he opened his first "McDonalds." In 1960 he bought the business for $1.5 million. His theory is that "part of being an entrepreneur is knowing what to give and when to give it."

Soichiro Honda founded the Honda Motor Company 30 years ago. He first brought motorcycles to the United States 20 years ago, and thus created a new product. His first task was to sell the United States on motorcycling; then he had to sell Honda. He is not sure that he is an entrepreneur, only that he is a man with imagination, creativity, and desire behind him.

1979 Recipients. John Eric Jonsson, 77, is the founder and former chairman of Texas Instruments. After graduating from Renssalaer Polytechnic Institute in 1922, he became interested in Texas Instruments, then Geophysical Services, Inc., in Newark, NJ. The outfit moved to Texas in 1934, and Jonsson and Eugene McDermott bought out what is now a billion-dollar concern.

Diane Von Furstenburg, president of DVF, Inc., came to the United States in 1969 and saw a great need in the fashion industry. She designed a basic dress, in a basic material called jersey. Her claim to success is that you can be a woman and mother and be in business, too, if you are willing to work, plan, and discipline yourself.

John H. Johnson is the founder of *Ebony* magazine. Poverty motivated him to work harder in high school, which earned him a scholarship to the University of Chicago. In his junior year, he worked on a company magazine, which gave him the idea to publish a *Negro Digest* similar to the *Reader's Digest.* The profits he received from the magazine enabled him to start *Ebony* magazine.

Thomas Mello Evans is the chairman of Crane Company, which manufacturers everything from steel to antipollution gear. He took over Crane Company in 1959, and more recently purchased 7.3% of the outstanding common stock of MacMilan, Inc. the broadly based purchaser. He has always shown a profit, and companies usually succeed under his management.

Byung Chull Lee, chairman of Samsung Group, started a rice cleaning plant in South Korea in 1935. After deciding that his country could prosper only through trade, he established the Samsung (Three-Start) export-import company in 1952. Today, as Korea's richest man, his fortune is over $500 million, and Samsung has become a 24-company conglomerate with sales of $2 billion per year.

1980 Recipients

1. Mary Wells Lawrence of Wells, Rich, Greene and Company.
2. L. Lehrman of the Rite-Aid and Lehrman Institute.
3. Mary Hudson of the Hudson Oil Company.
4. Peter Grace of W.R. Grace and Company.

Recipients for 1981. The 1981 inductees into the Babson College Academy of Distinguished Entrepreneurs represent four continents. All men of managerial enterprise, were honored on April 15, 1981.

Frank Perdue started raising chickens and selling eggs when he was 10 years old. In 1952 he took over control of Perdue Farms Inc. from his father and began marketing chickens along the eastern seaboard. His television marketing strategy, which includes a money-back guarantee, is one of the factors making the Perdue organization one of the five largest privately owned companies in the country.

Perdue interviewed over 40 advertising agencies before choosing one to represent his firm. At the agency's insistence he appeared in his own ads. The slogan, "It takes a tough man to make a tender chicken," helped his name recognition jump to over 50% within a few months.

Frank Perdue is most concerned with all aspects of his business and is known to make frequent spotchecks of his 5 plants from Maryland to North Carolina. Perdue is now opening a chain of restaurants in the New Jersey area, but is not ready for expansion into other chicken products.

The first Babson College alumnus to be named to the Babson College Academy of Distinguished Entrepreneurs, Gustavo Cisneros (Class of '68), is president of a Latin American conglomerate which is involved in banking, food retailing, communications and manufacturing.

The Organization Diego Cisneros (ODC) has extensive holdings in Venezuela and elsewhere in Latin America, its operations were recently expanded into Florida. ODC sales were close to $2 billion in 1980, the business employs more than 12,000 people.

ODC's major holdings include Venevision, 1 of 2 commercial TV networks in Venezuela; Circuito Nacional Radio-vision, a 13-station radio network which encompasses 80% of the country; C. A. Distribuidora de Alimentos, the largest supermarket chain in Venezuela; Pepsi-Cola and Hit De Venezuela, C.A., a soft drink corporation consisting of 24 bottling plants and 12 warehouses, and holder of the Pepsi franchise for Venezuela, the largest independent bottler in the world; and most recently, the Burger-King franchise for Venezuela. ODC has started renovating 30 of the soda fountain style restaurants within its super-market chain.

Married, with three children, Cisneros is a director of many organizations and corporatons. He is presently president of the Simon Bolivar Foundation of New York. Among his many awards, Mr. Cisneros holds the Order of Isabel la Catolica from the King of Spain.

Wang Labs was started by An Wang in 1951 in the Lowell-Tewksbury section of Massachusetts. By its 25th anniversary in 1976, Wang Labs showed a compounded sales growth of about 40% . . . in 1980 it posted a 66% growth rate. According to *Financial World's* tabulation of high-growth companies, Wang ranks fifth in earnings per share growth.

A leader in the microcomputer and word processing field, Wang employs 14,000 people. They are in direct competition with IBM and Burroughs in selling directly to customers. Wang stock is traded on the AMEX because Dr. Wang feels that NYSE requirements are too cumbersome.

Dr. Wang came from Shanghai, China after World War II to study at Harvard. In 1954 he became a naturalized citizen. While a staff-member of the Harvard Computation Laboratory, Wang developed the patent for the memory core and sold it to IBM. He has worked closely with Lowell in its renewal efforts and is now rehabilitating a Boston building. His plans are to open a new plant in Chinatown to employ Chinese-Americans in the computer industry. Dr. Wang is married and has three children.

Dr. Marcus Wallenberg, of Sweden, is the prime mover behind a $13 billion business empire which include Scandinavian Airlines Systems (SAS). The Wallenberg dynasty has had complete or partial control of 8 of the country's top industrial companies, a leading bank, and numerous smaller concerns, totaling 33% of Sweden's economy.

Dr. Wallenberg made the family bank, founded by his sea captain grandfather, into the brain and nerve center as well as financial guide and advisor to the best in modern Swedish business which has been called the Wallenberg Group. His directorships on company boards as the bank's representative has enabled him to influence and hand-pick managers who are considered among the best in Europe.

Through stock control of a few companies which have controlling interest in other firms, Marcus was able to build an empire which includes SKF, the world's largest ball-bearing manufacturer; L.M. Ericcson, a telephone equipment supplier which is the only substantial competition to ITT; Electrolux; SAAB-Scania car; ASEA, a truck and aircraft maker; and the Swedish answer to General Electric.

Dr. Wallenberg has managed to retain control of the $13 billion sales empire through accepting the heavily-socialized Swedish government and labor unions as partners in the complex Swedish system. Wallenberg found time for

THE TWO MOST COMMON EXEMPTIONS
FROM REGISTRATION OF SECURITIES ACT OF 1933

Requirments in General	Less than $100,000 in any rolling 12 month period. Rule 240 (§3(b))	Sophisticated investors Rule 146 (§4(2))
requirements apply to offerings	rule applies to each individual sale, not to an offering pursuant to which many sales are made	required; see Attachment (1) hereto, for definition of "offering" and of "safe harbor".
advertisements to general public	prohibited	prohibited
commission by issuer	prohibited	no restriction
limit on aggregate sales price	maximum of $100,000 in twelve months preceding sale (sales to promotes, executive officers, employees are excluded from aggregate price); includes *any* form of consideration	no limit
limit on number of beneficial owners	maximum of 100 before and after any transaction in reliance on Rule 240	maximum of 35 purchasers in any offering
transfers to underwriters; documentation required	prohibited, therefore issuer must: 1. inquire for whose account purchaser acquires 2. place legend on certificate re: resale restrictions* 3. inform buyer of resale restrictions	prohibited, therefore issuer must: 1. inquire for whose account purchaser acquires 2. place legend on certificate re: resale restrictions* 3. issue stop-transfer order to transfer agent (or note in records) 4. obtain written agreement from purchaser not to sell without registration 5. obtain letter of investment from offeree
character of offers and purchasers	no restriction*	1. issuer, on reasonable belief, to ascertain prior to offer that:

availability of information re: issuer and offering	not required**	a. offeree has knowledge re: risks/merits of investment, and
		b. issuer, *on reasonable inquiry*, to ascertain prior to sale that:
		  a. same as 1a. above, and
		  b. same as 1b. above.
		3. ***
		
		specific information, as listed in Attachment (3), is required to be available to offeree as well as an opportunity to offeree to question and verify the information.

written disclosures to offeree, prior to sale, by issuer	none required**	issuer required to disclose to offeree, prior to sale: 1. any material relationship between issuer and offeree representative. 2. the restrictions, pursuant to Rule 144, on subsequent sales or transfers of securities (if no disclosure of effect of Rule 144, issuer may be subject to charge of violation of prohibition of fraudulent transfers). 3. that the offeree must be able to bear the economic risk of the investment, due to the restrictions on transfers or sales.
notice and filing requirements	Form 240—after first $100,000 of sales; prior to first subsequent sale; thereafter once a year, within one month after first sales pursuant to 240—Form 240 which must be filed is shown below.	Form 146—at time of first sale of securities in offering—Form 146 which must be filled is shown below.

**"securities have not been registered under the Securities Act of 1933 and are subject to the Act's restrictions on sale or transfer."

**"therefore issuer must be able to demonstrate exercise of prudent business judgment.

*"securities have not been registered under the Securities Act of 1933 and are subject to the Act's restrictions on sale or transfer."

***such offeree has access to statutorily required information by reason if its family, or employment relationship or its economic bargaining power position, with respect to the issuer, enables it to obtain said information from the issuer.

various public activities including service to the domestic and international business communities. Retired from his position as Chairman of the Board of SAS in 1976, Wallenberg previously served in capacities such as President of the International Chamber of Commerce and a member of the board of the Nobel Foundation.

G. EXEMPTIONS FROM THE HOW TO RAISE CAPITAL LEGAL RESTRICTIONS

There are several commonly used exemptions from the securities act of 1933, which is the cornerstone of the legislations regulating how to raise capital. The first is rule 146, which provides an exemption because the purchasers are informed investors, whereas the exemption under rule 240 does not require the purchasers to be "sophisticated," it allows the exemption when the aggregate purchase price of the securities sold in any consecutive twelve month period meets a statutory limit, presently $100,000. These are the two federal exemptions to remain in compliance with the securities and exchange laws for raising new capital. Remember, when you are raising capital for an entrepreneurial venture, you must also meet the requirements of the state. Simply meeting the federal laws does not assure state compliance. The chart on pp. 162-3 highlights requirements of both rule 146 and rule 240. In addition, a copy of the form to be filed in both cases is also offered.

Attachment (1)

RULE 146 REQUIREMENT

Definition of offerings, for the purpose of determining the number of purchasers per offering:

Rule 146(b)
1. There is a "safe harbor" of six months before and after any offer or sale pursuant to the Rule: if no sales within those six month periods, no prior or subsequent sales or offers will be drawn into the definition of an offer and the limit on the number of offerees/purchasers per offering.
Preliminary Note 3 to Rule 146
2. In the event the issuer does not qualify under 1. above for the "safe harbor," an offering will be defined to include (for the purpose of determining the number of purchasers) offerings where all offerings are
   a) part of a single plan of financing
   b) same class of security
   c) made at or about the same time
   d) for the same type of consideration
   e) for the same general purpose.

Attachment (2)

FORM 240

Securities and Exchange Commission
Washington, D.C. 20549

NOTICE OF SALES OF SECURITIES PURSUANT TO RULE 240
OF THE SECURITIES ACT OF 1933

1. Name, address and telephone number (including area code) of the issuer of the securities to be sold:
2. Names (in full) of the executive officers, directors and promoters of the issuer (or of persons serving in similar capacities for noncorporate issuers) and of any persons beneficially owning 10 percent or more of the equity securities of, or equity interest in, the issuer:
3. Title of class of securities sold:
4. Aggregate sales price of unregistered securities sold within the preceding twelve months, computed in accordance with paragraph (e) of the rule:
5. Number of persons who are beneficial owners of securities of the issuer as of the date of filing this Notice, computed in accordance with paragraph (f) of the rule.

Pursuant to the requirements of Rule 240 under the Securities Act of 1933, the issuer has duly caused this notice to be signed on its behalf by the undersigned duly authorized officer or person acting in a similar capacity.

Date of Notice: _____   Issuer_____

_____

Attachment (3)

FORM 146

SECURITIES AND EXCHANGE COMMISSION
Washington, D.C. 20549

REPORT OF OFFERING MADE IN RELIANCE UPON RULE 146

1. (a) Name, address, and telephone number (including area code) and date and state (or other jurisdiction) of incorporation or organization of the issuer of the securities offered and sold:
   (b) Type of business (check one).

   _____ Oil/Gas   _____ Real Estate   _____ Other (specify)
   (c) Full name of chief executive officer, general partner(s), promoter(s) and controlling person(s).

Instruction: If the general partner(s), promoter(s) or controlling person(s) is (are) not a natural person(s), so state and provide similar information for a natural person(s) having primary responsibility for the affairs of the issuer.

(d) Names and addresses of all organizers, promoters and sponsors of, and of all offeree representatives (as that term is defined in Rule 146(a) (1) involved in, the offering reported on this form, indicating the capacity in which they acted.

2. With respect to securities sold or to be sold in this offering in reliance upon Rule 146, state the title of the class and the aggregate dollar amount of sales to date and sales to be made in the future in this offering.

Instruction: As to any securities sold or to be sold other than for cash or partly for cash and partly for other consideration, state and nature of the transaction and the source and aggregate amount of consideration received or to be received by the issuer.

3. Has the issuer made any previous filings with the Securities and Exchange Commission under

Rule 146 (if so, specify the number of such filings)?

_____ Yes   _____ No

The Securities Act of 1933 or the Securities Exchange Act of 1934 as an issuer of securities?

_____ Yes   _____ No

Pursuant to the requirements of Rule 146 under the Securities Act of 1933, the issuer has duly caused this report to be signed on its behalf by the undersigned officer or person acting in a similar capacity.

Date of Report _____   _____

(Issuer)

_____

(Signature)

H. EXPORTING

If you feel that your firm's production capacity warrants looking into foreign markets for your products, the U.S. Commerce Department has three excellent programs to offer.

Sales Representatives

To find an agent or distributor, you must complete an application form that includes a brief description of the products for sale and the qualifications required by an agent or distributor (type of customers served, products handled, etc.) This information is relayed to the relevant U.S. Foreign Service post, which attempts to identify up to six agents or distributors (in the country or countries you have specified), who are interested in your proposal. In about 60 days, you will receive the names and addresses of potential sales agents to contact and a description of their operations.

Sales Inquiries

The Trade Opportunities Program (TOP) helps in developing sales leads for United States suppliers. The one-time fee is $37.50 to have your business's individual registered code entered into the TOP computer in Washington. This code includes the products you sell, the countries in which you want them to be sold, and whether you want to deal directly with a buyer or through an agent or distributor. The inquiries are originated by the employees in 200 American embassies and consulates located in over 120 foreign countries who continually send data on foreign buyers' needs to Washington, D.C. You will receive a listing of the inquirers' names and addresses when one of the foreign sales inquiries matches your code.

Mailing Lists

The Export Contact List Service will help you compile a mailing list. This is a computerized version of the Commerce Department's old "trade lists." It includes information on over 140,000 manufacturers, service organizations, agents, distributors, retailers, and cooperatives in 143 countries. The cost of a list is $10.00 for set-up and 6 cents per name. One or two duplicate mailing lists may be obtained at $3.00 each. For an additional charge, the names can be printed on gummed mailing labels. Look in your telephone book for the Commerce Department nearest you or write to the U.S. Department of Commerce, Washington, D.C.

Other Sources of Help

"Market Match" in New York conducts a trade lead service similar to the Commerce Department's TOP. This program is also an online computerized directory of buyers and sellers worldwide. Write to:

Gerald Lieberman
World Trade Center
New York, NY 10048
(212) 466-3067

If you have a question concerning selling your products abroad, you can call Export-Import Bank on its new toll-free hot line (800) 424-5201, which was set up to help small business exporters contact an expert in the field to develop questions on doing business overseas.

Export Loans from SBA

The Small Business Administration (SBA) has $100 million available for loan guarantees for small business exporters. If your firm cannot secure bank debt on its own and would like to begin or expand into foreign markets, it is eligible for these loans. The money is actually distributed by the bank or financial institution, and the SBA offers its usual percentage type of guarantee. The use of the funds is extremely discretionary, including trips abroad or visiting trade shows. Application for this type of loan should be made through a local bank. Furthermore, the SBA has a new export program for the Procurement Automated Source System. It's known as PASS, and its purpose is to inform United States suppliers of export programs and seminars. You can register at your local SBA office with the Procurement Assistance Division for this PASS program.

Howard V. Perlmutter, professor of the University of Pennsylvania's Wharton School, an expert on multinational organizations, says that "... a wild game is about to begin. It's called how many of our companies can make it in world markets and how do we get them there?" (*Business Week,* July 2, 1979)

If you, as a venturesome entrepreneur are considering the foreign market, the following sources of information can be used to explore most areas of such an undertaking. Write:

Director, Bureau of Export Development
U.S. Department of Commerce
Washington, D.C. 20230

Programs to write for from the Dept. of Commerce include the following:

Foreign Trader's Index
Trade Opportunities Program (TOP)
Export Contact List Service
World Traders Report
Commerce Business Daily

Director
Export Trade Services Division
Foreign Agricultural Service
U.S. Dept. of Agriculture
Washington, D.C. 20250
(202) 447-6343

Federal Trade Commission
Public Reference Branch
6th Street & Pennsylvania Ave.
Room 130
Washington, D.C. 20580
(202) 523-3830

Department of the Treasury
U.S. Customs Service
1303 Constitution Ave. N.W.
Washington, D.C. 20520
(202) 566-8195

Export-Import Bank of the U.S.
811 Vermont Avenue, N.W.
Washington, D.C. 20571

Office of Commercial Affairs
Bureau of Economic and Business
  Affairs
Room 33-34
U.S. State Department
Washington, D.C. 20520
(202) 632-8097

Market Match
Gerald Lieberman
World Trade Center
New York, NY 20048
(212) 466-3067

Publications

Government and Business: A Joint Venture in International Trade (free booklet published by the U.S. State Department's Office of Commercial Affairs). To order, write to:

Office of Public Affairs
U.S. State Department
Room 48-27A
Washington, D.C. 20520
(202) 632-6575

Guide to United Nations Conference of Trade and Development (UNCTAD) Publications (free catalog published by UNCTAD). Write:

United Nations Sales Section
Editorial & Document
    Section
Palais Des Nations 1211
Geneva 10, Switzerland

Lorna M. Daniells,
    *Business Information
    Sources,* (Berkeley, CA;
    University of California
    Press, 1976) publishes a
    list of reference data
    sources for exporters.

*Quarterly Economic
    Review* (London,
    England: Economist
    Intelligence Unit),
    reviews 45 countries
    quarterly.

OECD *Economic Surveys*
    (Paris, France:
    Organization for Economic
    Cooperation and Development),
    individual, annual reviews listed
    by country.

*Investing, Licensing and Trading
    Conditions Abroad,* (New York,
    NY: Business International),
    two volumes.

The Department of Commerce provides free consultation with an expert trade specialist who can help answer questions about the feasibility of exporting your product to other countries, govenment regulations, cultural mores, and competition. Bankers in the international departments of major city banks are also good contacts to help assess a foreign market. A third source of information about export possibilities is foreign students at your local universities who can suggest marketing potential and possible cultural and governmental limitations.

I. GRANTS

In 1979 over 26,000 United States foundations gave away close to $3 billion in grants. The federal government, mostly the Department of Health, Education and Welfare, gave away over $60 billion. Very few of these grants were awarded to small businesses. Although it is true that 95% of the grant proposals submitted are rejected, it is also true that small businesses seldom seek or receive financial grants.

A special exemption is needed to give a grant to profit-seeking business, but it is not uncommon for a grant to be awarded for a project to a nonprofit organization (such as a college or university) and that an entrepreneur will be a subcontractor on the project. It may be very much in your interest, therefore, to support the efforts of local nonprofit institutions to obtain funds. Information on oraganizations that give grants can be obtained by consulting the following sources.

1. The Foundation Center, an information clearing house that maintains national libraries in Chicago, New York City, and Washington, D.C. as well as regional libraries in 48 states, Mexico, and Puerto Rico. These libraries are open to the public at no charge.

2. The *Foundation Directory,* a reference work which lists 2,800 foundations that awarded $1.8 billion in grants in 1976. The directory gives the following data on the foundations it lists: names and addresses (by state); founders' names; total assets; officials' names; purposes and activities; and the number and dollar amount of grants awarded during the year. This directory is available at any large library.

3. The *Foundation Grants Index,* which lists grants of more than $5,000 made by the 300 major foundations. It lists the names of the recipients, the purposes of the grants, and the dollar amounts awarded. A separate "Key Word & Phrase" index is especially useful in determining the current real interests of each foundation. This book is also available in most large libraries.

4. The *Catalog of Federal Domestic Assistance and the Annual Register of Grant Support.* This is the single best starting point for research on grants. For information on obtaining a copy write:

Marquis Who's Who
4300 West 62nd Street
Indianapolis, IN 46206

The Register lists procedures for requesting grants; programs; names of agency officers; and the total number of applications received and awarded by programs each years.

J. INFORMATION ABOUT PREMIUM AND INCENTIVE BUYING

Many products can be sold to companies or organizations that will use them as premiums or giveaways, or in incentive buying programs. Perhaps your product(s) can be used in this way. For a list of such buyers, there are several sources you can contact:

The Salesmen's Guide
1182 Broadway
New York, NY. 10001

Incentive Marketing
633 Third Avenue
New York, NY 10017
(212) 986-4800
Circulation: about 35,000

Premium/Incentive Business
1515 Broadway
New York, NY 10036
(212) 869-1300
Circulation: about 24,000

NPSE Newsletter
1600 Route 22
Union, NJ 07083
(201) 687-3832
Circulation: about 2,000

Free Publicity

Rather than launching a marketing program with a series of paid-for advertisements, consider the advantages of a publicity release program. Your firm may be eligible for news releases or product releases or literature releases, all of which are free. Doesn't it make sense to have all initial effort directed toward the free material? Entrepreneurial managers obtain all the available free products releases before they succumb to paid-for advertisements.

The procedure for contacting the various trade journals varies from industry to industry. Some journals require black-and-white photographs, others require color photographs, and others accept no photographs. To obtain specific information on how to obtain publicity and to obtain a list of relevant trade journals, these four publishers offer you directories and publicity release programs.

Ayer's Directory of Newspapers and Periodicals
William J. Luedke, Publisher; Ayer Press
210 West Washington Square
Philadelphia, PA 19106
(215) 829-4472

Ayer's Directory is the most comprehensive source of newspaper information.

Bacon's Publicity Checker
14 East Jackson Boulevard
Chicago, IL 60604

For an excellent overall list of periodicals, use the *Standard Periodical Directory* published by:

> Oxbridge Publishing Company
> 383 Madison Avenue,
>   Room 1108
> New York, NY 10016
> (212) 689-8524

Ulrich's Directory of Periodicals is usually available in public libraries and as a reference in college libraries. It is published by:

> R. Bowker Company
> 1180 Avenue of the Americas
> New York, NY 11036
> (212) 764-5100

Clipping Services

Below is a partial list of services that will clip newspaper and magazine articles about your company or about a product area. This can be a valuable service to keep you posted on the advertising and public relations efforts of your competitors as well as your own company's programs. *Note:* This list is only a partial list because no organization keeps this information on a national basis. We suggest that you inspect your local Yellow Pages to determine if such an organization exists in your geographical areas.

> Allen's Press Clipping Bureau
> 657 Mission Street
> San Francisco, CA 94105
>
> Bacon's Clipping Service
> 14 East Jackson Boulevard
> Chicago, IL 60604
> (312) 922-8419
>
> Florida Clipping Service
> Box 10278
> Tampa, FL 33679
> (813) 831-0962

> Luce Press Clipping Service
> 912 Kansas Avenue
> Topeka, KS 66612
> (913) 232-0201
>
> New England Newsclip Service
> 5 Auburn Street
> Framingham, MA 01701
> (617) 879-4460

Marketing Sources

The National Research Bureau is a subsidiary of the Automated Marketing Systems, Inc. It offers the *Gebbie House Magazine Directory,* which lists company house organs, newsletters, and internal company information. It is an often overlooked source of publicity. This directory is a part of the *Working Press of Nations,* a five-volume set of invaluable aids to over 100,000 prime media contacts available from:

National Research Bureau
  Headquarters
104 S. Michigan Avenue
Chicago, IL 60603
(312) 641-2655

Editorial and Production
424 North Third Street
Burlington, IA 42601
(319) 752-5415

Washington Bureau
1141 National Press Building
Washington, D.C. 20045
(202) 638-4746

Conventions and trade show listings are compiled and offered by:

Exhibits Schedule
144 East 44th Street
New York, NY 10017

The Hendrickson
  Publishing Company
91 North Franklin Street
Hempstead, NY 11550
(516) 483-6883

International Association
  of Fairs and Exhibits
77 Arbor Road
Winston-Salem, NC 27104

Sales Meeting Magazines
144 East 44th Street
New York, NY 10017

Trade Show Week
1605 Cahuenga Boulevard
Los Angeles, CA 90028
(213) 463-4891

K. MANUFACTURER'S REPRESENTATIVES

How to select the proper manufacturer's representative for your product line is
one of the most difficult questions facing an entrepreneurial venture. The
following sources list several organizations and directories that will help find
competent sales representatives for small businesses.

Albee-Campbell
806 Penn Avenue
Sinking Springs, PA 19608
(215) 678-3361

Representative Resources, Inc.
Drower Avenue
Thorndale, PA 19372
(215) 383-1177

L. H. Simmonds, Inc.
60 East 42nd Street
New York, NY 10017
(212) 889-1530

United Association of
  Manufacturers Agents
808 Broadway
Kansas City, MO 64105
(816) 842-8130

Anthony J. Zinno Associates
2 Park Avenue
Manhasset, NY 10030
(516) 627-2642

A group of nearly 100 firms engaged in selling products and services to consumers, primarily in their homes, lists several directories of members that are available to member firms.

> Direct Selling Association
> 1730 M Street N.W.
> Suite 610
> Washington, D.C. 20036
> (202) 293-5760

The Manufacturers Agents National Association is a 30-year-old industry association of manufacturers' agents and an excellent source of information. Write:

> Manufacturers Agents National Association
> 2021 Business Center Drive
> Box 16878
> Irvine, CA 92713

Pacific International (President Gordon Strickler) takes the guess-work out of appointing reps. They have in their files a list of reps and rep companies in 42 major marketing areas in the United States and all foreign countries

> Pacific International
> P.O. Box 894
> Escondido, CA 92025
> (714) 745-7361

A directory listing more than 2,000 U.S. electronic representative firms and branches, indexed by geographical region and cross-indexed alphabetically, can be obtained from:

> Electronic Representatives Association
> 233 East Erie Street
> Chicago, IL 60611

They also offer a service including a listing in the ERA *Lines Available Bulletin,* issued monthly to some 1,500 members, designed to help manufacturers establish representation. In addition, they maintain a hotline service that enables manufacturers looking for reps in one or two markets to get their messages, within 36 hours, to representatives serving the defined territories.

Your ad in the *Manufacturers' Agents' Newsletter* reaches manufacturers throughout the United States and Canada and in some foreign countries whose principal method of selling their products is through manufacturer's representatives. Your ad in the newsletter can let these manufacturers know who you are, where you are, which territory you cover, and which product lines you are looking for.

Manufacturers' Agents' Newsletter, Inc.
23573 Prospect Avenue
Farmington, MI 58024

The Rep Information Service offers a wide range of assistance in securing manufacturer's representatives. The three fundamental publications offered are listed
below. Write:

Rep Information Service
5521 Reseda Boulevard,
    Suite 17
Tarzana, CA 91356

Agent Edition, a published lead service giving sales agents in excess of
1,000 "Agents Wanted" leads during life of subscription, plus personal
assistance in locating new product lines.

Agent Edition—Rep Information Service
5521 Reseda Boulevard,
    Suite 17
P.O. Box L
Tarzana, CA 91356
(213) 705-1222

Manufacturers Edition is a lead service to help manufacturers find agents, manufacturers' representatives, and trading companies on a worldwide basis, plus
regular mailings of published "Lines Wanted" listings, plus personal referral
services to assist them in locating agents in specific territories.

Manufacturers' Edition—Rep Service (same as above) is a directory listing
1,235 moneymaking opportunity advertisements, complete with explanation of
what was received in experience of answering all these offers, plus detailed
explanation of illegal offers, postal regulations, schemes, chain letters, and how
moneymaking opportunity offers work.

Directory of 1,235 Opportunity Offers
J.E. Distributing, Inc., Publisher
5521 Reseda Boulevard,
    Suite 17
Tarzana, CA 91356
(213) 705-1222

Rep World is a quarterly publication to about 5,000 which focuses on manufacturers' representatives.

Rep World
578 Penn Ave.
Sinking Spring, PA 19608

Specialty Salesmen and Business Opportunities is a monthly magazine on direct mailing and direct-to-consumer selling. A directory of agents is also available.

Speciality Salesmen and Business Opportunities
307 North Michigan Avenue
Chicago, IL 60601
(312) 726-0743

For a free ad in a weekly bulletin that goes to rep members in all fields, world-wide, write:

United Association Manufacturers' Reps
808 Broadway
Kansas City, MO 64105
(816) 842-8130

Verified Directory of Manufacturers' Representatives is published biennially by Manufacturers' Agent Publishing Company. It presents a geographic listing of about 15,000 manufacturers' representatives (domestic and export) serving all industries, except food products, for the United States and Canada. It gives principal lines carried and trading areas covered.

A second publication lists more than 11,500 manufacturers who distribute through agents. Classified by industry, it includes name, address of manufacturer and principal products, credit ratings, and name and title of sales executives.

Manufacturers' Agents' Guide, $27.50.
National Association Diversified Manufacturers' Representatives
Manufacturers' Agents' Publising Company, Inc.
663 Fifth Avenue
New York, NY 10022
(212) 682-0326

Who's Who in Electronics lists 7,500 electronic manufacturers, 2,500 industrial electronic parts and equipment distributors, 3,300 independent electronic representative firms, together with a separate product index section with 1,600 product breakdowns, their manufacturers and distributors, It has information about products, sales, volume, marketing areas, key personnel, research facilities, telephone numbers, plant sizes, and new firms and information concerned with the electronics field.

B. Klein Publications
Box 8503
Coral Springs, FL 33065
(305) 752-1708

The National Directory of Manufacturers' Representatives is a directory that will help you find reps on your own. The alphabetical listing of reps includes size of staff, geographic territories, products represented, markets served, and special services. A second section, listed by state, indicates the Standard Industrial Classification (SIC) codes for all the industries called on by reps in that state. Write:

McGraw-Hill Publishing Company
1221 Avenue of the Americas
New York, NY 10020

L. NEW ISSUES STOCK MARKET

The new issues market is on the rise once again after a roller coaster ride during the 1970's. Many professionals involved in bringing new stocks into the market are suggesting that this revived interest could last for several years. Others caution prospective investors to be extremely selective as many entrepreneurs see the new issues market as an alternative in raising capital for start-up companies.

The volume of new issues this year remains below historic high levels, yet market analysts claim the new issues boom is still in its earliest stages. The new issues market is dependent on the general health of the entire market, and could face disaster if investor speculation falls short.

Nearly all of the new issues in the current market have been in the area of energy or computer related technology, however, the entertainment and food industries are in second place. The SEC claims that during the fiscal year ending September 30, 1980, 450 companies filed to go public through its main office in Washington, D.C.

Much of the most speculative new-issues action has taken place in Denver's market for shares in infant oil and gas. No one market has felt the new issues boom as much as Denver—where both the biggest risks and rewards are being found. Many of the new offerings have been in existence less than two years and frequently have limited assets backing their stock. New companies with few assets, little revenue, and no production are represented strongly among the firms that have gone public this year.

Although many of the new issues are highly speculative, the current trend has been founded on some genuine success stories.

Two examples of successful new issues stock investments are; Apple Computer and Genetech. Apple Computer is a producer of personal computers whose sales are upward to $200 million. Incidentally, in the State of Massachusetts, the sales of Apple Computer shares was curtailed by the Attorney General who believed the cost to be outrageous. He later reversed the ruling and the Attorney

General sanctioned the sale of Apple Computer stock in the Massachusetts marketplace.

Genetech is a genetic engineering company, whose gene-splicing research went public at $35 a share in October increasing to $89 after the first day on the market. Since then, Genetech shares have dropped to $43.75 per share, but still maintain a margin over the offering price.

Both Apple Computer and Genetech have received several rounds of venture capital, but with the new issues marketplace so receptive now, they have also chosen to go public. These quality, rapid growing companies could go in any market, but in a hot market, they really boom.

There are differences between the new issues boom of a decade ago, and the present boom. The high quality and growth records of many of the young companies going public now also encourage market optomists. Underwriters are anxious to handle new issues from which they take 10% to 15% commission of the money they raise. Of 300 underwriters surveyed, 115 have brought new issues to market in 1980.

The underwriter guarantees an offering by buying all the shares offered by a company and reselling them to the public. Many of the penny stocks underwritten (for example in the Denver market) are brought out as "best efforts" offerings in which the underwriter buys none of the stock itself, therefore assuming no risk. The proceeds are then held in escrow until a given number of shares are sold. If the minimum number of shares are not sold, the entire offering is withdrawn.

Some brokerage firms publish weekly calendars of forthcoming offerings for client information on the subject of new issues. Most brokers also subscribe to the "Investment Dealers' Digest", also a weekly publication that covers the new issues market.

The company sales and earning record, profit margins, accounting methods, competitive position, and other vital information on which an investor would form his opnion of the value of an issue appears on a prospectus. Other suggestions to aid the investor are:

1. A reputable underwriter: will not market the stock of any company likely to damage their reputation. Among these are, Blyth Eastman, Paine Webber, Dean Witter, Goldman Sachs, all of New York. A list of underwriters is available from Howard & Company.

2. If the stock holdings of top officers are being sold, the investor should carefully examine the appeal of the issue.

3. If there is the strong financial support of a venture capital firm, this indicates that the company has been well groomed for the public marketplace, and could be considered a "promising" investment.

4. Check the balance sheet to see if the company's finances are strong enough to keep it going if profits don't meet forecasted figures. Also notice if profit growth is on target, and the risks of plans for continued expansion.

How to Go Public

There are four ways to file a registration statement with the Securities Exchange Committee (SEC) to go public.

1. S-1—especially suited for companies dealing with oil, gas, and mining ventures. This is the SEC's general filing registration which requires maximum disclosure and reporting in both the offering and quarterly reports. This can be extremely demanding for small firms and start-up companies and should be used only if any other alternative registration statement is not applicable.

2. S-2—Intended for the use of start-up companies with no substantial sales or net income for the past 5 years. This special filing procedure requires detailed information about what the proceeds will be used for, and the credibility of the individuals who support the business venture.

3. S-18—To help businesses raise relatively large amounts of money (up to $5 million) without filing with SEC headquarters in Washington. These S-18's are processed by regional offices and have the following specific criteria to be met: (1) securities must be sold for cash; (2) the company must be incorporated in and operate in the U.S. or Canada; and (3) the firm may not be an investment company or offer limited partnerships.

4. Regulation A. This is an exemption from certain filing requirements, such as the 10-K, 10-Q, or interim 8-Q forms if the company has fewer than 500 shareholders and less than $1 million in assets. Regulation A offerings can be filed through SEC regional offices, but the company cannot raise more than $1.5 million.

If you don't have the stomach to invest directly into one of these entrepreneurial ventures, why not consider investing in a mutual fund which does invest in a new issues. Here is a list.
Some reliable sources of information to check are:

The 44 Wall Street Equity Fund, 150 Broadway, NY, NY 10038; (212) 227-0512.
Dreyfus Number Nine Fund, P.O. Box 600, Middlesex, NJ 08846; (1-800) 345-8501; in PA (1-800) 662-5180.
Oppenheimer Special Fund, 2 Broadway, NY, NY 10004; (1-800) 331-1750; in OK (1-800) 722-3600.

Fidelity Trend Fund, 82 Devonshire St., Boston, MA 02109; (800) 225-6190; in MA collect (617) 726-0650.

Nautilus Fund, Eaton Howard Vance Sanders, 1660 L St., N. W. Washington, D.C. 20036; (800) 424-9234.

Going Public:
The IPO Reporter*

If you are interested in the idea of going public, but would like more information before making the jump into the public offering market, "IPO REPORTER" is a monthly publication that can help you to make a well informed decision. The IPO Reporter is a complete reference guide with information from: investment bankers, brokers, attorneys, accountants, financial consultants and venture capitalists. The information is bound in a three-ring binder, making updated material easily inserted as a complete reference. We have printed sample pages below for your review.

The "IPO REPORTER" is prepared and published by Howard and Company, 1529 Walnut Street, Philadelphia, PA 19102 or call: (215) 563-8030.

Advest, Inc., 6 Central Row, Hartford, CT 06103 (203) 525-1421. Randolph Guggenheimer, VP-CF & Synd. 1980 IPOs: None. 1979 IPOs: Bank of New Haven (F $4.0), Greate Bay Casino (S $25.7). 1978 IPOs: None.

Allen & Company Incorporated, 711 Fifth Ave., New York, NY 10022 (212) 832-8000. Harold Wit, EVP-CF; Paul A. Gould, VP-Synd. 1980 IPOs: None. 1979 IPOs: None. 1978 IPOs: L. Luria & Son (F $4.6).

Alstead, Strangis & Dempsey, Inc., 609 Second Ave. S., Minneapolis, MN (612) 339-2800. Jerry A. Alstead, Pres. 1980 IPOs: Flight Transportation (BE $1.8). 1979 IPOs: None. 1978 IPOs: None.

Alta Investment Company, 10 Seventeenth St., Denver, CO 80202 (303) 573-7244. Robert W. Sneed, Principal. 1980 IPOs: None. 1979 IPOs: None. 1978 IPOs: Petro Mineral (BE $1.2).

American Growth Fund Sponsors, Inc., 650 Seventeenth St., Suite 800, Denver, CO 80202 (303) 623-6137, Robert D. Brody, Pres; Thomas H. Bock, EVP. 1980 IPOs: None. 1979 IPOs: Poly Co. of America (BE $1.8). 1978 IPOs: None.

American Investors of Pittsburgh Inc., 1380 Center City Tower, Pittsburgh, PA 15222 (412) 227-3500. John J. Bruno; Pres; John W. Mendicino, EVP. 1980 IPOs: Agripost (F & BE $1.15). 1979 IPOs: None. 1978 IPOs: None.

American Western Securities, Inc., 360 S. Monroe St., 6th Fl., Denver, CO 80209 (303) 399-0176. Jack D. Kelley, Pres; Dee Knoblauch, VP-Synd. 1980 IPOs: None. 1979 IPOs: Westwind Financial Services (BE $1.2). 1978 IPOs: Greenwood Resources (BE $1.1), Marine Nutritional

*Going Public. The IPO Reporter, © 1980 Howard & Company, Philadelphia, PA 19102 (215) 735-2815. Cost $500.00.

(BE $1.2), Pacer Technology (BE $1.0), Thermatron (BE $1.5). T.O.N.M. Oil & Gas (BE $1.0).

Arnhold and S. Bleichroeder, Inc., 30 Broad St., New York, NY 10004 (212) 943-9200. Stanford Warshawsky, CF Mgr; Chales R. Treuhold, Synd Mgr. 1980 IPOs: None. 1979 IPOs: Kevex (F $7.6). 1978 IPOs: None.

Bache Halsey Stuart Shields Incorporated, 100 Gold St., New York, NY 10038 (212) 791-1000. Raymond J. O'Connor, Sr VP-CF; Peter A. Bernard, Sr VP-Synd. 1980 IPOs: None. 1979 IPOs: Empire of Carolina (F $9.8). 1978 IPOs: None.

Baker, Watts & Co., 100 Light St., Baltimore, MD 21203 (301) 685-2600. N. Clark Moran, Synd Mgr. 1980 IPOs: None. 1979 IPOs: Antennas for Communications (F $2.3). 1978 IPOs: None.

Bateman Eichler, Hill Richards Incorporated, 700 S. Flower St., Los Angeles, CA 90017 (213) 625-3545. Frank L. Bryant, CF Mgr; John S. DeGroot, VP-Synd. 1980 IPOs: None. 1979 IPOs: Applied Solar Energy (F $7.0), Harken Oil & Gas (F $6.8), Thousand Trails (F $1.8). 1978 IPOs: Compact Video (F $4.5).

Bear, Stearns & Co., 55 Water St., New York, NY 10041 (212) 952-5000. Raphael Bernstein, CF Mgr; Livio M. Borghese, Synd Mgr. 1980 IPOs: None. 1979 IPOs: Bally's Park Place (S $58.5), The Western Pacific Railroad Co., a/k/a Newrail (F $14.0). 1978 IPOs: None.

You will also receive, as an added free bonus, complete cumulative data on all 81 companies that went public in 1979 plus a two-page profile on each company.

1. MONTHLY REPORTS for 1980 on all the companies going public during the month, analyzing over 20 different aspects of each offering, including:

company names, address, & phone number	company counsel
line of business	underwriters' counsel
revenues	auditor
date filed & date effective	underwriting fees
registration form (S-1, 2, 3, or 18)	cash expenses
offering type	aggregate fees & expenses
security offered	start-up IPOs
price per share	price/earnings ratio
dollars raised	stockholders' equity
managing underwriter(s)	price/equity ratio
underwriting syndicate	aftermarket performance

2. 1980 IPO PROFILES (updated monthly) which include key excerpts from the prospectus and a concise analysis of each offering.

3. CUMULATIVE REPORTS (updated periodically) on the initial public offering activity in 1980 enabling you to spot trends in the IPO market and make easy comparisons.

4. REFERENCE SECTIONS (updated periodically) that include:

A comprehensive Guide to IPO Underwriters listing the name of each investment banking firm which has underwritten an initial public offering since 1978; its address and telephone number; the name of the Corporate Finance Manager and Syndicate Manager; the name of the companies it has underwritten; and the offering type and dollar amount raised for each company.

A Guide to IPO Experts listing the law firms and accounting firms involved with initial public offerings since 1979.

Articles on various aspects of going public and an invaluable booklet on the advantages, disadvantages, procedures and consequences of going public.

The most current and comprehensive IPO Bibliography and reading list available today.

Each month in 1980 you will receive a new report on the previous month's IPO activities and new profiles on the companies that went public during the month.

THE AFTERMARKET PERFORMANCE
OF SELECTED NEW ISSUES (1980)

Company	Issue Date	Offering Price	Price (as of 10/3/80)	% Change
Advanced Systems	7/24	$12.75	$12.75	0%
Alcogas	6/6	2.50 (unit)	1.50	− 40
Andrew Corp.	6/19	18.50	25.63	+ 36
Applicon	7/22	22.00	51.50	+134
Brock Hotels	6/18	12.25	23.50	+ 92
Cado Systems	3/11	18.00	35.00	+ 94
China Trade	1/11	10.00 (unit)	7.75	− 22
Codenoll Technology	9/4	5.50 (unit)	5.63	+ 2
Eagle Exploration	9/24	5.00	4.50	− 10
General Nutrition	6/19	15.00	15.25	+ 2
Geokinetics	4/30	7.50	8.63	+ 15
High Stoy Technology	7/29	7.25 (unit)	7.25	0
Keith Collins Petroleum	3/24	.10	.53	+530
Mid Pacific Airlines	9/16	5.00	4.75	− 5
Mitral Medical	5/30	3.00 (unit)	15.75	+525
Optimum Holding	7/16	9.00	12.25	+136
Sci-Tex	5/21	11.00	34.50	+214
Siltec	3/11	20.00	22.50	+ 13
Solar Electric Engineering	5/1	.05	.04	− 20
Up-Right	5/21	11.00	14.25	+ 29

"Wall Street West"

The Denver, 17th Street investment marketplace has been nicknamed "Wall Street West." The Denver market is having a particularly profitable year due to the current boom with new issues and penny stocks. Denver brokers have become very selective in the sotcks they underwrite. Many new securities are dealing with energy issues and the use of gas and oil. This energy-concerned market stimulates a great deal of patriotism among brokers, as well as profits for selective investors.

For information on the Denver market, check *Denver Business World*—a weekly news and financial publication, cost $26 per year. Telephone (303) 744-1800, 701 South Logan, Denver, CO 80209. Or check:

IDWA Marketing Corp.
Penny Stock Preview
1901 N. Olden Ave.
Trenton, NJ 08618
609-882-6880

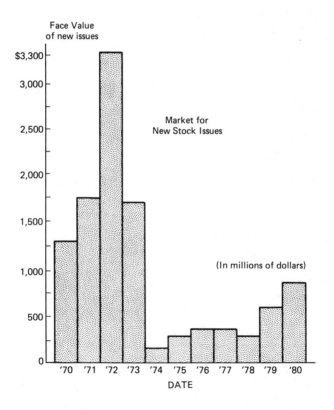

Sources of Information

New Issues Newsletter

3471 North Federal Highway
Ft. Lauderdale, FL 33016
Monthly publication, cost $100

"Underwriters of Initial
Public Offerings"
and
Going Public, The
IPO Reporter
Growth Stock Outlook

published by Howard and Company
1529 Walnut Street,
Philadelphia, PA 19102 or call
(215) 563-8030.
A bi-monthly publication, cost $60
per year. Also, Jr. Growth Stock
newsletter at $54.00 per year.
(Prices subject to increase in
February). Write or call for sample
package. Growth Stock Outlook,
P.O. Box 9911, Chevy Chase, MD
20015 or call (301) 654-5205.

Sources of Investment/Venture Capital

Chief Counsel for Advocacy
Small Business Administration
1411 L Street N.W.
Washington, D.C. 20005
(202) 653-6998

National Association of Business
    Development Associations
Industrial Development Corporation
    of Florida
801 North Magnolia Avenue, Suite 218
Orlando, Florida 32803
(305) 841-2640

American Assoc. of MESBICS
(Minority Enterprise S.B. Invest. Co.)
1413 K St., N.W. 13th Floor
Washington, D.C. 20005
(202) 347-8600

Office of Business Development
Economic Development Administration
Room 7876 14th and Constitution Ave., N.W.
Washington, D.C. 20230
(202) 377-2000

M. PATENTS, INVENTIONS, TRADEMARKS, AND LABORATORIES

How to Get a Patent is about America's patent law. For a copy of the booklet, write:

Consumer Information Center
Department 126E
Pueblo, CO 81009

The Inventors News, published by the Inventors Club of America, offers information on protection before patent, marketing and manufacturing, and development. The Inventors Club of America is a non-profit organization established to help inventors who are willing to help themselves. They show you ways to develop and market your ideas yourself. Write:

    Inventors News
    Box 3799
    Springfield, MA 01101
    (413) 737-0670

    Inventors Club of America
    National Headquarters
    1562 Main Street
    Box 3799
    Springfield, MA 01001
    (413) 737-0670

Action is published regularly to serve as a medium of communication between members of the Association for the Advancement of Invention and Innovation. It is open to inventors, entrepreneurs, research directors, business people, scientists, engineers, lawyers, patent attorneys and agents, educators, patent examiners, economists, and others who support the objectives of the Association. Write:

    The Association for the Advancement of Invention
        and Innovation
    Suite 301, Crystal Mall 1
    1911 Jefferson Davis Highway
    Arlington, VA 22202

New Products and Processes Newsletter, a publication of *Newsweek Magazine, Inc.,* is a source for the most comprehensive, timely, and usable new product information available anywhere. Each issue contains reviews of 75 to 100 new products and processes, including complete product descriptions, many with illustrations, availability for manufacturing, and sales of licensing arrangements. Write:

    New Products and Processes
    Newsweek International
    444 Madison Avenue
    New York, NY 10022

The United States Trademark Association is a nonprofit organization dedicated to the protection, development, and promotion of the trademark concept. USTA is the only organization in the United States totally devoted to trademarks, protecting the rights of trademark owners as well as communicating with business educators, the press, and the public to foster understanding and appreciation of the role of trademarks. The services offered by USTA concern all aspects of the trademark field: federal, state, and foreign legislation; education, promotion advertising, and merchandising; publicity and use by the press; proper handling of trademarks by corporate personnel, sales staff, dealers; and more. An important caveat: The services of USTA do not purport to substitute for or duplicate in any way the advice of legal counsel. To obtain information about ordering any of their publications, write:

> The United States Trademark Association
> 6 East 45th Street
> New York, NY 10017

Where to Get Help on Patents and Licensing

Have a good idea? Is it patentable? Where can you turn for help? Here is a comprehensive listing of help available.

Inventors' associations.   Arrange meetings with inventors to educate them in aspects of the patenting process and the seeking of licenses:

Institute of American Inventors
635 F Street, NW
Washington, DC 20004
(202) 737-6616

Inventors Assistance
  League, Inc.
1815 W. 6th Street
Los Angeles, CA 90057
(213) 483-4850

Mortic Corp.
2030 E. 4th Street
Suite 149
Santa Ana, CA 92705
(714) 835-4353

The United Inventors and
  Scientists of America
2503 W. 7th Street
Los Angeles, CA 90057
(213) 389-3003

Alexander T. Marinaccio
Inventors Club of America
1562 Main Street
Box 3799
Springfield, MA 01101
(413) 737-0670

Invention brokers. Firms specializing in getting licensor and licensee together:

Battelle Development Corp.
505 King Avenue
Columbus, OH 43201
(614) 424-6424

Control Data Technotec, Inc.
8100 34th Avenue South
Minneapolis, Minn.

Dr. Dvorkovitz and Associates
P.O. Box 1748
Ormond Beach, FL 32044
(904) 677-7033

Eurosearch Marketing, Inc.
663 Fifth Avenue
New York, NY 10022
(212) 355-5633

International Inventors, Inc.
Suite 309
4900 Leeburg Pike
Alexandria, VA 22303
(703) 931-3130

Invention Marketing, Inc.
701 Smithville Street
12th Floor, Arott Building
Pittsburgh, PA 15222
(412) 288-1300

Invention Marketing, Inc.
Suite L-5 The Vendome
160 Commonwealth Avenue
Boston, MA 02116
(617) 266-7696

Kessler Sales Corp.
Kessler Bldg.
1247 Napoleon Street
Fremont, OH 43420
(419) 332-6496

Licensing Management Corp.
80 Park Avenue
New York, NY 10016
(212) 682-5944

Arthur D. Little, Inc.
Invention Management Corp.
Acorn Park
Cambridge, MA 02140
(617) 864-5770

L and M Product Finders
752 Guinda
Palo Alto, CA 94301
(415) 322-7082

Promotional Marketing, Inc.
615 Milwaukee Avenue
Glenview, IL 60025
(312) 729-6100

REFAC Technology
  Development Corp.
122 E. 42nd Street
New York, NY 10017
(212) 687-4741

Research Corporation
405 Lexington Avenue
New York, NY 10016
(212) 695-9301

University Patents, Inc.
2777 Summer Street
Stamford, CT 08905
(203) 325-2285

Publications. Several specialized publications seek to match products offered for license with licensors:

American Bulletin of
  International
  Technology Transfer
International
  Advancement
5455 Wilshire Blvd.
Suite 1009
Los Angeles, CA 90036
(213) 931-7481

International New Product
  Newsletter
Box 191
390 Stuart Street
Boston, MA 02117
(617) 631-3225

New Products and Processes
Newsweek International
444 Madison Avenue
New York, NY 10022
(212) 350-2000

Technology Mart
Thomas Publishing Co.
One Penn Plaza
New York, NY 10001
(212) 695-0500

Technology Transfer Times
Benwill Publishers
167 Corey Road
Brookline, MA 02146
(617) 212-5470

Institute for Inventions
and Innovations, Inc.
85 Irving Street
Box 436
Arlington, MA 02174
(617) 646-0093

One publisher produces two excellent newsletters on patents and inventions that may prove of interest to you:

1. *Invention Management.* An informational and educational journal for individuals and companies concerned with intellectual property. This is published monthly and costs $60.00 annually. It is excellent in the area of patents, technology transfer, and inventions.

2. *Copyright Management.* This is also published monthly. It deals with copyrights, licensing, and trademarks.

If you are interested in either monthly newsletter, write:

Richard A. Onanian
Institute for Invention & Innovation, Inc.
85 Irving Street
Arlington, MA 02174
(617) 646-0093

The Federal Laboratory Consortium (FLC) consists of the 180 federal research and development laboratories. In each there is a person with the title "technical transfer representative," whose job is to respond to questions from businesses. The good news is that there is no charge. A directory is available from:

FLC Headquarters
Federal Laboratory Program Manager
National Science Foundation ISPT
Washington, D.C. 20050
(202) 634-7996

A more expensive source of information exists at seven university-based technical information centers. An industrial application study costs between $5,000 and $10,000, but literature searches are also available. These centers draw on a vast array of business, government, and trade organizations data. The locations are:

New England Research
Applications Center
Mansfield Professional Park
Storrs, CT 06268

North Carolina Science
and Technology
Research Center
P.O. Box 12235
Research Triangle Park,
NC 27709

Knowledge Availability Systems
Center
University of Pittsburgh
Pittsburgh, PA 15260

Aerospace Research
Application Center
Administration Building
1201 E. 38th Street
Indianapolis, IN 47401

Technology Use Studies Center
Southeastern Oklahoma
State University
Durant, OK 74701

Technology Application Center
University of New Mexico,
Albuquerque, NM 87131

Western Research
Application Center
University of Southern California
University Park
Los Angeles, CA 90007

N. RESOURCE ORGANIZATIONS SERVING SMALL BUSINESS

National Federation of
Independent Business
490 L'Enfant Plaza East, S.W.
Washington, D.C. 20006

National Small Business
Association
1604 K Strret, N.W.
Washington, D.C. 20006

Center for Small Business
Chamber of Commerce of U.S.
1615 H Street, N.W.
Washington, D.C. 20062

Cosiba Members

Council of Smaller Enterprises
Mike Benz
690 Union Commerce Bldg.
Cleveland, OH 44115
(216) 621-3300

Independent Business Association
of Wisconsin
Jack Gardner
7635 Bluemound Rd.
Milwaukee, WI 53213
(414) 258-7055

National Association of Small
Business Investment Companies
Walter Stults
618 Washington Bldg.
Washington, D.C. 20005
(202) 638-3411

National Business League
Sylvester Bass
4324 Georgia Avenue, N.W.
Washington, D.C. 20011
(202) 726-7600

National Federation of
Independent Businesses
James D. "Mike" McKevitt
490 L'Enfant Plaza East, S.W.
Washington, D.C. 20006

National Small Business
Association
John Lewis
1604 K Street, N.W.
Washington, D.C. 20006

Small Business Council
Sandy Chadwick
One MONY Plaza, Suite 1500
Syracuse, NY 13202

Smaller Business Association
of New England
Lewis Shattuck
69 Hickory Drive
Waltham, MA 02154
(617) 890-9070

Smaller Manufacturers Council
Leo McDonough
339 Boulevard of Allies
Pittsburgh, PA 15222
(412) 391-1622

Small Business Legislative Council
Herbert Liebonson
1604 K Street, N.W.
Washington, D.C. 20006
(202) 296-7400

Select Staff, SBA Office of Advocacy

Office of Advocacy
Small Business Administration
1441 L Street, N.W.
Room 1010
Washington, D.C. 20416

David K. Voight
Executive Assistant
(202) 653-6984

Thomas A. Gray
Administrative Officer
(202) 653-6808

Jere Glover, Director
Office of Interagency Policy
(202) 653-6213

David Metzger, Director
Office of Small Business Service
Management
(202) 653-6579

Fred A. Tarpley, Director
Office of Economic Research
(202) 634-5886

Sally Bender, Director
Office of Women in Business
(202) 634-6087

Robert E. Berney
Chief Economist
(202) 634-4886

Chief Counsel for Advocacy
(202) 653-6984

Christopher Burke
Advocate for Energy & Natural
Resources
(202) 653-6986

Victor M. Rivera
Advocate for Government
Industry Relations
(202) 653-6840

John S. Satagaj
Assistant Chief Counsel for State
& Local Affairs
(202) 653-6808

Susan M. Walthall
Field Activities Coordinator
(202) 653-6808

Janice Somers
Trade Association Coordinator
(202) 653-6808

Staff of the House Small Business Committee

A reference list of people and committees in government who play major roles in the everyday operation of a smaller enterprise follows.

Thomas G. Powers
General Counsel
2361 Rayburn House Office Bldg.
(202) 225-5821

Raymond S. Wittig
Minority Counsel
B-343 Rayburn House Office Bldg.
(202) 225-4038

Carol Clawson
Communications Specialist
2361 Rayburn House Office Bldg.
(202) 225-6020

Subcommittee on SBA
and SBIC Authority
and General Small
Business Problems

Thomas G. Powers,
General Counsel (see above)

Jordan Clark
Minority Subcommittee Counsel
2361 Rayburn House Office Bldg.
(202) 225-4038

Subcommittee on General
Oversight and Minority
Enterprise

George Neidich
Subcommittee Counsel
2361 Rayburn House Office Bldg.
(202) 225-4601

Subcommittee on Antitrust and
Restraint of Trade Activities
Affecting Small Business

Mark Rosenberg
Subcommittee Professional Staff
Member
B-363 Rayburn House Office Bldg.
(202) 225-8944

Karen Davis Hoppe
Minority Subcommittee
Professional Staff Member
B-363 Rayburn House Office Bldg.
(202) 225-4541

Subcommittee on Energy,
Environment, Safety and
Research

Mark Rosen
Subcommittee Counsel
B-363 Rayburn House Office Bldg.
(202) 225-6026

Gregory S. Dole
Minority Subcommittee Counsel
B-363 Rayburn House Office Bldg.
(202) 225-4541

Subcommittee on Access
to Equity Capital and
Business Opportunities

David E. Franasiak
Subcommittee Counsel
B-363 Rayburn Building
(202) 225-7797

Harold L. Aronson
Minority Subcommittee Counsel
B-363 Rayburn House Office Bldg.
(202) 335-4541

Subcommittee on Special Small
Business Problems

Stephen P. Lynch
Subcommittee Professional Staff
Member
B-363 Rayburn House Office Bldg.
(202) 225-9368

Washington Information Sources

The Division of Information Services, Bureau of Labor Statistics has data ava.
able on employment, living conditions, prices, productivity, and occupational
safety and health.

441 G Street, N.W.
Washington, D.C. 20212
(202) 523-1239

The Bill Status Office will provide you with current status of any legislation or tell you if legislation has been introduced on a topic.

3669 HOBA #2
The LEGIS Office
Washington, D.C. 20515
(202) 225-1772

The National Referral Center will find an organization willing to provide free information on any topic, for free.

Library of Congress
10 First Street, S.E.
Washington, D.C. 20540
(202) 426-5670

The Federal Information Center will locate an expert in the federal government to tell you how the federal government can help you.

General Services Administration
7th and D. Streets, S.W.
Washington, D.C. 20407
(202) 755-8660

Reference Section, Science and Technology Division offers both free and fee reference on bibliographic services.

Library of Congress
10 First Street, S.E.
Washington, DC 20540
(202) 426-5639

Data Users Services Division will identify census data on your topic.

Bureau of the Census
U.S. Department of Commerce
Washington, DC 20233
(301) 763-7662

Economics, Statistics, and Cooperative Service can provide the latest production and stock estimates for agricultural products as well as the supply-demand-price relationships and other economic factors.

U.S. Deperment of Agriculture
Information Staff
Washington, DC 20250
(202) 447-4230

Bureau of Domestic Business Development 100 industry analysts can provide or
guide you to information on a company or industry.

U.S. Department of Commerce
Washington, DC 20230
(202) 377-2786

Information Central will identify an association that can help with your problem, if you cannot find help in Gale's "Encyclopedia of Associations."

American Society of Association Executives
1101 16th Street, N.W.
Washington, DC 20036
(202) 659-3333

Energy information sources are:

National Energy
    Information Center
Energy Information
    Administration
1726 M Street, N.W.
Washington, DC 20461
(202) 566-9820

National Solar Heating
    and Cooling
    Information Center
P.O. Box 1607
Rockville, MD 20850
(800) 523-2929

Technical Information Center
U.S. Department of Energy
Oak Ridge, TN 37830
(615) 483-8611, ext. 34271

U.S. Civil Service Commission, Bureau of Manpower Information Systems has
this material available: Civil Service employment, payroll information, and payroll information, and paydays (particularly useful in scheduling campaigns for
consumer goods in Washington).

Manpower Statistics Division
1900 E Street, N.W.
Washington, DC 20415
(202) 655-4000

U.S. Department of Commerce Census Bureau has this material available: General Census statistics, Census of Business, educational demographics, statistics on construction and other businesses in Washington area

> Social and Economic Statistics
>   Administration
> Washington, DC 20233
> (202) 655-4000

U.S. Department of Labor has this material available: Cost of Living Index, monthly reports on employment by state and metro area, and general labor statistics.

> Bureau of Labor Statistics
> 441 G Street, N.W.
> Washington, DC 20210
> (202) 393-2420

District of Columbia Government has this material available: General employment information and occupational make-up of the District of Columbia.

> Department of Manpower
> Community Relations and Information Division
> 500 C Street, N.W.
> Washington, DC 20011
> (202) 393-6151

Metropolitan Washington Council of Governments has this material available: General statistical data and planned development information for the metropolitan Washington area.

> Information Services
> 1225 Connecticut Avenue, N.W.
> Washington, DC 20036
> (202) 223-6800

Washington Center for Metropolitan Studies has this material available: Population demographics and updated 1970 Census information.

> 1717 Massachusetts Avenue, N.W.
> Washington, DC 20036
> (202) 462-4868

Useful Government Data

Materials that can be very beneficial to you are published by all the Nader groups. A wide variety of reports and publications is available. To obtain copies of the following free citizen action materials, send a self-addressed, stamped envelope to P.O. Box 19404, Washington, DC, 20036 (unless another address is indicated).

1. Public Citizen, Reports and Publications. A complete list of all reports and publications by Ralph Nader and other well-known consumer advocates.

2. Public Citizen Action Projects. A list of many citizen action projects that can be undertaken by any interested group.

3. Public Citizen Health Research Group's list of reports and publications includes information in the areas of food and drugs, occupational safety and health, pesticides, product safety, health care delivery, and how to get a copy of your health records.

4. Toll-free hotline numbers. A complete guide to all federal agencies designed to help and inform consumers.

5. Airline Passenger Rights. Information on your rights as an airline passenger, including how to deal with an airline-related problem. Write to ACAP (Aviation Consumer Action Project), P. O. Box 19029, Washington, D.C. 20036.

6. Freedom of Information. Pamphlet on the Freedom of Information Act and how to use it. Send SASE (self-addressed stamped envelope) to Freedom of Information Clearinghouse, P.O. Box 19367, Washington, D.C. 20036. Pension Rights. Information on the rights of employees, retirees, and spouses under the new private pension reform law. Send SASE to the Pension Rights Center, 1346 Connecticut Avenue, N.W., Room 1019, Washington, D.C., 20036.

7. Human Rights and the Elderly. Information on programs involved with agism and other special projects. Send a first-class stamp to the Grey Panthers, 3700 Chestnut Street, Philadelphia, PA, 19104.

8. *People and Taxes.* Monthly newspaper of the Public Citizen's Tax Reform Group. Include a first-class stamp.

9. *Critical Mass.* Newspaper covering nuclear power information and activity. Write to *Critical Mass*, P.O. Box 1538, Washington, D.C., 20013. Please include a first-class stamp.

10. People and Energy, CPSI Quarterly, The Nutrition Newsletter, and publications list. Newsletter from the Center for Science in the Public Interest. Send SASE to Center for Science in the Public Interest, 1757 S. Street, N.W., Washington, D.C., 20009.

In addition to the aforementioned publications, the following are some other helpful publications:

A monthly newsletter, *Cose Update,* is offered by:

Council of Smaller
  Enterprise of the
  Greater Cleveland
  Growth Association
690 Union Commerce Building
Cleveland, OH 44115
(216) 621-3300

The Family Business Forum is the newsletter of the National Family Business Council. As the "voice of family business," this publication discusses important issues that affect the small business owner/managers. It also keeps its membership informed of the happenings within the organization on a local and national level. Write:

National Family Business Council
3916 Detroit Boulevard
W. Bloomfield, MI 48033

National Memo is a monthly newsletter that provides timely information on economic and business issues and events. *The Corporate Guide to Minority Vendors* is a resource manual for use by corporate executives and minority entrepreneurs to strengthen the communications network between the two sectors. The NBL also maintains a file of minority vendors and a comprehensive list of corporate procurement and purchasing agents for constitutents. Write:

National Business League
4324 Georgia Avenue, N.W.
Washington, D.C. 20011
(202) 829-5900

The Voice of Small Business is a monthly newsletter for small business owners/ managers in all industries, trades, or professions. It deals generally with news of interest to small business relating to legislative and governmental activities in Washington. It is the membership newsletter of the National Small Business Association, a nonprofit and nonpartisan organization dedicated to the preservation and expansion of the small business sector of the economy. Write:

National Small Business Association
1225 19th Street, N.W.
Washington, D.C. 20036

For the newsletter, *Voice of Small Business,* write:

Voice of Small Business
1605 K Street, N.W.
Washington, D.C. 20006
(202) 296-7400

The newsletter of the Chamber of Commerce of the United States is called *Washington Report*. Most of its subscribers are business people, and the majority of its articles are geared to information about federal policies and programs that can affect their firms and the economy. Write:

> Washington Report
> Chamber of Commerce of the United States
> 1615 H Street, N.W.
> Washington, D.C. 20062

Your local chamber of commerce can also be a source of valuable assistance, including information about plant or storage locations and financing. It is most quickly located via the local telephone directory.

O. SMALL BUSINESS AIDS

Improvement to SBA Guaranteed Loans

The Bank Certification Program hands the financial decision-making for Small Business Administration Guaranteed Loans over to professional lenders. Processing time for these loans will be cut to 2 to 4 weeks when the loan is obtained from a certified lending institution. The SBA has authorized some large nationwide financial service organizations to provide and prepare guaranteed loans, in addition to many banks. Credit Financial Corporation, a subsidiary of Control Data Corporation, was incorporated for the sole purpose of lending under the SBA Guaranteed Loan Program. Their loans are being made via 13 Control Data Business Centers and 30 Satellite Centers.

The following list provides information on the 13 Control Data Business Centers, they will supply you with information with regard to their Satellite centers too.

COMMERCIAL CREDIT SERVICES CORP.
BUSINESS CENTERS*

Location	Contact Person	Telephone Number

ATLANTA, GA
  Business Center
  180 Interstate North
  Suite 115
  Atlanta, GA 30339
	G.M. Turner	404/952-7284

BALTIMORE, MD
  Business Center
  22 W. Padonia Road
  Timonium, MD 21093
	R.W. Hoover	301/561-1800

COMMERCIAL CREDIT SERVICES CORP.
BUSINESS CENTERS* (continued)

Location	Contact Person	Telephone Number
CHARLOTTE, NC Business Center Arnold Palmer Center P.O. Box 34189 3726 Latrobe Drive Charlotte, NC 28234	T.H. Hardy	704/365-1420
CHICAGO, IL Business Center 2001 Midwest Road Suite 105 Oak Brook, IL 60521	N.J. Mika	312/629-7991
CLEVELAND, OH Business Center Western Reserve Bldg. 1468 W. 9th St., Suite 100 Cleveland, OH 44113	J.A. Dahl	216/523-1570
DALLAS, TX Business Center Control Data Bldg. 14801 Quorum Drive, Suite 101 Dallas, TX 75240	H.L. Luper	214/385-5577
DENVER, CO Business Center 8000 E. Prentice Avenue Building D Englewood, CO 80111	T.E. Atwell	303/771-0805
LOS ANGELES, CA Business Center 18831 Von Karman Avenue Suite 300 Irvine, CA 92715	W.R. Franks	714/851-5620
LOUISVILLE, KY Business Center Triad East, Suite 150 10200 Linn Station Road Louisville, KY 40223	D.D. Witten	502/423-1660
MINNEAPOLIS, MINN Business Center 5241 Viking Drive Bloomington, MN 55435	D.W. Hackett	612/893-4200
SAN FRANCISCO, CA Business Center One Bay Plaza, Suite 330 1350 Old Bayshore Highway Burlingame, CA 94010	G.L. Cervantez	415/342-7622

COMMERCIAL CREDIT SERVICES CORP.
BUSINESS CENTERS* (continued)

Location	Contact Person	Telephone Number
KANSAS CITY, KA Business Center Executive Hills Office Park 11011 Antioch Shawnee Mission, KS 66210	D.E. Wille	913/648-1422
TAMPA, FL Business Center Suite 285 4511 N. Himes Avenue Tampa, FL 33614	W.T. Crawford	813/877-5523

*Information about Control Data Business Centers is also available from Commercial Credit Services Corporation, 300 St. Paul Place, Baltimore, MD 21202 (301) 332-3000.

Sources: Other SBA Non-Bank Lenders

1. Money Store Investment Corporation, Springfield, NJ (201) 467-9000. Offers SBA Guaranteed Loans in branch locations in 12 states.

2. Merrill Lynch Small Business Lending Company, New York City, (212) 637-7455. Loan program will function nation-wide later this year.

3. Allied Lending Corporation, Washington, D.C. (202) 331-1112. SBA Guaranteed Loans for the Washington area.

4. NIS Capital Funding Corporation, White Plains, N.Y., (914) 428-8600. Provides SBA Guaranteed Loans locally.

5. Independence Mortgage Company, Inc., Odessa, Texas (915) 333-5814. SBA Guaranteed Loans for the Odessa area.

6. The First Commercial Credit Corporation, Los Angeles, California (213) 937-0860. Provides SBA loans in Los Angeles.

7. ITT Small Business Finance Corporation, Minneapolis, Minnesota (612) 540-8509. Waiting for authorization to offer SBA Loans on a national basis. (this is a subsidiary of International Telephone & Telegraph Finance Corporation.)

Q. SOURCES OF CAPITAL

How to raise capital for a growing enterprise is a fundamental question. The very nature of the venture capital industry has changed dramatically with the advent

P. SMALL BUSINESS PUBLICATIONS

Annual Subscription Price	Frequency	Magazine	Advertising Accepted	Hero
$48.00	Monthly	*The Business Owner* 50 Jericho Tpke. Jericho, NY 11753	No	Thomas J. Martin

The Business Owner is getting better editorially since the recent repurchase of the magazine by Tom Martin from the Transamerican Media Corporation, in Riverton, CT. Martin is now investing more editorial time to produce quality work, and doing a good job on his monthly magazine.

$15.00	Monthly	*Venture Magazine* 35 W. 45th Street New York, NY 10037	Yes	Joe Giarraputo

Venture Magazine is geared toward the individual who is starting his or her own business, and it best serves the $0 to $1 million business. Editorially it is excellent.

$18.00	Monthly	*Inc. Magazine* 38 Commercial Wharf Boston, MA 02110	Yes	Bernard Goldhirsh

The focus of *Inc. Magazine* is directed to the market of managers of small businesses in the range of $1 million to $25 million. In my opinion it is a serious competitor to *Business Week*.

Price	Frequency	Publication		Editor
$36.00	Monthly	*Entrepreneur* 631 Wilshire Blvd. Santa Monica, CA 90401	Yes	Chase Revel

Entrepreneur is an opportunity magazine focusing on retailing and the retail trades. To receive it, you must be a member of the International Entrepreneurial Association (IEA).

$48.00	Monthly	*Small Business Report* 550 Hartnell St. Monterey, CA 93940	No	Gene E. Mattauch

Small Business Report is a pleasant, helpful, and non-controversial magazine with an orientation to the people side of business.

$42.00	Monthly	*The Professional Report* 118 Brook St. Scarsdale, NY 10503	No	John L. Springer

The *Professional Report* is basically a tax and management newsletter of well-established quality. It has been around much longer than any of the newsletters, and it is an excellent value.

$14.00	Bimonthly	*In Business* 18 So. 7th Street Emmaus, PA 18049	Yes	Jerome Goldstein

Annual Subscription Price	Frequency	Magazine	Advertising Accepted	Hero

In Business is a new magazine with a combination of nature and small business, somewhat of an entrepreneur's "mother earth catalog."

$28.00	Bimonthly	*Journal of Applied Management* 1200 Mt. Diablo Blvd. Walnut Creek, CA 94596	Yes	John Stickler

Journal of Applied Management was originally founded by Bob Roth and is now owned by John Stickler. It is making a transition from being geared toward consultants to being geared toward the entrepreneur.

$48.00	Bimonthly	*New Venture Newsletter* George Spencer Observer Publishing Co. Canal Square Washington, D.C. 20007	No	George Spencer

New Venture Newsletter is geared toward successful business people who want to branch out into a wider range of business endeavors. It gives names and addresses to contact for information on promising ventures.

of Small Business Investment Companies (SBICs) launched by the Small Business Administration (SBA).

Locating sources of available venture capital can be both time consuming and frustrating if you don't know where to go or whom to contact. We have compiled the following comprehensive list of venture capital sources to aid you in your search.

Small Business Administration (SBA)

SBA. The United States Small Buinsess Administration is an independent, federal agency that was created by Congress in 1953 to assist, counsel, and champion American small businesses. The agency provides prospective, new, and established members of the small business community with financial assistance, management training and counseling, and help in getting a fair share of government contracts through over 100 offices throughout the nation.

SBIC. Small Business Investment Corporations are licensed, regulated, and in certain cases, financed by the SBA. They supply venture capital and long-term financing to small businesses for expansion, modernization, and sound financing for their organizations.

MESBIC. Minority Enterprise Small Business Investment Corporations have been incorporated into SBICs. They exist only to assist small business concerns owned and managed by socially or economically disadvantaged persons.

For more infomation about the services that the SBA provides, consult the Yellow Pages for the office nearest you or write:

SBA
1441 L Street, N.W.
Washington, D.C. 20005

SBIC Division
SBA
1441 L Street, N.W.
Washington, D.C. 20005

A Small Business Investment Company (SBIC) is a licensee of the federal government charged with making investments in small entrepreneurial ventures. A MESBIC is an SBIC that does the same thing for businesses with strong minority group interests. The way it works is simple. A pool of money is established (currently a minimum of $500,000 for an SBIC, $300,000 for a MESBIC), and then the manager of the pool of money applies to the SBIC division of the Small Business Administration (SBA) for an SBIC license. Once the pool of money qualifies for an SBIC license, you can accomplish the following:

1. A loan of between 3:1 and 4:1 times the amount in the pool of equity funds, you can leverage the equity by 3 or 4 times with an SBA loan.

2. The loan will be subordinated to bank debt. Consequently, with the total capital you should be able to borrow several million dollars on a short term basis from the banks.

3. The loan will be unsecured and all investors will have limited liabilities.

4. The loan will be a balloon payment loan with interest only payable.

5. The interest rate is currently three points under prime rate.

These features are a few of the incentives to reach the minimum targets of paid investment capital. There are some disadvantages to an SBIC and it is not a panacea, but the advantages often outweigh the disadvantages. One disadvantage is that any investment is limited to 20 percent of the paid-in capital ($500,000). Hence you could invest only up to $100,000 on any single deal. A second disadvantage is the paperwork that the SBA creates to prevent fraud in distribution of their funds.

Approximately 60 percent of the SBIC financing by number (and a little higher by dollars) are first or initial financings. This has been a fairly constant pattern for SBICs over the years. About half of the SBIC dollar financing is in the form of straight debt versus straight equity. The average interest on the debt in 1979 was just under 13 percent annually. The SBICs have an interest ceiling of 15 percent and rather than charge excessive interest, they are motivated to opt for equity in the form of warrants along with a debt financing.

The United States Small Business Administration (SBA) publishes on a quarterly basis a complete listing of SBICs as well as minority enterprise small business investment companies (MESBICs), listing name, address, and size category. Write:

SBA Investment Divisions
1441 L Street, N.W.
Washington, D.C. 20416

American Association of MESBICs
1413 K Street, N.W., 13th Floor
Washington, D.C. 20005
(202) 347-8600

The AAMESBIC newsletter is sent monthly to about 1,000 subscribers.

Banks

Foreign-owned banks. The rapid expansion of foreign-owned banks in the United States is due primarily to the devaluation of the United States dollar and their ability to avoid United States banking regulations. They are allowed to open branches outside of their countries (United States banks are not), and they are not required to tie up funds in the Federal Reserve system. These foreign-owned banks fall under state banking regulations. The banks are most often found in metropolitan areas. Suggested banks to contact are Britain's Barclay Bank, the Bank of Montreal, or the Japanese, Swiss, or French banks. We suggest you consult your local Yellow Pages for the foreign-owned bank nearest you.

Two-tier lending. A major change in commercial bank lending was triggered by the heroes of small business at the Mellon National Bank in Pittsburgh, PA. They began offering small businesses a borrowing rate below the prime rate. They did this in times of money shortages (now) to help entrepreneurs, and they deserve pioneering recognition! For an up-to-date list of banks that offer a two-tier lending rate that is revised monthly write:

Chief Counsel for Advocacy
SBA
1441 L Street, N.W.
Washington, D.C. 20005

Actually, Herbert A. Biern, chief counsel's assistant, compiles these lists; his telephone number is (202) 653-6998. The list dated January 22, 1979 had 33 banks that offered special deals to small companies.

T.H.E. Insurance Company. The role of T.H.E. Insurance Company is to write an insurance policy to protect a lender against bankruptcy. They essentially appraise the collateral asset and insure to repossess it from a lender at the assessed rates. The value of T.H.E. policy allows more capital to be secured from existing lenders. It often happens that an asset or inventory can be borrowed against although it was given zero valuation by a bank because of T.H.E. insurance.

Lending institutions prefer to loan money against collateral because they maintain the option of liquidating the collateral to repay the loan. The table below is the rule of thumb for what can be loaned against different forms of collateral from the balance sheet of an entrepreneurial venture.

	Percentage to be Loaned Against
Accounts Receivable	75% - 80% under 90 days
Inventory	10% − 20%
Fixed Assets	70% − 80% market values

In practice, the actual ratios are even more pronounced. In other words, banks prefer not to lend against inventory as contrasted to lending against receivables.

In turn, easily liquidated, fixed assets are the most attractive type of collateral (automobiles), and they usually command both a high percentage of their lendable market value as well as a subsequently lower interest rate.

A lender is basically unsure of an inventory's value until it is converted to cash by being sold. That's the underlying reason that lenders shy away from accepting inventory of certain types of fixed assets as collateral for a loan. Thus, the role of T.H.E. Insurance Company is to write an insurance policy to protect a lender against bankruptcy. They essentially appraise the collateral asset and insure to repossess it from a lender at the assessed rates. Rather than paying off the insurance policy on a death, the policy is paid upon default in the loan. Here's how it works:

1. T.H.E. appraises the assets to be pledged, including both inventory and fixed assets.

2. T.H.E. will then issue an insurance policy for the amount of their appraisal.

3. The company hands this policy over to the lender and then borrows 100 percent of the value of the policy in a loan.

4. If the company defaults, T.H.E. takes title to the collateral and sells it. The lender is paid in full using T.H.E.'s credit and capital to be reimbursed. What does all this insurance protection cost?

1. Appraisal fee: minimum amount: $1,000. This is for the appraisal and it is 1 percent of the appraised value of the collateral plus out-of-pocket (travel) expenses.

2. A 2 percent add-on interest rate on the outstanding loan balance, not on the full appraisal of the collateral. The premium interest rate of 2 percent is charged only on what's borrowed or what is at risk.

The value of T.H.E. policy allows more capital to be secured from existing lenders. On the one hand, a lender will typically allow only 10 percent of inventory value to be used as loan collateral, with a policy the inventory allowed as collateral might be above 50 percent of its value, depending upon T.H.E.'s assessment. This often allows a two or three times greater amount to be loaned against an asset.

An asset or inventory can often be borrowed against when it was given zero valuation by a bank because of the T.H.E. formula. On a theoretical basis, the lending interest rate can be reduced if you can convince the lender of the merits and security of the guarantee. In effect, given the policy, the lender should advance funds on T.H.E.'s credit, not the credit of your entrepreneurial venture.

In practice, you are seldom ever able to negotiate the bank interest rate lower by securing a T.H.E. guarantee and, in total, you are paying 5 to 6 percent above prime rate for this type of lending. If your entrepreneurial venture can service debt, write:

Mr. Ed Shifman, V.P.
T.H.E. Insurance Company
52 Church Street
Boston, MA 02116
(617) 357-5220

Farmers Home Loan

The SBA is supposedly the government agency charged with helping the entrepreneur, but in practice other federal agencies also provide a great deal of help. The FmHa is the loan program of the Farmers Home Administration which offers guaranteed loans to growing businesses. Unlike the SBA's program with a $500,000 ceiling, the FmHa loan program has no ceiling. In fact, loans have ranged from $7,000 to $33 million with an average of about $900,000.

The FmHa loan gives preference to distressed areas and rural communities of less than 25,000 inhabitants. It will loan money for any worthwhile business purpose. The minimum equity requirement is 10 percent and, if your venture can be shown to be job-creating, your loan has a greater chance of approval. Unlike the SBA, you do not have to prove to be an unbankable company to secure a FmHa loan. The loans are for fairly long terms, 30 years for construction, 15 years for equipment, and 7 years for working capital. The interest rate is about the same as can be negotiated with a bank, but the FmHa has a one-time fee that is calculated by multiplying 1 percent of the principal loan amount by the percentage of the guarantee. Even given the one-time fee, the good standing of the U.S. government stands behind the guaranteed portions of the loan, and the interest rate eventually negoitated often effects these favorable considerations.

Why not write the FmHa in care of the (USDA) United States Dept. of Agriculture, Washington, DC 20250, or you could look in your nearest largest city Yellow Pages for one of the 1800 county offices. Look under US Government—Agriculture.

EDA Funds

If your company needs funds to expand or strengthen an existing business, you may be eligible for federal funds without knowing it. The federal government has designated two-thirds of all counties in the U.S. as "economically depressed." If you're located in one of these areas, you may apply for a loan under the special program of the Economic Development Administration. To qualify for such a loan, a company must show that it has been unable to borrow under similar terms and conditions from other sources. There is no limit on the amount that may be requested. Most of the loans are under $1 million, or $10,000 per job created or saved.

On direct loans for fixed assets, or where there is mortgagable collateral, the interest rate is currently under 10 percent. EDA would provide up to 65 percent of the total funds, but the applicant has to put at least 15 percent of his own and get 5 percent from his state or a nongovernmental community organization, such as Community Development Corporation. The repayment time is usually the useful life of the fixed assets. The interest rate on a direct loan for working capital or for less mortgagable assets is usually on a ¼ percent higher than fixed assets.

A list of economically depressed areas, the loan application form, and other details of the loan program can be obtained from any of EDA's six regional offices. For the address of the office nearest you, write or call:

Office of Business Development
Economic Development Administration
Room 7876
14th & Constitution Avenue, N.W.
Washington, D.C., 20230
(202) 377-2000

Business Development Corporation

The purpose of Business Development Corporations is to attract and retain business in their respective states, and thus increase employment. Although they sound like government agencies, they are not. BDCs operate within a state. Business development corporations are specifically designed to provide long-term capital to small businesses. With capital tough to get today, it is a good idea to become familiar with your state BDC. For further information contact your local chamber of commerce or write to:

Industrial Development
  Corporation of Florida
801 North Magnolia Avenue
Suite 218
Orlando, FL 32803

First Arkansas Development
  Finance Corporation
910 Pyramid Life Building
Little Rock, AR 72201
(501) 374-9247

Alaska State Development
  Corporation
Pouch D
Juneau, AK 99811

Statewide California
  Business & Indus. Dev. Corp.
717 Lido Park Drive
Newport Beach, CA 92663
(714) 675-8030

Connecticut Development Credit
Corporation
99 Colony Street
P.O. Box 714
Meriden, CT 06450
(203) 235-3327

Business Development Corporation
of Georgia, Inc.
822 Healey Building
Atlanta, GA 30303
(404) 577-5715

Iowa Business Development
Credit Corp.
247 Jewett Building
Des Moines, IA 50309
(515) 282-9546

Kansas Development Credit Corp.
First Natinal Bank Tower
Suite 620
One Townsite Plaza
Topeka, KS 66603
(913) 235-3437

Business Development Corp.
of Kentucky
1940 Commonwealth Bldg.
Louisville, KY 40202
(502) 584-3519

Development Credit Corp. of Maine
P.O. Box 262
Manchester, ME 04351
(207) 724-3507

Development Credit Corporation
of Maryland
1301 First National Bank Bldg.
Baltimore, MD 21202
(301) 685-6454

Massachusetts Business
Development Corp.
One Boston Place
Suite 3607
Boston, MA 02108
(617) 723-7515

First Missouri
Development Finance Corp.
302 Adams Street
P.O. Box 252
Jefferson City, MO 65101
(314) 635-0138

Development Credit
Corp. of Montana
P.O. Box 916
Helena, MT 59601
(406) 442-3850

Business Development Corporation
of Nebraska
Suite 1044, Stuart Bldg.
Lincoln, NE 68508
(402) 474-3855

New Hampshire Business
Development Corp.
10 Fort Eddy Road
Concord, NH 03301
(603) 224-1432

New York Business
Development Corp.
41 State Street
Albany, NY 12207
(518) 463-2268

Business Development Corp.
of N. Carolina
505 Oberlin Rd.
P.O. Box 10665
Raleigh, NC 27605
(919) 828-2331

North Dakota State Dev.
Credit Corp.
Box 1212
Bismark, ND 58501
(701) 223-2288

Oklahoma Business
Development Corp.
1018 United Founders Life Tower
Oklahoma City, OK 73112
(405) 840-1674

RIDC Industrial
Development Fund
Union Trust Building
Pittsburgh, PA 15219
(717) 234-3241

Southeastern Pennsylvania
Development Fund
3 Penn Center Plaza
Philadelphia, PA 19102
(215) 568-4677

Business Development Co.
of Rhode Island
40 Westminster Street
Providence, RI 02903
(401) 751-1000

Business Development Corp.
of S. Carolina
Palmetto State Life Bldg.
P.O. Box 11606
Columbia, SC 29211
(803) 252-3759

Virginia Industrial
Development Corp.
201 Mutual Building
P.O. Box 474
Richmond, VA 23204

Business Development Corp.
of Eastern Washington
417 Hyde Building
Spokane, WA 99201
(509) 838-2731

R. SOURCES OF HELP

1. "Basic Information on Treasury Bills", write for free booklet to Federal Reserve Bank of New York, 33 Liberty Street, New York, NY 10045.

2. Bargains on New Issue Stocks: underwriters offer package deals to give investors a bargain. Write or call: Richard Whitman, Vice President, John Muir & Company, 61 Broadway, NY, NY 10006 1-(800) 221-5814, (212) 747-8300, or ask your own investment broker for more information.

3. Small Business Bosses: Small Business executives usually determine their own salaries. These salaries are often considered too high by the IRS and bankers when loans are sought. The first series of annual national surveys of compensation for executives among manufacturing, technology and service companies whose annual sales are from $250,000 to $20,000,000 is available. This report includes information on salaries, bonuses, company cars, benefits etc. The Small Company Officer Compensation Report" costs $250 postage paid and is available through: Growth Resources, Inc. One Newbury Street, Peabody, Mass. 01960. It is a good companion to the CEM Survey Remuneration, Perquisites, Incentives & Compensation for Entrepreneurial Ventures—$100—CEM 311 Main St. Worcester, MA 01608.

4. The Planning Book: 100 pages of comprehensive information covering such subjects as: estate planning for a family business, timing deductions, tax shelters, real estate syndications, retirement planning and much more. For your free copy, write: "Personal Tax and Financial Planning—1980", Delotte, Haskins & Sells, 144 Avenue of the Americas, NY, NY 10036 or the local branch in your community.

Facts and Figures

A loss deduction is available to shareholders for costs incurred in preparation for a public offering of corporate stock where unfavorable market conditions or other reasons, cause the offering to be abandoned. (Rev. Rul. 79-2, CB 1979-1, 98)

Have You Considered Incorporating?

From a legal standpoint, incorporation is a tax advantage for smaller businesses. For businesses with an income exceeding $100,000 going the corporate route provides attractive tax incentives, after allowing for a reasonable salary. There are four points in summarizing the important tax breaks.

1. Income left in the corporation is taxable on each $25,000 level beginning at 17 percent increasing to 46 percent. See table below.

CORPORATE INCOME TAX RATE

The corporate income tax rate structure is as follows:

Taxable Income	Rates effective January 1, 1979
$0 – $25,000	17%
$25,000 – $50,000	20%
$50,000 – $75,000	30%
$75,000 –$100,000	40%
Over –$100,000	46%

The alternative tax rate on corporate capital gains has been reduced from 30 percent to 28 percent. However, a portion of capital gains may continue to be a tax preference item for purposes of the minimum tax.

This means a corporation with taxable income of:

$50,000 pays $9,250 in taxes for an effective rate of 18½%
$75,000 pays $16,750 in taxes for an effective rate of 22-1/3%
$100,000 pays $26,750 in taxes for an effective rate of 26¾%

Hence, only about one-quarter of profits up to $100,000 are taxed and retained earnings can now be the preferred method of financing growth.

2. The Keogh plan contribution for an individual owner or partner is limited to $7,500 with the exception of large partnership. The limit is much higher for a corporate employee. The allowable contribution can be several times the Keogh limit. All money put in the Keogh plan or corporate pension plan is tax sheltered until paid out and the unpaid balance at death can avoid estate taxes.

1244 Stock

3. If a small company fails, the entrepreneur can still offer his stockholders one benefit-provided that his lawyer was on the ball in the beginning and used Section 1244 of the Internal Revenue Code. This section, established to encourage investments in small business, gives stockholders the right to write off against ordinary income up to $100,000 on a joint return ($50,000 on a single return) of any loss due to the failure of such a company during any tax year. Prior to the tax act of 1978, these numbers were $25,000 on a single return and $50,000 for a joint return. If the loss is sustained by a partnership, the $50,000 (or $100,000) limit is determined separately for each partner.

The ordinary loss deduction is treated as a business loss—it can be carried back three years and forward seven years. Any loss over the $50,000 (or $100,000) limit comes under the less favorable rules for capital losses. An individual can only write off up to $3,000 annually as a capital loss against ordinary income.

4. Nondiscriminatory medical reimbursement plans for corporate employees can permit the owner employee to receive medical reimbursement tax free from his corporation. This eliminates the 3 percent "waste" which would occur if the individual had to pay his own medical expenses.

Check with your accountant or contracted tax counselor for more complete information concerning the advantages of a business incorporating.

Installment Tax Rule

In selling a business, real estate, securities or collectable items, it will now be easier to comply with the capital gains tax. Under previous ruling, the total gain on an installment sale becomes taxable immediately when the down payment was equal to 30 percent or more of the entire sale price. Retroactive to January, 1980, the new installment sale ruling allows the seller to collect any part of the sale price as a down payment and still take advantage of the installment formula. With the new installment tax rule, it is possible to sell the physical assets to a buyer who may not wish to buy the business intact.

To illustrate this concept, property sold for $100,000, that was purchased at $20,000, leaves 80 percent or $80,000 of the sale price as taxable gain, while 20 percent is returned of your initial capital investment. If you collected $40,000 down payment, the old rule taxes the entire $80,000 gain immediately. Now, only 80 percent of the down payment (in this case $32,000) is immediately taxable. Each subsequent payment thereafter has capital gains tax on 80 percent of the total amount.

For more details on capital gains tax, check with your personal accountant and or investment adviser. This can alter the method of buying or selling assets.

Lost in the Mail

At one time or another, everyone seems to experience something missing or lost in the mail. Before panic takes over, call the U.S. Postal Service for help in locating your mail. The Postal Service's Transportation Management Office is responsible for monitoring mail as it moves across the country. If you have a problem, try contacting the regional office. Your local post office can direct you to the correct regional office for help in locating missing mail. Listed below are some helpful numbers to aid the process.

Northeast Region:
  Boston, (617) 223-1160
  New York City, (212) 660-5630
Western Region:
  Denver, (303) 327-4471
  Los Angeles, (213) 793-9610
  Salt Lake City, (801) 588-4516
  San Francisco, (415) 467-9234
Southern Region:
  Atlanta, (404) 214-3180
  Jacksonville, (904) 346-1386
  Memphis, (901) 222-4547

Central Region:
  Chicago, (312) 353-2101
  Detroit, (313) 226-4700
  St. Louis, (314) 279-7209
Eastern Region:
  Philadelphia, (215) 481-7054
  Washington, DC (202) 763-6215

S. TRIBUTE TO ROYAL LITTLE

Best known as the founder of Textron, Royal Little has also founded Narragan-sett Capital Corporation and Amtel Inc., and co-founded Indian Head, Inc., American Television and Communications Corporation, and All American Beverages. He has established a special endowment at the Harvard University Graduate School of Business Administration, where the Royal Little Chair of Business Administration was named in his honor, and has lent financial assistance to the governments of East Africa for creating national parks in Tanzania and Kenya. A member of the Business Hall of Fame and the Babson Academy of Distinguished Entrepreneurs, Royal Little is well known throughout the business community, where his extraordinary talents and business philosophy make him a sought-after speaker to business groups and financial editors—invariably to advise his audience on how not to follow his example.

How to Lose $100,000,000
and Other Valuable Advice*

Dedication. To the future entrepreneurs ot America whose courage to risk, whose ability to create, and whose determination to achieve will assure the survival of the free enterprise in this country.

"No businessman in the past has ever written such a book possibly because no one else has compiled such an impressive record of errors," entrepreneur Royal Little writes in the introduction to *How to Lose $100,000,000 and Other Valuable Advice.* In this candid, tongue-in-cheek business memoir, Wall Street's famed "father of conglomerates" recalls how he became involved in dozens of disastrous business ventures during nearly sixty years in the business community.

It all began in 1923, when Little took out a loan for $10,000 to start the first synthetic-yarn processing plant in New England. The tiny plant eventually led to the formation of Textron and, thirty years after its inception, revolutionized the concept of a conglomerate with Little's theory of "unrelated diversification." Textron today boasts such top names in their fields as Gorham silverware, Bostitch staplers, Homelite chainsaws, Fafner bearings, and Talon zippers.

As the director of some thirty businesses and charitable organizations over the subsequent three decades, the intrepid entrepreneur gambled on enterprises dealing in woolens, hardware, helicopters, cement, cable television, outboard motors, fiberglass, and pharmaceuticals, as well as in ventures with printers, booksellers, and promoters of golf courses. His more unlikely, and unprofitable, risks included a Nebraska cattle ranch, bowling alleys in suburban Rhode Island, and a resort development in the Bahamas.

The dizzying number and variety of things that can—and did—go wrong in Little's distinguished association with finance prompt his droll conclusion, "It isn't necessary to have an MBA from Harvard to lose $100 million!" A wry tribute to America's free enterprise system, with its equal opportunities for fame and infamy, *How to Lose $100,000,000 and Other Valuable Advice* will delight and instruct businessmen and laymen alike.

Shoestring Financing. This country must encourage its entrepreneurs. We must find ways to help the creative people who wish to develop their new ideas, processes, and products. There are not too many sources of capital for start-up situations available today. The reason this is so important is that we must plant the seeds of our future important businesses today to reap the benefits of their expansion and growth in the future.

*From *How to Lose $100,000,000 and Other Valuable Advice* by Royal Little. Copyright © 1979 by Royal Little and Harvard University Graduate School of Business Administration. By permission of Little, Brown & Co.

Most readers may feel it unusual that Textron could have built up a $3,000,000,000 business form its humble beginning in 1923 with a $10,000 bank loan and no equity capital—not even a shoestring. People do not realize that practically every large corporation in the country was originally started by some entrepreneur with very limited capital. Many of our large corporations today resulted from mergers during the 1920s when the stock market was booming, but if one could go back to the origins of these companies we would find that some entrepreneur started with very limited capital to create the original business. The replies I have received to my inquiries from these companies indicate how frequently this has occurred. It's true, however, that one could not start a railroad, a public utility, or a steel mill on a shoestring.

Since no one has yet published a summarized list of who started many of today's billion dollar corporations and how they were financed, I would like to. I have received some most interesting information from sixty-one companies that were started on a shoestring, each with current sales in excess of $1 billion. However, because of space limitations, I am limiting the story to sixteen.

Avon. David H. McConnell started Avon in 1886 with a $500 loan from a friend. In 1977, sales were $1,648,000,000 with profits of $191,000,000. The total market value of the company as of Aug. 15, 1978, was $3,486,000,000.

Campbell Soup. Campbell Soup was founded in 1869 in Camden, New Jersey, as a partnership of Joseph Campbell and Abraham Anderson, with no specified capital. In 1977, sales were $1,769,000,000 and earnings were $107,000,000. The market value as of August 15, 1978, was $1,213,000,000.

Coca-Cola. An Atlanta druggist, Dr. John Pemberton, produced the first Coca-Cola syrup in 1886, and he had earnings that year of $50. In 1977, sales were $3,560,000,000 and profits were $326,000,000. The market value as of August 15, 1978 was $5,510,000,000.

Digital Equipment. Kenneth H. Olsen, his brother Stanley, and Harlan E. Anderson started Digital Equipment when American Research and Development Company purchased 70 percent of the stock for $70,000 in August 1957. In 1977, sales were $1,059,000,000 and profits were $108,000,000. The market value as of August 15, 1978, was $1,941,000,000.

Du Pont. Eleuthere Irenee du Pont organized the company in 1802 with eighteen shareholders providing $36,000 equity. In 1977, sales were $9,435,000,000 and profits were $545,000,000. The market value of the company as of August 15, 1978, was $6,152,000,000.

Eastman Kodak. Eastman Kodak was founded by George Eastman a few days before Thanksgiving in 1880, with a $3,000 investment. In 1977, sales were

$5,967,000,000 and profits were $643,000,000. The market value of the company as of August 15, 1978, was $10,625,000,000.

Ford Motor. Henry Ford and eleven associates filed incorporation papers for Ford Motor on June 16, 1903, with only $28,000 in cash invested. I was amazed to learn that on October 26, 1909, General Motors offered to purchase Ford Motor Company for $8,000,000 with $2,000,000 down and the balance in the future. Henry Ford held out for all cash, and since William Durant was unable to raise the money, that acquisition fell through. In 1977, sales were $37,842,000,000 and profits were $1,673,000,000. The market value of the company as of August 15, 1978, was $5,513,000,000.

Gillette. On September 28, 1901, King Camp Gillette founded Gillette with $5,000 of equity. In 1977, sales were $1,587,000,000 and profits were $80,000,000. The market value of the company as of August 15, 1978, was $896,000,000.

Goodyear. Frank Seiberling started the Goodyear Tire and Rubber Company on August 29, 1898, with $13,500 of borrowed money. Sales in 1977 were $6,628,000,000 and profits were $206,000,000. The market value of the company as of August 15, 1978, was $1,277,000,000.

Hewlett-Packard. In 1939, William R. Hewlett and David Packard invested their personal savings of $538 in Hewlett-Packard. In 1977, sales were $1,360,000,000 and profits were $122,000,000. The market value of the company as of August 15, 1978, was $2,486,000,000.

McDonald's. In 1954, Ray Kroc obtained the exclusive franchise rights from the McDonald brothers to start hamburger drive-ins, using their name, throughout the country. Since then, Kroc has built McDonald's into the leading fast-food business in the country. In 1977, sales were $1,406,000,000 and profits were $137,000,000. The market value of the company as of August 15, 1978, was $2,366,000,000.

Pepsico. Caleb Bradham originally incorporated Pepsi Cola in North Carolina in 1902, and produced the first drink in his drugstore. He had no equity capital. In 1977, sales were $3,546,000,000 and profits were $187,000,000. The market value of the company as of August 15, 1978, was $2,779,000,000.

Proctor and Gamble. William Proctor and James Gamble organized the company on October 31, 1837, in Cincinnati, with equity capital of $7,192. In 1977, sales were $7,284,000,000 and profits were $461,000,000. The market value of the company as of August 15, 1978, was $7,311,000,000.

Sears, Roebuck. Richard Warren Sears started the company in the fall of 1886 at North Redwood, Minnesota, to sell watches. In 1977, sales were $17,224,000,000 and profits were $838,000,000. The market value of the company as of August 15, 1978, was $7,846,000,000.

Singer. Isaac Merrit Singer, with $40 in borrowed capital, invented the first practical sewing machine in 1850. In 1977, sales were $2,285,000,000 and profits were $78,000,000. Market value of the company's shares on August 15, 1978, were $327,000,000.

Xerox. Xerox Corporation was founded in 1906 in Rochester, New York, by Joseph C. Wilson, Sr., and three other businessmen under the Haloid name. In 1977, sales were $5,077,000,000 and profits were $407,000,000. The market value of its shares on August 15, 1978, was $4,931,000,000.

Advice. After reading about all these shoestring-financed companies, don't say, "That all happened in the past. I can't be done again." Under our free enterprise system, it will continue to be possible for entrepreneurs to duplicate in the future what has been done in the past; but it will just be more difficult to do so. It's up to the younger people of this country to have the vision and determination to accomplish it. More power to them—they'll need it.!

T. VENTURE CAPITAL RESOURCE PUBLICATIONS

The Capital Publishing Company was originally started by the late Stanley Rubel in 1961 and was recently acquired by Stanley Pratt. It has been the single clearinghouse for most industry-wide information on venture capital. They offer several publications, including a monthly newsletter entitled *Venture Capital*, which highlights a number of useful areas of what's happening within the industry. *The Guide to Venture Capital Sources*, 4th edition, is the most valuable single source on venture capital every published. Besides a nicely indexed listing of venture capital sources by state and by product group interest, the front half of this guide has several valuable articles. About $550 million is invested annually by about 450 professional venture capital firms with assets of about $3,000,000,000. The directory lists 600 sources and is available for $49.50.

The Source Guide for Borrowing Capital by Leonard Smollen, Stanley Rubel, Mark Rollinson (1977) tells how to raise capital without having to give up any equity. There are 50 federal programs for financing small business handled by nine different government agencies. This includes the SBA, the FHA, and others. The directory also lists state agencies, commercial banks, insurance companies, commercial finance companies, leasing companies, and investors in industrial revenue bonds. It is a valuable directory.

The Guide to Selling a Business by Stanley Rubel (1977) lists about 1,500 acquisition-oriented corporations. In addition, about 100 companies as seeking leveraged buy-outs; also about 500 professional merger intermediaries are listed. This unique and valuable book available for $49.50.

For more information on these publications, write:

The Center for Entrepreneurial Management
311 Main Street
Worcester, Massachusetts 01608
(617) 755-0770

Capital Publishing Corporation
2 Laurel Avenue, Box 348
Wellesley Hills, MA 02181
(617) 235-5405

The Center for Community and Economic Development (CCED), along with the Institute for New Enterprise Development (INED), has compiled *Sources of Capital for Community and Economic Development,* an excellent sourcebook on capital. In addition, the CCED offers a free bimonthly newsletter for interested parties. This group works to promote the concept of community based economical development. Write:

CCED/Cynthia Rose
639 Massachusetts Avenue
Suite 316
Cambridge, MA 02139
(617) 547-9695

The Directory of State and Federal Funds is a single source for basic data on the financial assistance programs of the 50 states and 12 federal agencies. This concise directory is the starting point for any business, large or small, that seeks to relocate or expand. The book helps management to "shop," compare, select, and discard a wide range of aid programs without collecting and sorting through mountains of promotional literature. Write:

Directory of State and Federal Funds for
    Business Development
Pilot Books
347 Fifth Avenue
New York, NY 10016

How and Where to Raise Venture Capital by Ted Nicholas (1978) is an excellent 68-page pamphlet on venture capital. Write:

Enterprise Publishing Company
1300 Market Street
Wilmington, DE 19801

Another booklet by Ted Nicholas is *Where the Money Is and How to Get It.*

How to Finance a Growing Business by Royce Diener is a book on capital security written from the viewpoint of the businessman-borrower. It not only describes what is available in the field of finance but also provides insight into what goes on in the lender's mind and by what standards the funding source operates. This is an exceedingly readable and understandable basic work on finance, including the more serious business of raising capital to start a company, keeping a growing concern solvent, financing the purchase of other companies, issuing securities and international finance. It is written from the viewpoint of the businessman. Write:

Frederick Fell Publishers, Inc.
386 Park Avenue, South
New York, NY 10016
(212) 685-9017

The Business Research and Service Institute of the College of Business at Western Michigan University publishes a spiral bound book entitled *Johnson's Directory of Risk Capital for Small Business,* edited by James M. Johnson, Ph.D., a member of the finance faculty. This several hundred page listing and categorizing of venture capital lists 373 venture firms. Write:

Professor James Johnson
Faculty of Finance
Western Michigan University
Kalamazoo, MI 49008

Venture Capital by John R. Dominquez (1974) includes a list of venture capital firms by investment limits. Write:

D.C. Heath Company
125 Spring Street
Lexington, MA 02173
(617) 862-6650

Howard and Company publishers an excellent guide for borrowing capital. The *1978 Market for Risk Capital Directory* is $25.00 and the *Program for Successful Bank Borrowing* is $50.00. This is not a well-known source of venture capital information, but it is a good one. Write:

Graham Howard
Howard and Company
1529 Walnut Street, 5th Floor
Philadelphia, PA 19102
(215) 603-8030

How to Raise Money to Make Money (The Executive's Guide to Financing a Business) is an excellent book that is easy to read and extremely comprehensive. The Institute for Business Planning, a subsidiary of Prentice-Hall, has some excellent material available for entrepreneurs. A monthly newsletter called *Closely Held Business* contains almost every known way to boost profits and generate personal wealth from a closely held business. Business, financial, and tax implications of buying, operating, expanding, selling, or terminating a business are discussed in this newsletter. Write:

Institute for Business Planning
IBP Plaza
Englewood Cliffs, N.J. 07632
(201) 592-2040

A source of international venture capital offers a newsletter, *Finance International,* and several directories on venture capital. One of the directories is called *Guide to Corporate Borrowing: Source and Rates.* Write:

Institute for International Research
95 Madison Avenue
New York, NY 10016

If you've ever tried to raise capital for a business venture, consider this book, *A Guide to Money Sources and How to Approach Them Successfully,* which covers such topics as various sources of loans, preparation of loan requests, government financing, and financial data and analysis as it relates to loans. The book is available from:

Kephart Communications, Inc.
901 Washington Street
Suite 200
Alexandria, VA 22314

The following three books are available from B. Klein Publishing Company: (1) *Business Capital Sources:* Lists hundreds of firms, banks, mortgage lenders, etc., having capital available for business loans. Also gives many hints on running a business successfully. (2) *How and Where to Get Capital* gives information on over 4,500 organizations and foundations that make capital loans, with requirements for borrowing. It also supplies information on raising capital through venture and risk capital sources. (3) *Small Business Investment Company Directory and Handbook* lists more than 400 small business investment companies interested in various businesses; also gives recommended procedures for running a profitable business. Write:

B. Klein Publishing, Inc.
P.O. Box 8503
Coral Springs, FL 33065
(305) 752-1708

The Money Market Directory lists the 4,600 largest institutional funds, their addresses, telephone numbers, amounts of money managed, and the money managers and investment counselors for each. These investors own securities with a market value of $1 trillion, with annual investment purchases and sales of $200 billion.

Money Market Directory
Money Market Directories Inc.
370 Lexington Avenue
New York, NY 10070

The National Association of Small Business Investment Companies (SBICs) offers a twice-monthly newsletter from Washington, D.C. It is one of the better sources of what is happening within the venture capital industry.

NASBIC News
512 Washington Building
Washington, D.C. 20005

The NASBIC membership directory of 21 pages is free as well. The directory lists names, addresses, telephone numbers, key executives, and a code to distinguish: preferred limit for loans or investments, investment policy, industry preference. About 5,000 of these directories are given away annually. The approximate circulation of the semimonthly newsletter is 500. The newsletter is extremely helpful for keeping up with legislation effecting venture capital industry.

The New England Venture Capital Directory, written by John McKiernan, is similar to the original book, but much more current, with a 1978 copyright. It lists about 100 of the most popular sources of venture capital around the country. However, its real strength lies in its commentaries about the Northeast venture groups. The second half of the book discusses entrepreneurs, business plans, and venture capitalists. Write:

John McKiernan
Management Association
Box 230
Chestnut Hill, MA 02167

A 134-page study by the Management Department at Boston College, entitled *Venture Capital—A Guidebook for New Enterprise,* is especially good for Northeastern United States businesses. Write:

Superintendent of Documents
U.S. Government Printing Office
Re: Committee Print No. 75-292
Washington, D.C. 20416

Venture Capital in the United States: An Analysis (1972) is an excellent guide on risk capital and venture management as practiced by large corporations. Write:

Venture Development Corporation
One Washington Street
Wellesley, MA 02181
(617) 237-5080

Western Association of Venture Capitalists—Directory of Members, San Francisco, provides a list of members and periodic bulletins on West Coast ventures. Write:

Directory of Members
244 California Street
Room 700
San Francisco, CA 94111
(415) 781-6897

A Handbook of Business Finance and Capital Sources. This hard cover handbook has 460 pages and an excellent reference book on more than 1,000 capital sources. It contains information on financing techniques and instruments for both private and government sources of capital. It is a very detailed and well-presented reference book. It would be useful for anyone trying to raise capital. The price is $50.00 per copy. The author/editor is Dileep Rao, Ph.D., who was also India's number one ranked junior table tennis player. Not only is the author an academician, but also an entrepreneur by way of his self-published book. Write to:

Dileep Rao
InterFinance Corporation
305 Foshay Tower
Minneapolis, MN 55402
(612) 338-8185

Sources of Corporate Venture Capital

Kenneth W. Rind, the principle in the Xerox Development Corporation, states that there has been a resurgence in corporate venture capital. The following list contains the industrial firms that have been most active in this resurgence:

Textron	Johnson & Johnson
Xerox	3M
Gould	Corning
Time	Dun & Bradstreet
Innoven-Monsanto/Emerson	Fairchild Camera
Exxon	CTS
Standard Oil of Indiana	Control Data
General Electric	Burroughs
Syntex	NCR
Motorola	TRW
Bolt Beranek & Newman, Inc.	National City Lines
Arthur D. Little	Telescience
Inco	

Foreign-based companies are also active in venture capital. They include:

Northern Telecom	Fujitsu
Siemens	Robert Bosch
Nippon Electric	Lucas Industries
Seiko	Jaegar
Oki	VDO
Mitsui	

U. WOMEN ENTREPRENEURS

One of the great changes in the 1980s has been the emergence of the woman entrepreneur. The Women's Liberation Movement has brought women out of the home and into the work force. Now women understand the value and the importance of the start-your-own-business process, and they are beginning to become entreprenurs at a much faster rate. A recent study indicated that 10 percent of all businesses were owned by women. However, more than half of the United States wealth is in the hands of females. Sources of help for women entrepreneurs are listed here; however, don't disregard the other sources of information tht are equally valuable.

Women have specialized needs to help combat some of the natural forces that work against a woman in business. These sources of information are offered to help a woman combat these problems.

American Women's Economic Development Corporation
250 Broadway
New York, N.Y. 10007

The Businesswoman's Letter
P.O. Box 337
Wall Street Station
New York, NY 10005

Organizations

The National Association for Female Executives, Inc. seeks out opportunities, provides information, arranges special offers, and offers information on extending your money power. Write:

NAFE Executive Office
32 East 39th Street
New York, NY 10016

NAFE Administrative Office
31 Jeremys Way
Annapolis, MD 21403
(301) 267-0630

National Association of Women Business Owners
200 P Street, N.W.
Suite 511
Washington, D.C. 20036
(202) 338-8966

More and more women are becoming entrepreneurs. Other sources of help are available.

New England Women Business Owners
c/o SBANE
69 Hickory Drive
Waltham, MA 02154
(617) 890-9070

New York Association of Women Business
   Owners/Enterprising Women
525 West End Avenue
New York, NY 10024
(A monthly newsletter is offered to subscribers.)

Publications

*Small Business Ideas for Women and How to Get
   Started,* by Terri Hilton
Pilot Books
347 Fifth Avenue
New York, NY 10016

The Woman's Guide to Starting a Business, by Claudia Jessup and Genie Chipps, 1978. This two-part guide is concerned with the special problems that women face when establishing a business. Part I consists of basic information on getting started, and Part II is a collection of interviews of successful women entrepreneurs. Write:

Holt, Rinehart & Winston
383 Madison Avenue
New York, NY 10017

A monthly, 12-page digest of affirmative action news, *Womanpower* is a newsletter designed to keep employers up to date with the laws, government regulations, suits, and court decisions that affect the employment of women of all races, ages, religions, and ethnic origins. Write:

Betsy Hogan Association
222 Rawson Road
Brookline, MA 02146
(617) 232-0066

Women Entrepreneurs
P.O. Box 26738
San Francisco, CA 94126
Contact: Sue Easton,
   (415) 474-3000

Women-Owned Businesses, 1972, 1976, provides basic economic data on businesses owned by all women and on minority firms owned by women. Data include number of firms, gross receipts, and number of paid employees, listed geographically by industry, size of firm, and legal form of organization of firm.

   The Entrepreneurial Woman. Newsweek Books, is a new book recently written by Sandra Winston. It is a 740-page easy reader. Sandra is both a marriage counselor and a business consultant. Her book focuses on the people side of the issue with a great understanding of women but with less insight into the process of launching entrepreneurial ventures. One of the chapters, entitled "How to Be Assertive", leads the reader to believe she is talking to would-be entrepreneurs who are presently housewives. Her writing style is excellent, and she does have a good bibliography.

Speaking of bibliographies, here is a great one on the subject. The title is *Women in the Economy*, a 40-page bibliography compiled in 1979. It is a source of information on careers and education in business for women. It was prepared as a project by the Empire State College Center for Business and Economic Information with the assistance of the Hauppauge unit of the Empire State College. Write:

> George S. Dawson, Director
> Empire State Colege
> Long Island Regional Center
> Old Westbury State
> University of New York
> Box 130
> Old Westbury, NY 11568

Septima Palm has a range of services for the female entrepreneur including a new book called *The Cinderella Syndrome*. Write:

> Success Series
> Box 2096
> Sarasota, FL 33578
> (813) 349-4634

Dottie Walters is another woman who has been extremely successful in promoting the female entrepreneur. Write:

> Dottie Walters
> 600 West Foothill Blvd.
> Glendora, CA 91740
> (213) 335-0218

INDEX